PHILOSOPHY AND MYTH IN
KARL MARX

The philosopher, *himself an abstract form of alienated man, sets himself up as the* measure *of the alienated world.*   KARL MARX (1844)

TO MY PARENTS AND
EVGENIA

PHILOSOPHY AND MYTH
IN
KARL MARX

BY

ROBERT C. TUCKER
Professor of Politics, Princeton University

SECOND EDITION.

CAMBRIDGE
AT THE UNIVERSITY PRESS
1972

Published by the Syndics of the Cambridge University Press
Bentley House, 200 Euston Road, London NW1 2DB
American Branch: 32 East 57th Street, New York, N.Y.10022

© Cambridge University Press 1961, 1972

Library of Congress Catalogue Card Number: 70-180022

0 521 08455 5 hard covers
0 521 09701 0 paperback

First puplished 1961
Reprinted 1961 (twice)
1964
1965
1966
1967
1969
1971
Second Edition 1972

Printed in the United States of America

CONTENTS

CONTENTS

PREFACE TO THE SECOND EDITION

The only part of *Philosophy and Myth in Karl Marx* that I have revised to a considerable extent for this second edition is the concluding chapter. The Introduction has not been changed, nor have any basic revisions been made in the fifteen following chapters that comprise the substance of the work. These chapters offer what is essentially an extended exegesis of Marx, and I remain persuaded both of their interpretation of the philosophical genesis of Marxism and of their argument for the underlying continuity of Marx's thought from the early writings to *Capital* and the centrality of the alienation theme throughout.

Only in two places in these chapters are there revisions that go beyond textual corrections and minor changes of wording. At the end of chapter XIII, a passage stressing Marx's lack of concern with socialism as a quest for community-forms in society has been altered to eliminate the inferential criticism of him on this score. The reason is that his insistence on conceiving socialism in terms of world-change no longer appears a weakness of his futurology. In a more recent context I have put the point as follows: 'In our time, any serious utopia must be, like Marx's, a new state of the world.'*

Secondly, I have taken the opportunity afforded by a new edition to clarify fully something that appears not to have been made sufficiently plain in the original edition. This is the fact that my phrase 'Marx's myth of the warfare of labour and capital' (in chapter XV) is not at all meant to deny that social conflicts have taken place in Marx's time and after which could properly be described in class terms and as a warfare of labour and capital. My point was not, and is not, that class struggle itself is a myth, but that Marx's special *vision* of an ongoing titanic battle between labour and capital contained a mythic element deriving from the projection upon society of a drama of conflict out of the inner life of man—a drama prefigured in the picture of an alienated species-man in Marx's manuscripts of 1844.

The concluding chapter of the first edition went beyond the interpretative enterprise of the rest of the book to essay an assessment of Marx in relation to the concerns of our time. This

* *The Marxian Revolutionary Idea* (New York, 1969), p. 223.

consisted of a critique on his treatment of alienation, and a general comment on the moot question of the continuing relevance of his economic and social thought. As indicated above, my views on the latter question have changed somewhat in the intervening years, in the direction of perceiving relevance where I did not do so before, and I have tried to reflect this more mature view (as I would like to think of it as being) in revising this chapter. The concluding critique of Marx on alienation has not, however, undergone any significant change.

In one of his books and in a subsequent personal communication, Dr Erich Fromm pointed out an inadvertent mistranslation, in the first edition, of a passage in Marx's 1844 manuscripts on the role of the idea of 'greed' in the classical theory of political economy. My analysis does not rest on the meaning of this passage, but I have of course taken the opportunity to correct the translation and am grateful to Dr Fromm for calling the matter to my attention.

In the decade since this book first came out, many friends, colleagues, students and in some instances strangers have given me their reactions to it, and I am indebted to them all for doing so. If this is now a less imperfect piece of work, they have all contributed to making it so. My friends Stephen Cohen, Kenneth Harline and Norman Moscowitz are among those to whom I am particularly grateful for advice in the course of work on the new edition. My thanks go too to the officers of the Cambridge University Press for their editorial help.

R.C.T.

PRINCETON, NEW JERSEY
August 4, 1971

PREFACE TO THE FIRST EDITION

This book seeks to carry forward the still unfinished work of reinterpretation and basic critical analysis of the thought of Karl Marx.

The need for reinterpretation has become apparent since the publication some years ago of a set of previously unpublished manuscripts in which Marx, as a young man of twenty-six, set forth a first systematic sketch of Marxism. Here the economic interpretation of history and the conception of communism have as their setting a comprehensive scheme of thought that is philosophical in character. Its subject is man and the world—self-estranged man in an 'alienated world' as Marx called it. The world revolution is conceived as the act by which estranged man changes himself by changing the world. Instead of being divided against himself as always in the past, man is to be restored to his human nature—and this is what Marx means by 'communism'. The origins of this *Weltanschauung* in earlier German philosophy from Kant to Feuerbach, its genesis in Marx's mind during the early 1840's, and its evolution into the more familiar, seemingly unphilosophical Marxism of the *Communist Manifesto* and other later writings by Marx and Engels, form the main subject-matter of this book. An underlying continuity of Marx's thought from the early philosophical manuscripts to the later stage is demonstrated. In the concluding part, this demonstration becomes the basis for a new analysis of the element of myth in Marx's vision of the world-process as recorded in *Capital*.

Many were generous with encouragement and assistance while I was in the process of writing, expanding and then re-writing the book over a period of seven years. Paul Kecskemeti, Maurice Mandelbaum, Morris Watnick, Rulon Wells, Morton White and John Wild read it in the original version, which was submitted to Harvard University in 1958 as a doctoral dissertation, and offered valuable criticisms and suggestions. I am very grateful too for comments received from Daniel Bell. Moreover, discussion with my students of ideas contained in the book has contributed much to the shaping of the finished product.

PREFACE TO THE FIRST EDITION

My indebtedness to R. A. Becher and the staff of the Cambridge University Press is very great. Among the many others who were more than helpful with advice on various matters concerning the book I should like to mention Justinia Besharov-Djaparidze, Edward Buehrig, Byrum Carter, Robert Ferrell, Richard Hare, Frank Ross and P. Vatikiotis. Melvin Croan and Erich Goldhagen assisted me in exploring the writings of Moses Hess. H. W. Theen provided expert counsel on points of translation. The Research Division of the Indiana University Foundation furnished a grant for the final preparation of the manuscript for the press, and Miss Rosalie Fonoroff and Mrs Laura Murray rendered able assistance with the typing at different stages.

I owe a special debt of gratitude to Robert Adamson for his criticisms and suggestions with reference to the substance of the book, his friendly interest in it all along, and his wise advice on every aspect of it. Finally, my deepest thanks go to my wife for helping in all the ways that she did to make this work possible.

R.C.T.

BLOOMINGTON, INDIANA
March 1961

INTRODUCTION

MARX IN CHANGING PERSPECTIVE

*The criticism of religion ends with the precept that the supreme
being for man is man . . .*   MARX (1844)

To many people in our time Marxism means the Communist
ideology, a body of doctrine derived in part from the ideas of
Karl Marx and professed by members of the Communist parties
of the world. This is not, however, the usage that will be followed
in these pages. Here Marxism will mean the thought of Marx.
Our subject is Marx's own Marxism—its pre-history in German
philosophy before Marx, its genesis and evolution in Marx's
mind, and its basic meaning.

The recent rise of interest in this circle of problems springs in
part from the discovery of an early philosophical Marx about
whom next to nothing was known until the second quarter of the
twentieth century. Only then did we obtain access to certain
previously unpublished materials of Marx's formative period
that enable us to learn how he created Marxism. The most
important of them is a set of manuscripts written by Marx in
Paris in 1844. These *Economic and Philosophic Manuscripts of 1844,*
as they have been named, contain a first version of Marxism
seemingly quite different from the mature Marxian system, to
which Marx and his collaborator Friedrich Engels gave the
title 'Materialist Conception of History' or alternatively
'scientific socialism'. They resurrect for us a young philosophical
Marx whose central theme of human self-alienation shows
affinity with the thought of our own later age and thus confers
upon the first system (which I have called 'original Marxism') a
curious modernity across the gap of years.*

* The circumstances underlying the unwillingness of Marx and Engels to publish
the first system are discussed in chapter XI of this book. The manuscripts were
originally published in an incomplete Russian translation in 1927. They first
appeared in German in 1932 in volume III of Marx and Engels, *Historisch-Kritische
Gesamtausgabe* (ed. D. Rjazanov and V. Adoratski), usually cited as *MEGA*. Some
parts of the manuscripts are missing, but the bulk of the material has survived. A

The discovery of Marx's first system has reinforced a trend of thought about Marxism that had been growing independently for a long while, especially in the West. It seems fair to say that a change in the generally accepted view of Marx has been taking place in the twentieth century. In the new image he appears not as the scientist of society that he claimed to be but rather as a moralist or a religious kind of thinker. The old assumption that 'scientific socialism' is a scientific system of thought has tended more and more to give way to the notion that it is in essence a moralistic or religious system. It appears now, at any rate to very many of us, as the single most influential expression of a modern socialist movement that was inspired by fundamentally religious impulses and represented, in Martin Buber's phrase, a 'socialist secularization of eschatology'.[1]

The change of perspective is radical, as a brief glance at some representative earlier opinions on Marx and Marxism will show. The basic question in the mind of an older generation of students and critics of Marx's system was simply: is it true? The underlying assumption was that 'scientific socialism', as its name suggests and Marx and Engels always maintained, was essentially a scientific system of thought. It followed that the chief problem with regard to it was the problem of verification. The crucial issue was its validity or non-validity as a scientific theory of the historical process, and particularly as an economic theory of the inevitable revolutionary breakdown of the capitalist system. The moral content of Marxism—not to mention the religious content—was thought to be nil. Thus Werner Sombart spoke of the 'purely theoretical character of Marxism' in an article of 1892, and contrasted it in this respect with what he called 'ethical socialism'. 'Marxism is distinguished from all other socialist systems', he declared, 'by its anti-ethical tendency. In all of Marxism from beginning to end, there is not a grain of ethics, and consequently no more of an ethical judgment than an ethical postulate'.[2] Sombart's statement was quoted with emphatic approval by young Lenin in one of his early writings.

The philosopher Croce, writing at that time as a sympathetic critic of Marx, casually dismissed the ethical issue. What was the 'philosophical opinion' of Marx and Engels in regard to

number of English translations are now available, including Karl Marx, *Early Writings* translated and edited by T. B. Bottomore (New York, Toronto, London: McGraw-Hill, 1964).

morality? The question, he said, 'is of no great importance, and is even somewhat inopportune, since neither Marx nor Engels were philosophers of ethics, nor bestowed much of their vigorous ability on these questions'. True, their ideas presented 'no contradiction of general ethical principles, even if here and there they clash with the prejudices of current pseudo-morality'. However, this did not warrant any attempt to discover a moral meaning in Marxism: 'And, in truth, even if some may be able to write on the theory of knowledge according to Marx, to write on the principles of ethics according to Marx seems to me a somewhat hopeless undertaking.'[3]

Among the many who shared this position was Karl Kautsky, the leading theorist of German Marxism after Engels' death. At the beginning of this century, Kautsky wrote a little treatise for the express purpose of supplementing Marxism with the 'moral ideal' that, as he saw it, the Social Democratic workers' movement required but scientific socialism did not provide. Marxism was strictly a demonstration of certain historical cause-and-effect relations. All it could say was that 'Socialism is inevitable because the class struggle and the victory of the proletariat are inevitable'.[4] It had no way of saying or showing that the inevitable was something that the workers should regard as desirable. For assistance in his attempt to construct a Marxist ethic on non-Marxist ground, Kautsky turned to Charles Darwin's theory of the social instinct in animals and men. The teachings of his master Marx appeared to him to be ethically empty.

Such was the older trend of thought. The change of view that has been taking place since then, and especially in the middle years of the present century, scarcely requires documenting. The contemporary Western literature on Marxism abounds in statements that would have bewildered the earlier generation of authorities from whose writings we have just quoted. We now frequently read that Marxism is essentially a moralistic system, that it stands or falls as ethical, that *Capital* is a moral or even metaphysical treatise in economic disguise, that the Materialist Conception of History is a form of eschatology, that Marxism is a religion of the age of industrialism, and so on. Even the Soviet Marxists deny that Marxism is ethically empty, although they cling to the tenet that it is essentially a scientific system of thought.*

* The official Soviet position has recently been summarized as follows: 'Marxism-

In the non-Communist part of the world, on the other hand, the view that Marxism is a scientific system has come to seem less and less tenable. This statement must be qualified by the admission that Marxism has been one of the influential shaping forces in the evolution of modern social science, that we owe in part to Marx our present heightened awareness of the economic factors in the history of civilization, and that some particular elements within his system may be of enduring scientific interest and value. The point in question is simply that 'scientific socialism', viewed as a whole, is not a scientific system of thought. It is non-scientific in some of its basic aspects of substance and structure. For example, the Materialist Conception of History, with its scheme of successive world-periods from primitive communism through the Asiatic, ancient, feudal, and bourgeois historical epochs to final world communism, is not constructed on the plan of a scientific theory, but rather on the plan of a philosophy of world history in the classic Western sense.

In the non-Communist part of the world, widespread abandonment of the supposition that Marxism is essentially scientific in character has helped to reorient the study of Marx. It has stimulated the tendency to examine his system from other points of view. If it is not the scientific theory that it claimed to be, may it not be comprehended as basically an ethical or religious system? As already indicated, this is the question that increasingly determines the direction of present-day non-Communist inquiry into the thought of Marx. The search for understanding of the deeper springs of his world-view increasingly becomes a search for its moral or religious meaning. However, the work of systematic analysis of Marxism from this point of view still remains in its early stages.

[2]

Approaches to Marxism from the new point of view diverge. If some students of Marx's thought interpret it in religious terms, others prefer the hypothesis that Marxism is fundamentally an ethical system. It seems to them more feasible to analyse Marx

Leninism sees the supreme criterion of communist morality in the struggle for communism' (A. Shishkin, *Osnovy kommunisticheskoi morali*, p. 95). It is based on a change in Lenin's own view after the revolution of 1917. 'Morality for us is subordinated to the interests of the class struggle of the proletariat', he said in a speech to the third All-Russian Congress of the Russian Young Communist League in 1920 (*Selected Works*, vol. II, p. 668).

as a moral philosopher than as a religious thinker. It appears, perhaps, less radical, less in contradiction with what Marx thought of himself, and more likely to yield definite positive results. And an apparent justification for it lies close at hand.

An attentive reader of Marx quickly becomes aware of the intensely moralistic tone of his thought. Although he disclaims the intention to moralize, his portrait of the world in the *Communist Manifesto, Capital,* and other writings is manifestly the portrait of a world felt to be wrong and evil in its basic constitution. It is a world that stands morally condemned in the eyes of the portrait-painter, a world awaiting merited destruction at the hands of its 'grave-digger', the proletarian. On occasion Marx found imagery of compelling power to express this moral condemnation. For example, in a speech given in London in 1856, he said that there existed in Germany in the Middle Ages a secret tribunal called the *Vehmgericht,* and went on: 'If a red cross was seen marked on a house, people knew that its owner was doomed by the *Vehm.* All the houses of Europe are now marked with the mysterious red cross. History is the judge—its executioner the proletarian.'[5] Here he presents the proletarian revolution as history's mighty act of retributive justice against a society so criminal in character that it deserves capital punishment.

The deep-dyed moralistic texture of his thought is obvious. If by moralist we mean simply a person whose thought moves in the orbit of prime concern with values of good and evil, a person whose thought-process is decisively governed by a basic value judgment, then Marx is unquestionably a moralist. But this still leaves open the question whether he is a moral philosopher. As conceived and practised in the Socratic tradition in the West, moral philosophy is a form of inquiry. It is inquiry into the nature of the supreme good for man or the criterion of right conduct. Now a distinguishing mark of inquiry, whether in moral philosophy or other branches of philosophy or in science, is that thought proceeds from a methodological doubt, a suspension of commitment. We may feel that we know the correct answer, but we recognize the rational possibility of different answers from our own. Thus moral philosophy, as inquiry, presupposes recognition that the nature of the supreme good for man is problematic. It begins, as Aristotle began his *Ethics,* with the raising of the question: what is the highest good or proper supreme end of man's activity?

Marx is a moralist, but does not fit this description of a moral philosopher. He is concerned above all else with an issue of good and evil, but not in the sense of inquiry. His system, comprised within the comprehensive framework of the Materialist Conception of History, is not constructed in the manner of a system of ethics. It is not an example of ethical inquiry. It does not start by raising the question of the supreme good for man or the criterion of right conduct; these questions are not raised by Marx *as questions*. What is more, he is adamantly opposed to raising them. He will have nothing to do with ethical inquiry, and shows contempt for the very idea of it, as, for example, in the following passage in *The German Ideology:* 'The communists in general preach no *morality*, which Stirner does too much. They do not make moral demands upon men—to love one another, not to be egoists, etc. On the contrary, they know well that egoism as well as self-sacrifice is, in certain circumstances, a necessary form of the self-assertion of individuals.'[6] The moralist Marx is radically opposed to moral philosophy.*

The effort to interpret Marxism as a system of moral philosophy is also beset with other serious difficulties. In the modern history of moral philosophy, a number of ethical positions have become familiar. Those who look on Marx as a moral philosopher naturally tend to ascribe one or another of them to him. Marx lived in an age of Utilitarian ethics, which put forward the pleasure principle or the doctrine of greatest happiness. He was also associated with the modern European socialist movement, in which the principle of distributive justice has figured as an exceedingly important ethical idea. To some it has seemed plausible to suppose that Marx, in so far as he was a moral philosopher, adhered to one of these two principles.† But testimony to be found in Marx's writing speaks against them.

---

* Understandably reluctant to face this fact squarely, those who wish to view him as a moral philosopher tend to advance extraneous explanations for his attitude. Thus Sidney Hook writes: 'In combatting the excesses of ineffective and sentimental "moralizing" Marx leaned so far backward that, soon after his death, the myth became current that he had no place for any ethics in his philosophy of social activity' (*From Hegel to Marx*, p. 51). This treats Marx's opposition to moral philosophy as a tactical expedient in socialist controversy. A different position is taken by K. R. Popper. 'Marx, I believe, avoided an explicit moral theory because he hated preaching', he writes. 'Deeply distrustful of the moralist who usually preaches water and drinks wine, Marx was reluctant to formulate his ethical convictions explicitly.

From his German philosophical predecessors, Kant and Hegel, Marx imbibed a scorn for hedonism and related philosophies that always remained with him. His longest discussion of this question occurs in *The German Ideology*, where he writes that the philosophy of pleasure has never been anything but the 'clever phraseology' of certain social circles that have enjoyed the privilege of pleasure. And departing from the economic interpretation for a moment, he goes on to say that the Greeks in antiquity and the French in modern times have been the leading proponents of this philosophy, in both instances because of a temperamental predisposition to the pursuit of pleasure. More recently, he continues, the philosophy of pleasure has been elaborated in a new form by the bourgeoisie—Utilitarian ethics. Here the philosophy of pleasure is generalized and becomes 'a flat and hypocritical moral doctrine', hypocritical because it groundlessly presumes to generalize for all individuals regardless of differences in what they view as pleasureable. And he concludes: 'The pleasures of all hitherto existing classes and estates have inevitably been either juvenile and tedious or else coarse because they have always been divorced from the over-all life-activity of the individuals.'[7]

Elsewhere Marx interprets the Utilitarian ethics of Bentham as a monetary moral philosophy, a philosophical generalization of the pecuniary relations prevailing in bourgeois society. In *Capital*, he graciously introduces Jeremy Bentham to the reader as 'the insipid, pedantic, leather-tongued oracle of the commonplace bourgeois intelligence of the nineteenth century'.

The principles of humanity and decency were for him matters that needed no discussion, matters to be taken for granted' (*The Open Society and Its Enemies*, vol. II, pp. 187–8). Here the explanation is sought in Marx's personal character. Neither of the two views cited reckons with the possibility that Marx's antipathy for moral philosophy was rooted in the very structure of his thought.

† Rebecca Cooper explicitly imputes a Utilitarian ethic to Marx: 'Armed revolution and the proletarian dictatorship are ethically justified as necessary means toward the greatest amount of human happiness' (*The Logical Influence of Hegel on Marx*, p. 180). Herbert Marcuse, suggesting a similar interpretation, writes that in the transition from Hegelianism to Marxism 'The idea of reason has been superseded by the idea of happiness', which 'denoted an *affirmative* materialism, that is to say, an affirmation of the material satisfaction of man' (*Reason and Revolution*, pp. 294, 295). Among the writers who ascribe the principle of justice to Marx are A. G. Lindsay and E. H. Carr. According to Lindsay, 'His fundamental passion is a passion for justice' (*Karl Marx's Capital*, p. 114). According to Carr, 'In *Capital*, published twenty years after the *Communist Manifesto*, Marx demonstrated for the first time that the victory of the proletariat would be the victory not only of brute force, but of abstract justice' (*Karl Marx: A Study in Fanaticism*, p. 83).

Bentham did not invent the principle of utility; he only repro-
duced in dull and spiritless fashion what Helvetius and other
Frenchmen of the eighteenth century had said before him
brilliantly. He was a purely English phenomenon, and 'I do not
even except the German philosopher, Christian Wolff, when I
declare that at no time and in no country has the most trivial
commonplace ever before strutted about with such appalling
self-satisfaction.' Having thus vented his feelings, Marx goes on
to remark that the principle of utility is quite useless apart from
a definite conception of the nature of the creature concerned:
'To know what is useful for a dog, we must study dog nature.
This nature cannot be excogitated from the "principle of
utility".' If man is in question, human nature and its historical
transformations must be studied. 'But Bentham makes short
work of it. In his arid and simple way, he assumes the modern
petty bourgeois, and above all the modern English petty
bourgeois, to be the normal man. Whatever seems useful to this
queer sort of normal man and to his world, is regarded as useful
in and by itself.'[8]

Many people, doubtless including numerous followers of
Marx, have assumed that distributive justice is the value underlying his value judgment against existing society. His indictment
of capitalism and call for its replacement with communism have
been attributed to a concern for justice in the sense of a fair
distribution of material goods. It must be said that such an
assumption has at least a superficial plausibility. Not only was
the demand for justice an important theme in the European
socialist movement of Marx's time. It seems to lurk behind his
analysis of capitalism as a system of production founded on
'wage labour'.

Wage labour, according to Marx, is labour performed in the
service of the capitalist's hunger for 'surplus value'. Surplus
value results from surplus working time, during which the
worker produces beyond the amount whose monetary equivalent
he receives as his day's wage. Given Marx's labour theory of
value and the fact that labour power under capitalism is a commodity like any other, the day's wage, or value of a day's use of
the worker's labour power, is equivalent to the amount of labour
incorporated in the labour power, i.e. the amount of the
necessities of life required to maintain the worker for a day. The
wage is a subsistence wage. This much the worker produces in a

part of the working day, and receives in recompense for the whole day. What he produces in the remainder of the working day is surplus value appropriated by the capitalist for his own enrichment. Now Marx condemns wage labour and holds that it is the mission of the proletarian revolution to destroy it forever. Many have inferred that he condemns it on the ground that the worker is being robbed of something that rightfully belongs to him, viz., the full proceeds of his labour. They have concluded, with Lindsay, that 'his fundamental passion is a passion for justice'.

Such an inference, however, collides with a cascade of explicit negative testimony from the pens of both Marx and Engels. First, they assert quite emphatically that *no injustice whatever is involved in wage labour*. The subsistence wage, they argue, is precisely what the worker's labour power for a day is worth under capitalism. The worker is receiving full value for his services despite the fact that the employer extracts surplus value at his expense. To quote Marx: 'It is true that the daily maintenance of the labour power costs only half a day's labour, and that nevertheless the labour power can work for an entire working day, with the result that the value which its use creates during a working day is twice the value of a day's labour power. So much the better for the purchaser, but it is nowise an injustice (*Unrecht*) to the seller.'[9] It is nowise an injustice because the subsistence wage is precisely what the commodity labour power, sold by the worker to the employer, is worth according to the laws of commodity production. But is there no higher standard of justice than that implicit in these laws? Is there no abstract idea of justice in relation to which wage labour, though perfectly just on capitalist principles, could be adjudged as unjust *per se*? Marx and Engels are absolutely unequivocal in their negative answer to this question. 'Social justice or injustice', writes Engels, 'is decided by one science alone—the science which deals with the material facts of production and exchange, the science of political economy.'[10] 'Right', says Marx in his *Critique of the Gotha Program,* 'can never be higher than the economic structure of society and its cultural development conditioned thereby.'[11]

The latter work, consisting of marginal notes that Marx penned in 1875 on a draft programme for a united German workers' party and published posthumously, contains a furious diatribe against the whole idea that fair distribution is a socialist

goal. Marx points out sarcastically that socialists cannot agree
on any criterion of distributive justice: 'And have not the
socialist sectarians the most varied notions about "fair" distribution?' He speaks of 'ideological nonsense about "right" and
other trash so common among the democrats and French
socialists'. He dismisses the notions of 'undiminished proceeds of
labour', 'equal right' and 'fair distribution' as 'obsolete verbal
rubbish' which it would be a 'crime' to adopt as a party programme. It is here that Marx quotes, for the only time, the old
French socialist slogan, 'From each according to his ability, to
each according to his needs.' But in the very next breath he
declares that 'it was in general incorrect to make a fuss about
so-called *distribution* and to put the principal stress upon it'. To
present socialism as turning principally on distribution was
characteristic of 'vulgar socialism', Marx says, and he concludes
by asking: 'Why go back again?'[12] It should be clear in the light
of all this that a fair distribution of the proceeds of labour is not
the moral goal for Marx. The ideal of distributive justice is a
complete stranger in the mental universe of Marxism. The
underlying reason will be shown later in this study.

The difficulty of analysing Marx's thought by reference to one
or another of the conventional positions in modern Western
moral philosophy has impelled some to impute unconventional
ethical positions to him. A notable example is provided by
K. R. Popper, whose book *The Open Society and Its Enemies*
(volume II) contains perhaps the most vigorous critical assault on
the problem of Marxist ethics to be found in the recent scholarly
literature. As already mentioned, Popper believes that Marx
deliberately avoided an 'explicit moral theory' because he hated
preaching. He argues, however, that Marx's writings contain an
ethical theory by implication, and this he calls an 'historicist
moral theory' or, alternatively, 'moral futurism'.

This term is used to distinguish Marx's position from Hegel's,
which is 'moral positivism'. Hegelian moral positivism, according to Popper, holds that whatever historically *is* is right,
whereas Marxist moral futurism holds that whatever inevitably
will be in history is, for that very reason, right. In other words,
Marxism as moral philosophy is said to be based upon the
principle of historical inevitability. Imagining what Marx
himself might have said if he had been asked why he desired the
future proletarian revolution, Popper formulates for him the

following moral futurist reply: 'I am able to see that the
bourgeoisie, and with it its system of morals, is bound to disappear, and that the proletariat, and with it a new system of
morals, is bound to win. I see that this development is inevitable.
It would be madness to attempt to resist it, just as it would be
madness to attempt to resist the law of gravity. . . . In this way,
I adopt the facts of the coming period as the standards of my
morality.'[13]

Overlooking some of the complexities of Popper's analysis,
let us simply ask whether the principle of historical inevitability
plays the part of a basic ethical norm in Marx's scheme of
thought. There is no evidence that it does. There is nothing to
indicate that Marx morally affirmed the future world revolution
on the ground of its presumed inevitability. Far from deciding
that a communist revolution would be desirable after discovering
that it was inevitable, he became convinced as a young man of
its desirability and then embarked on a life-long effort, materialized in *Capital*, to prove that it must come. And how could the
hypothesis before us explain the burning intensity of Marx's
moral rejection of the existing world, his readiness to pronounce
death sentence upon it in the name of the *Vehmgericht* of history?
How, indeed, could anyone become imbued with a fierce
antagonism to the existing social order merely on the basis of an
intellectual perception or proof that it is doomed to give way to
a different order in the future? One might just as logically,
depending on one's values, start to appreciate the doomed
society all the more and reserve one's condemnation for the
inevitable future. In short, inevitability *per se* is scarcely a
plausible candidate for anyone's moral value. The hypothesis
that the principle of historical inevitability served Marx as an
implicit ethical norm is not seriously tenable.

[3]

If, as the preceding discussion suggests, efforts to interpret
Marxism as a special expression of moral philosophy lead into
an analytic *impasse*, a different approach is needed. If Marx was
a moralist opposed to moral philosophy, may he not have been
a moralist of the religious kind? In general, men who create
myths or religious conceptions of reality are moralists in the
sense in which this term has been used here. They may in fact be
obsessed with a moral vision of reality, a vision of the world as

an arena of conflict between good and evil forces. If so, ethical inquiry is entirely foreign to their mental makeup. For them there is no possibility of the suspension of commitment that ethical inquiry presupposes. They are passionately committed persons. The good and evil forces in the world are present before their mind's eye with such overwhelming immediacy, and the conclusions for conduct follow with such compelling force, that ethical inquiry must seem to them pointless or even perverse. It is to this class of minds, as the following study will endeavour to show, that Karl Marx's belongs.

The religious essence of Marxism is superficially obscured by Marx's rejection of the traditional religions. This took the form of a repudiation of 'religion' as such and an espousal of 'atheism'. Marx's atheism, however, meant only a negation of the trans-mundane God of traditional Western religion. It did not mean the denial of a supreme being. Indeed, as shown by his words in the epigraph to this chapter, denial of the transmundane God was merely a negative way of asserting that 'man' should be regarded as the supreme being or object of ultimate concern. Thus his atheism was a positive religious proposition. It rules out consideration of Marxism as a religious system of thought only if, with Marx, we equate the traditional religions with religion as such.

From a structural viewpoint, moreover, Marxism invites analysis as a religious system. It follows in certain ways the pattern of the great religious conceptions in Western culture. In particular, it has a number of basic characteristics in common with the Christian system in its Augustinian and later medieval expression. One of these is the aspiration to totality of scope. Like medieval Christianity, Marx's system undertakes to provide an integrated, all-inclusive view of reality, an organization of all significant knowledge in an interconnected whole, a frame of reference within which all possible questions of importance are answered or answerable. It does not limit itself to some one province of reality. Thus Marx defies classification under any one of the accepted modern specialized headings, such as 'economist', 'sociologist', 'historian', or even 'philosopher'. This, of course, indicates a source of his system's appeal to some modern men in whom the hold of traditional religion has loosened but the craving for an all-inclusive world-view remains alive and strong.

Like the Christian religious system again, Marxism views all existence under the aspect of history; it fundamentally tells a story that has a beginning, middle, and end. 'Theology in the thirteenth century presented the story of man and the world according to the divine plan of salvation', writes Carl Becker. 'It provided the men of that age with an authentic philosophy of history.' And further: 'Paradise lost and paradise regained— such was the theme of the drama of existence as understood in that age. . . . Theology related and expounded the history of the world.'[14] Marx too aims to provide the men of his age with an authentic philosophy of history. His all-inclusive world-view is historical in essence.

The Materialist Conception of History is the matrix of his thought. It is notable that each of his four general formulations of Marxism—in the Paris manuscripts of 1844, in *The German Ideology*, in the *Communist Manifesto*, and in the preface to the *Critique of Political Economy*—takes the shape of an exposition of world history. The notion of a division of the Marxist theoretical structure between a 'dialectical materialism' treating of nature and an 'historical materialism' that applies the laws of dialectical materialism to man's history is utterly foreign to Marx's thought. For him, nature and its transformations belong to the historical process; the comprehensive category is history. The concept of a 'dialectical materialism' dealing with nature apart from human history takes its rise from some of the later writings of Engels. The phrase itself was introduced by the Russian Marxist Georgi Plekhanov.

For Marx, the drama of mankind's historical existence is framed by a temporalized pre-history at one end (primitive communism) and a temporalized post-history at the other (future communism). Communism lost and communism re-gained—such is the plot of world history as he expounds it. Between the one and the other intervenes a series of world-periods stamped with a fundamental antagonism, as are the six successive world-periods of strife between the City of God and the City of Man in Augustine's scheme. And just as Augustine portrays the present as the last of the historical world-periods before the Judgment, so Marx finds that the present bourgeois epoch is the 'closing chapter of the pre-historic stage of human society',[15] the time of the deepest suffering, and the prelude to the final revolution.

Thirdly, there is far more than a formal analogy here. For deeply embedded in Marxism is a theme that corresponds to the master-theme of salvation of the soul in the Christian theology of history. Marx, of course, does not use the word 'salvation'. Yet, he has the concept of a total regeneration of man. In his system, it is the mission of the final revolution to bring about a radical transformation of human nature or 'change of self', whereby man will become a wholly new man. In his later and better known writings he has very little to say in concrete detail about the expected change of self, other than describing it as a change from a condition of 'enslavement' to a new condition of 'freedom'. Nevertheless, the meaning of Marxism turns in a crucial way upon this idea. It is the thread that holds the entire system together.

Man, according to the Christian scheme, exists all through history in the state of sin and is redeemed from it only at the end. According to Marx, man exists all through history in the state of enslavement, and the great change of self—deliverance from enslavement and entry into freedom—occurs only through the revolution with which the present final world-period is scheduled to close. Thus, for Marx the communist revolution is the means of attaining not material abundance (though that, in his view, will come too) and not justice in the distribution of goods, but the spiritual regeneration of man. This he expresses in his 'Theses on Feuerbach'—a set of notes written in 1845 in which he sketched the Materialist Conception of History—by saying that the change of circumstances effected by revolutionary activity will coincide with 'self-change' (*Selbstveränderung*). And in the text of *The German Ideology* he repeats: 'In revolutionary activity, change of self coincides with change of circumstances.'[16] There is no possibility of comprehending the system of Marx at all deeply unless this redemptive idea is seen to lie at the core of it.

A fourth basic characteristic that Marxism has in common with religious systems in general and the medieval Christian system in particular is the 'unity of theory and practice', or the integral relation between the world-view as such and a set of prescriptions for action in accordance with it. Sombart was profoundly mistaken in speaking of the 'purely theoretical character of Marxism'. Marx himself took great pains to point out the contrary. He sharply distinguished Marxism from all merely philosophical systems of thought on the basis of its combined theoretical-practical character. 'The philosophers have only *interpreted* the world in various ways', he declared in the last of the 'Theses on Feuerbach'. 'The point is, to *change* it.'[17]

Although the fact has not been generally recognized, this way of thinking belongs to the religious pattern. It is not as a 'pragmatist' or man of scientific temper that Marx takes issue with the 'contemplative' posture of the philosopher and issues the call for action to change the world. Albeit unwittingly, he does so in the Western religious tradition. Philosophy and science, being activities of inquiry, have no necessary nexus with action, but religion in Western experience generally does. The crux of this connection is the idea of *participation* in the drama of history that the religious system represents as objectively taking place in the world. Thus medieval Christianity did not simply portray existence as a drama of the original fall and ultimate redemption of man. It bid the believer to participate, to contribute his bit by faith and good works to an outcome that was predestined. It was constructed around the idea of the unity of theory and practice in this sense.

This too is the sense in which Marx proclaims the unity of theory and practice. Here the historical process is a revolutionary drama; the way of salvation is the way of revolution. Marxism on the theoretical side is primarily the theory of this revolution. It offers the proof; it presents the world communist revolution as the far-off event towards which the whole history of the world has been moving inexorably ever since the original division of labour, which corresponds to original sin in the Christian scheme. And Marx, although he holds the outcome to be irrevocably predetermined, calls upon the proletarians, Marxism's believers, to participate actively in the process, to shorten the birth-pangs of the new world that is to be inhabited by the new man with the changed self. As in the traditional Christian religious system, a practical injunction is integrally associated with the theoretical credo. It is an injunction to participate in the drama supposed to be in process of enactment in history. Here, of course, the 'good works' are revolutionary works— 'revolutionary praxis' in Marx's own phrase. The way to salvation is revolutionary action to overthrow existing society.

The central task of a critical elucidation of Marxism as a religion of revolution is to clarify the largely hidden master-theme of the system, the idea of a radical 'change of self' that is to be effected through world revolution and the establishment of communism. For this purpose it is necessary to approach the mature Marxian system via an analysis of the original philosophical Marxism, and to examine the latter in its relation to previous German philosophy, particularly that of Hegel. It was not, as we shall see, primarily through the study of economics that Marx was led to his economic interpretation of history; he came to it by the philosophical path. Nor did he derive his notion of the communist revolution of self-change from earlier French and English doctrines of socialism and communism. Marx's doctrine of world revolution and communism has its origins in the movement of modern German philosophy from Immanuel Kant to Ludwig Feuerbach.

Extremely interesting testimony bearing on this essential point was left by Engels in a now generally forgotten early article of 1843, when he and Marx were but slightly acquainted associates in the circle of so-called Young Hegelian intellectuals in Germany. Having just taken up residence in Manchester, where he was to work in the family's firm, Engels wrote the article in his still imperfect English and published it in the Owenite paper *The New Moral World* under the title of 'Progress of Social Reform on the Continent'. Unlike the practically minded English and the politically minded French, it said, the Germans had arrived at communism by the philosophical path. There had recently appeared in Germany a philosophical party of communists, 'unconnected in its origin with either French or English communists and arising from that philosophy which, since the last fifty years Germany has been so proud of'.[18] One of its members was a Dr Marx.

Engels explained further that German philosophy had reached its zenith in the all-embracing system of Hegel, which was invulnerable from without and could only be conquered from within by Hegel's own disciples. Starting as republicans and atheists, some of these 'New Hegelians' had, by 1842, come to the conviction that communism would constitute the fulfillment of Hegelian philosophical principles. Now their task was to demonstrate this fact to the German people:

. . . the Germans are a philosophical nation, and will not, cannot abandon Communism, as soon as it is founded upon sound philosophical principles; chiefly if it is derived as an unavoidable conclusion from their *own* philosophy. And this is the part we have to perform now. Our party has to prove that either all the philosophical efforts of the German nation, from Kant to Hegel, have been useless—worse than useless; or, that they must end in communism; that the Germans must either reject their great philosophers, whose names they hold up as the glory of their nation, or that they must adopt communism.[19]

In the following year, the 'philosophical communism' that Engels here described as the unavoidable outcome of German philosophy received its full elaboration in Marx's first system.

PART I

THE PHILOSOPHICAL
BACKGROUND

I

THE SELF AS GOD IN
GERMAN PHILOSOPHY

All of which is only another way of saying that . . . it is our affair to participate in this redemption by laying aside our immediate subjectivity (putting off the old Adam), and getting to know God as our true and essential self.   HEGEL

The movement of thought from Kant to Hegel revolved in a fundamental sense around the idea of man's self-realization as a godlike being or, alternatively, as God. A radical departure from Western tradition was implicit in this tendency. The centuries-old ruling conception of an unbridgeable chasm of kind between the human and the divine gave way to the conception of a surmountable difference of degree. It is hardly surprising that out of such a revolution of religion there issued, among other things, a religion of revolution.

The image of man striving to realize himself as a godlike being found earlier literary expression in the figure of Goethe's Faust. The Faust of the first part of Goethe's poem is absorbed in 'dreams of godlike knowledge'. He aspires to 'this soaring life, this bliss of godlike birth', and would 'prove in man the stature of a god'. Having become in his imagination a godlike being, the possessor of absolute knowing powers, he feels driven to prove himself in action in this capacity. In order to confirm that he *is* the all-knowing self, he must acquire an infinity of knowledge. The goal is reflected in his complaint to Mephistopheles:

> I have not raised myself one poor degree,
> Nor stand I nearer to infinity.[1]

Faust feels revulsion towards his very learned but withal less than omniscient empirical self; it is alien in its finitude. He must either actualize the exalted image of himself as absolute knower, or else confess his 'kinship with the worm'.

The Faust-theme is pride in the sense of self-glorification and the resulting search for self-aggrandizement to infinity. This is

31

the meaning that will be attached to the term 'pride' in the following pages. It does not refer to ordinary human self-esteem based on actual achievements or potentialities, but to self-deification. This special kind of pride, which may be called 'neurotic', is expressed in a person's creation of an idealized image of himself as a being of godlike perfection, in his presumption that this being represents his real self, and in his attempt to prove it in practice. The word 'godlike' connotes absoluteness, the transcendence of human limitations. The exalted self of the imagination is unlimited in its attributes and powers. It is *all*-good, *all*-knowing, or *all*-powerful, etc., and so may be described as an 'absolute self'.*

Pride may be viewed as a peculiar kind of religious phenomenon, for it involves a worship of the self as the supreme being. The godlike self displaces God. The religions of the Hebraic group (Judaism, Christianity and Islam) have, on this account, condemned pride as the radically faulty tendency in human nature or root of sin. They posit the infinite transcendence or otherness of God as eternally complete and perfect being. Man, by contrast, is understood to be limited and imperfect by nature. Thus, the Bible's myth of the Fall of Man contains the idea that man errs in transgressing the limits of the creature and striving to be 'like God'. This condemnation of pride is a fundamental element in the Hebraic-Christian religious tradition. I take it that Kierkegaard expressed the true sense of this tradition when he wrote: 'God and man are two qualities between which there is an infinite qualitative difference. Every doctrine which overlooks this difference is, humanly speaking, crazy: understood in a godly sense, it is blasphemy.'[2]

In the movement of German thought from Kant to Hegel,

---

* A noted psychiatrist, the late Dr Karen Horney, considers that self-deifying pride is the nucleus of the neurotic type of personality. A person who has been able to find a sense of identity only through pride transfers his energies into the drive to actualize his idealized image of himself; this is what self-realization comes to mean to him. He develops a set of coercive inner dictates by which he seeks to mould himself into the absolute self. Since he is only human, however, the effort necessarily falls short of its goal. A rift opens up in the personality, for the person is conscious of himself as two discordant beings: the god-like being of perfection on the one hand, and the imperfect actual being on the other. He regards the actual or empirical self as an alien being and starts to despise it. The rift in the personality becomes a raging inner conflict: 'And this indeed is the essential characteristic of every neurotic: he is at war with himself' (*Neurosis and Human Growth*, p. 112). Horney uses the phrase 'neurotic process' to describe this entire pattern of self-development growing out of the quest to actualize the superhuman self.

the Faust-theme entered into philosophy. That is, it was generalized. The absolute self was made into an abstract norm of
human nature, and man in general became a neurotic personality. Hegel in particular might be described as a Faust in
philosophical prose, for 'absolute knowledge' is the goal of man
in history as expounded in his *Phenomenology of Mind*. The source
of his doctrine of the absolute self lay in the moral philosophy
of Kant.

[2]

Kant undertakes to expound ethics as a requirement of the
practical reason. The ground of morality is not to be sought
in the 'particular constitution of human nature', but rather in
the formal nature of practical reason conceived in abstraction
from any image of man as man. Nevertheless, behind this façade
of ethical formalism, we find in Kant a conception of morality
as the expression of a compulsion in man to achieve absolute
moral self-perfection.

This theme recurs constantly in his ethical writings. He suggests, for example, that if there were any principle of human
nature which might serve as a respectable basis for moral
theory, it would be the 'ontological conception of *perfection*' or,
alternatively, 'absolute perfection'.[3] In point of fact, the logical
exposition of the categorical imperative coexists in Kantianism
with a doctrine of moral perfectionism. According to Kant,
morality has its theatre of manifestation in the relations between
men. However, the real moral drama is conceived as going on
behind the scenes of the theatre, in each man's relation with
himself in the effort to be absolutely good. We shall be concerned here solely with this psychological side of Kant's moral
philosophy.

He portrays man in a posture of anguished striving to actualize
an image of himself as divinely virtuous. He writes that there
would be no need for morality at all, no obligation or 'moral
compulsion', if man were in actual fact a 'holy being'.[4] This is
a manner of suggesting that morality is the compulsion to
become such a holy being in actual fact. It is a compulsion to
become godlike. For Kant holds that we derive our very conception of God from the idea of absolute moral perfection or
holiness. Yet man, as a merely finite rational being, who is
in part a fallible creature of the senses, cannot achieve holiness

in this life. Hence the moral situation of man assumes in Kant's philosophy the shape of a fundamental dilemma. Morality is man's compulsion to realize himself as a holy being. But his human nature stands in the way of success in this endeavour.

Kant's explanation is that man has a twofold nature, half godly and half human. He is a divided being, a dual personality: *homo noumenon* and *homo phenomenon*. The former is the godlike self of man; the latter, his merely human self. The terminology of this distinction is taken from Kant's epistemological dichotomy of noumenon and phenomenon as reality and appearance. The noumenon is the *Ding-an-sich* or thing as it is in itself. The phenomenon is the thing as it appears. Hence *homo noumenon* is man-in-himself, and *homo phenomenon* is man-as-he-appears. Further, man is conscious of himself in both capacities. He is aware of himself, on the one hand, as 'intelligence' and, on the other hand, as 'an object affected by the senses'. In the former or noumenal capacity, man is his 'real self', whereas, says Kant, 'as human he is only appearance of his self'.[5]

The noumenal 'real self' is a being of godlike moral perfection. In one place Kant describes it as an image that man is forced to form of himself as an 'idealized person'.[6] He claims that this is a requirement of practical reason. Leaving that argument aside for the moment, we may note simply that man, according to Kant, creates an idealized image of himself as absolutely virtuous, and identifies this 'idealized person' as his 'real self'. It becomes, then, the perspective from which he views himself, and the measuring rod by which he judges all his actions and inclinations. He discovers, when he does so, that his phenomenal or empirical self, i.e. the person that he observably is in much of everyday life, fails to conform to the godlike standards of virtue laid down by the noumenal self. He is conscious of himself as a dual self, as two different persons, the ideally perfect person on the one hand and the imperfect creature of the senses on the other. The latter appears as an alien being, a stranger, a 'me' who is not the real 'I'.

There is a war going on inside Kantian man. The moral life is a drama of ceaseless conflict within the dualized personality of the human being who is conscious of himself as half godly and half human. His duty, as he sees it, is to actualize the godlike noumenal self. This means that he must bend the phenomenal self to his moral will to be absolutely good. He must mould the phenomenal self into the being of absolute perfection. He attempts to do this by addressing himself in the stern language of the categorical imperative: Thou shalt be perfect. Morality is the system of commands of this order by which the godlike self in man attempts to compel the merely human self to be perfect. But the human self, *homo phenomenon*, resists the command. And so there arises in man, says Kant, a 'natural dialectic' in which the relentless compulsion to be perfect meets an 'urge to argue against the severe laws of duty and to question their validity'.[7] Sometimes he describes this as a war between duty and inclination. It is the inner conflict engendered by man's striving to actualize in conduct the absolute self. This situation of sharp and unending conflict inside moral man is reflected also in Kant's image of the phenomenon of conscience. He represents it as an internal 'tribunal' before which the idealized person arraigns the phenomenal self for harsh accusation and judgment as transgressor of the dictates of moral perfection.[8] The Kantian conception of the moral life is epitomized in this subjective courtroom scene. The implication is that man, having become in his imagination a being of complete perfection, turns against the imperfect empirical actuality of himself in a fury of self-accusation for violating the norm of holiness, for failure to be perfect.

Kant accepts the fact that there is no possibility of winning the war of the self this side of the grave. The phenomenal self regularly tends to violate the dictates of perfection, and so is always having to be arraigned before the internal tribunal. There is no prospect of completely eliminating the discrepancy between the noumenal and phenomenal selves. The only final victory conceivable is a posthumous victory in the event of personal immortality. Meanwhile, the only possible solution lies in the exertion of the moral will relentlessly toward a *progress* of self-perfection. If man cannot mould his phenomenal self into complete conformity with the idealized person, he can at any rate achieve a closer and closer approximation: 'For a rational but finite being, the only thing possible is an endless progress from the lower to the higher degree of moral perfection.'[9] Kant's solution of the dilemma of the dual self is, then, the idea of an endless progress toward a solution never to be reached. It is the idea of a process of infinite self-perfecting.

This doctrine yields the notion that freedom is inner bondage or successful self-coercion. Kant argues that man is unfree when subjected to coercion from without, or when he follows his spontaneous inclinations. He is free, on the other hand, when he acts under compulsion of the moral will to be perfect. Freedom means 'autonomy of the will', a condition in which man is subject to no outside commands but issues the moral law to himself. This is what Kant calls self-determination to action, which is his formula for freedom. The essential point is that self-determination means for Kant determination by the noumenal self. And this, as we have seen, is compulsive; it is a question of self-coercion to be perfect. Kant therefore not only admits, but continually insists upon, the identity of freedom and internal compulsion. He writes, for example: 'The less a man can be physically forced, and the more he can be morally forced (by the mere idea of duty), so much the freer he is.' He speaks too of 'free self-constraint'.[10]

According to this view, a man is never so free as when he acts under the greatest sense of inner bondage, self-constraint, compulsion. It is only when he feels morally driven to do something, when he experiences it as compulsory and himself as a slave to the self-imposed command to do it, that he is free at all. The soul of moral man becomes, therefore, a kind of dictatorship of the moral 'ought'. Kant himself calls it an 'autocracy'.[11] Man is free, he contends, in so far as he identifies himself with the internal autocratic authority (i.e. the noumenal self) and compels himself to obey all its perfectionist dictates. He is free in so far as he submits willingly to the internal autocratic order, unfree in so far as he acts in accordance with mere impulses or desires. There is an interesting analogy between this position and that of the political dictator who claims that his authoritarianism is the 'highest form of freedom' and that there is no real freedom in a democracy, where everyone does as he pleases.

[3]

A critique of Kant's position might well start at this point. Something is radically wrong with a doctrine which tells us that the more compulsive a person's conduct is, the freer he is, that life in a subjective autocracy of the moral 'ought' is the true life of freedom. Such a doctrine does violence to our understanding of freedom by divorcing it from the experience of freedom.

This is no less foreign to a subjective feeling of compulsiveness or involuntariness than it is to a sense of acting under compulsion of an external force or authority. Absence of compulsiveness is the basic mark of the experience of freedom. It is the experience of spontaneity in activity, of voluntariness, of not being coerced by anyone, including one's self.

Kant's perversion of the idea of freedom is a logical consequence of his identification of *homo noumenon* as the real self of man. We may agree with him that self-determination to action is the correct general formula for freedom, but there is a hidden corollary: the determining self must be a possible self. It must represent, in other words, a set of authentic potentialities of the individual, and thus be a self whose realization lies within the realm of genuine possibility. Only if this essential condition is met can man know the experience of freedom as spontaneous self-expression in activity. The experience of voluntariness in action is given only to the person who is giving expression to *himself*.

When, on the other hand, the self with which a man identifies himself is a godlike being of perfection, the experience of freedom evaporates and his actions are performed under an inner compulsion. For such a self is not a possible self. As Kant himself admits, it is not a self that any mere human being could ever really be or become. A man cannot become an impossible superhuman absolute self, but he can force himself to try and coerce himself endlessly in the attempt. This is what Kant pictures him as doing, and the logical but fallacious conclusion is that freedom means successful self-coercion. Kantian man cannot spontaneously (freely) determine himself to action in the capacity of *homo noumenon*; he can only strive to *compel* himself to action in this capacity. All his actions become compulsive.

The subjective system of bondage which may arise in man as a consequence is sharply etched in Kant's picture of the autocracy of the moral will to perfection. Although it is not his conscious intention to do so, he shows that self-glorification leads to the formation in man of a pride system that becomes autonomous and exerts, through its coercive imperatives, a tyrannical power over the individual. An internal 'autocracy' emerges. The individual becomes a subject of the godlike noumenal self in him which imperiously orders: Thou shalt comply with my standards of absolute perfection or else suffer torments of self-accusation for violating them. All his energies are canalized into the ceaseless effort to comply with the dictates of the internal autocracy. This is a system of slavery far more complete and severe than any external political autocracy. The human being becomes the slave of the force of pride that has arisen and grown autonomous within him. Kant's representation of this subjective system of bondage is drawn with great psychological accuracy. His error is a philosophical one. It expresses itself in the fact that he calls this bondage 'freedom'.

The error in his conception of freedom is only a manifestation of the deeper error in his conception of man. He maintains that practical reason compels man to form a picture of himself as a being of godlike perfection and to regard this 'idealized person' as his 'real self'. It seems, on the contrary, that reason cautions against this, and that pride is the force that leads man to reach out for the infinite and absolute, to confuse humanity in his own person with divinity. This *hubris* is the pathology of human selfhood. Man falsifies his identity as finite man when he arrogates to himself absolute attributes and powers. The absolute self that he becomes in his imagination is necessarily a pseudo-self, i.e. a self impossible of realization. In the attempt to realize the unrealizable, he necessarily becomes divided against himself. His soul becomes the arena of a war between *homo noumenon* and *homo phenomenon*. Pride dualizes man, and initiates a destructive conflict within him. Kant's image of self-divided man is a vivid if unwitting illustration of this fact.

Kant's philosophy transformed what had always been regarded as the radical fault in man, the pathology of selfhood, into a universal norm. It identified the neurotic personality as the normal man, and pride as the requirement of 'reason'. The consequences of this momentous step were reflected in the further development of German philosophy in the systems of Kant's immediate successors, Fichte and Hegel in particular. Here we encounter an exuberant affirmation of pride. The apotheosis of the human self that Kant had adumbrated was taken as the revelation of a great truth. The noumenal self was accepted as the authentic essence of man, and the urge to demonstrate its actualization became a driving force of philosophical thought. The field of its actualization was extended from the life-history of the self-deifying individual to the life-history of the human race. Man's self-realization as a godlike being became the theme of a philosophy of history. Hegelianism was the high point of this development.

[4]

In a letter to Schelling in 1795, the twenty-five-year old theology student Hegel declared that a great new creative movement was to grow out of the Kantian philosophy, and that the central idea in the movement would be the doctrine of the absolute and infinite self. In a series of unpublished writings of these early years,* Hegel groped toward the formula that would serve as the lever of this creative transformation of Kantianism. He found it at a time of acute spiritual crisis in his life, the year 1800, and then set about the elaboration of his vast system. The traditional distinction between theoretical and practical philosophy faded away in this system, which can best be described as a philosophical religion of self in the form of a theory of history. The religion is founded on an identification of the self with God.

In the first of the somewhat misnamed *Early Theological Writings*, Hegel makes a savage assault upon historical Christianity as a corruption of the teaching of Jesus. Jesus, in turn, is pictured as an exponent of Kantian self-perfection. More Kantian than Kant, Hegel has interpreted Kant's moral philosophy in religious terms. In the doctrine of *homo noumenon* he has found a 'virtue religion' of man's self-actualization as a divinely perfect being. The essence of this religion is that it locates God within man. Regarding Jesus as the teacher of such a religion, Hegel argues that his true message was lost when Christianity arose as a 'positive religion' founded on institutionalized authority and a dogmatic theology.

Hegel's objection to the Christian theology is that it severed human nature from the divine, allowing no mediation between the two save in 'one isolated individual' and reducing man's consciousness of the divine to the 'dull and killing belief in a superior Being altogether alien to man'. God, he says, was placed in another world, to which man contributed nothing by his activity, but into which, at best, he could beg or conjure his way. Man, in his misery, 'objectified' his own absolute self as an external deity:

* A collection of these writings was published in 1907. The title *Early Theological Writings* was bestowed upon them by their German editor, Hermann Nohl.

The despotism of the Roman princes had hounded the spirit of man from the face of the earth; deprived of freedom, he was forced to let that which was eternal in him, his absolute, flee into the deity; and the spread of misery forced him to seek and expect blessedness in heaven. The objectification of the deity went hand in hand with the corruption and slavery of man, and it is actually only a revelation and a manifestation of this spirit of the times.[12]

Jesus, according to Hegel, was one of those exceptional Jewish personalities 'who could not deny their feeling of selfhood or stoop to become lifeless machines or men of a maniacally servile disposition'. However, his new teaching was transformed by 'Jewish intellects' into 'something which they could slavishly serve. . . . Out of what Jesus said, out of what he suffered in his person, they soon fashioned rules and moral commands, and free emulation of their teacher soon passed over into slavish service of their Lord.'[13]

So ends Hegel's essay on 'The Positivity of the Christian Religion', written in 1795. In 'The Spirit of Christianity', probably written in 1799, he adumbrates his own new religion. Here, for the first time, he *contrasts* Jesus with Kant. He protests against what he calls the 'self-coercion of Kantian virtue'. Kant had remarked that there was no real difference in principle between the Shaman and the European prelate, between the Voguls and the Puritans, since all alike were obeying positive authorities, external commands, and not commands issued by man to himself. To this Hegel replies that 'the former have their lord outside themselves, while the latter carries his lord in himself, yet at the same time is his own slave.' The 'human being's division against himself' remains in force. Hegel is saying, in effect, that Kant has an erroneous conception of freedom as internal bondage, and that he offers no way out of the predicament of dual selfhood. Jesus, on the other hand, was 'a spirit raised above morality'.[14] Hegel sees in him a solution to the dilemma posed by Kant's image of man divided against himself and self-enslaved.

The question, he goes on, is whether man should put the divine *wholly* outside himself. The intellect does so, positing two natures of different kinds, a human nature and a divine one, each with personality and substantiality. It sees an absolute difference of essences. Hegel comments scornfully that the Jews took this 'intellectualistic point of view' when they refused to recognize the divinity of the man Jesus, to accept the fact that 'though born a man he made himself God'. He continues:

How were *they* to recognize divinity in a man, poor things that they were, possessing only a consciousness of their misery, of the depth of their servitude, of their opposition to the divine, of an impassable gulf between the being of God and the being of men? Spirit alone recognizes spirit. . . . The lion has no room in a nest, the infinite spirit none in the prison of a Jewish soul, the whole of life none in a withering leaf. The hill and the eye which sees it are object and subject, but between man and God, between spirit and spirit, there is no such cleft of objectivity and subjectivity; one is to the other an other only in that one recognizes the other; both are one.[15]

Hegel sees in the figure of Jesus a paradigm of the solution for the Kantian dilemma. To him, this figure is not God become man, but man become God. This is the key idea on which the entire edifice of Hegelianism was to be constructed: there is no absolute difference between the human nature and the divine. They are not two separate things with an impassable gulf between them. The absolute self in man, the *homo noumenon,* is not merely godlike, as Kant would have it; *it is God.* Consequently, in so far as man strives to become 'like God', he is simply striving to be his own real self. And in deifying himself, he is simply recognizing his own true nature. Such recognition is preceded by 'faith', which is a middle state between non-recognition and recognition of the self as divine; it is a 'trust in one's self'. Beyond it lies full scale recognition, 'when divinity has pervaded all the threads of one's consciousness, directed all one's relations with the world, and now breathes throughout one's being'.[16]

In 1800, shortly after making this 'breakthrough', Hegel wrote another essay of which we have only a short fragment ('Fragment of a System'). Here he no longer opposes the virtue religion of human self-worship to traditional theology. The reason is that by this time he has brought the concepts of man and God into the dialectical fusion just explained. Having supplanted the objectionable separation of man and deity with the idea of a dynamic unity of the two, he now proclaims as his own the point of view of 'religion', for which he offers the following formula: 'This self-elevation of man from finite to infinite life, is religion.'[17] In other words, religion is the action by which man elevates himself to the plane of divine life, realizes himself as God. We find a marvellously vivid metaphorical representation of this thought in a separate contemporaneous fragment of Hegel's:

If a spectator visits a temple and without any feeling of piety, regards it purely as a building, it may fill him with a sense of sublimity; but then its walls are too narrow for him. He tries to give himself space by stretching his arms and raising his head to infinity. The confines of the building which had roused the sense of sublimity thus lose their importance for him and he demands something more, namely, infinity.[18]

The essence of the Hegelian idea is revealed in this metaphor. The image of the man who finds the temple too small is a symbolic expression of Hegel's own rebellion against a religion that sets the Supreme Being above and beyond man. Hegel is the spectator who tries to give himself 'space' by raising his head to infinity. He feels driven to recognize God in his own person. A religion that makes God an other is intolerably confining to him. It conflicts with his urge to soar into the unlimited, to reach out in his own person for the absolute and the infinite, to make *himself* God. He finds that the only religion which can satisfy the grandiose urge and claim is a religion of the self as God, a religion which holds, in the words Hegel was to employ in his *Phenomenology*, that 'The Self is Absolute Being'.[19] This is the religion that he soon began to call 'philosophy'.

It hardly needs to be emphasized that an intensely personal drama was reflected in all this. Hegel had set out in search of a lever for the creative transformation of Kantianism. He wanted to overcome philosophically the predicament of dual selfhood in which Kant had left man. But it was by no means a purely intellectual impulse that drove him to the effort; powerful emotional forces were involved. Hegel himself was in the predicament of dual selfhood. He was engaged in a war of the self similar to the one represented in the Kantian philosophy, save that in Hegel the urge to be godlike expressed itself in a quest not for moral holiness but for omniscience, absolute knowledge. Consequently, the search for a solution for the Kantian philosophical dilemma was simultaneously a search for a solution for the Hegelian personal dilemma. Commenting on the 'Fragment of a System', Richard Kroner observes that here 'a triumphant victory was won over the powers about to destroy the unity of Hegel as a person', and he adds: 'The struggle of his life was directed toward an inner peace that would satisfy reason and soul by a gigantic metaphysical conception.'[20]

The image of the man who lifts his head through the temple to infinity reveals both the meaning of the gigantic metaphysical conception that Hegel created and the nature of the terms on which he found peace with himself: he had conceived himself as the particular man in whom God—the absolute self—finally achieves full actualization. God had come to himself completely in the philosophical person of Hegel. When he undertook to elaborate the doctrine of his philosophical religion of self, Hegel found different ways of formulating this crucial point. In 1801–2, he wrote a preliminary sketch of the future system, at the close of which 'The theoretical Ego finds itself as the Supreme Being'.[21] A few years later he presented the system again in the *Phenomenology*, which closes with 'spirit knowing itself as spirit' in the form of philosophical science or 'absolute knowledge'. As we have seen, 'spirit knowing itself as spirit' is a formula that Hegel earlier evolved for man's self-recognition as the divine being.

He began with a scornful rejection of Christianity as a religion for slaves, and dismissed its theology as erroneous through and through. Now, however, he speaks in the accents of a theologian. He adopts an attitude of benevolent condescension toward traditional or 'revealed' religion. He assimilates the conventional religious consciousness into his scheme of history as an anticipation in figurative form of the ultimate religious moment that is reached when the philosophical mind attains absolute knowledge in Hegelianism. Many students of Hegel have assumed, therefore, that Hegelianism, as Kroner puts it, is 'Christianity spelt by dialectic'.[22] They have treated Hegel as an unusual kind of Christian religious philosopher.

But if we assume that the condemnation of pride is basic to the Christian position, then Hegelianism must be pronounced radically anti-Christian. It is a religion of self-worship whose fundamental theme is given in Hegel's image of the man who aspires to be God himself, who demands 'something more, namely, infinity'. The whole system is spun out of the formula concerning man's self-elevation from finite to infinite life. The finite mind is seen as aggrandizing itself to infinity, becoming universal mind. Hegelianism is, therefore, a colossal embodiment and rationalization of pride. Hegel frankly recognizes this fact. For example, when he comments in his *Logic* on the myth of the Fall of Man, he says that man, having originally lost his harmony through the overweening desire to become like God in knowledge, must achieve a 'second harmony' through the philosophical quest for absolute knowledge. By pride he fell; by pride he shall rise again: 'The hand that inflicts the wound is also the hand that heals it.'[23] Consequently, the Fall of Man becomes an incident, as it were, of the Fall of God, and man's subsequent striving to realize himself as God is simply God's way of coming back to himself out of what Hegel calls his 'alienation'. Hegelianism carried the principle of pride to the final point of consummation in thought. It is pride become theological. It is the theology of a religion in which the self is apprehended as God.

II

HISTORY AS GOD'S
SELF-REALIZATION

Of the Absolute it must be said that it is essentially a result, that only at the end is it what it is in very truth . . . HEGEL

Hegel often remarks in his later writings that philosophy is circular, that it presupposes its beginning and reaches its beginning only at the end. This circularity is visible not only in the world process as projected in Hegel's philosophy. The procedure that he followed in the construction of the system shows it as well. He began by identifying man, in his own philosophical person, with God, and his system represents a prodigious effort to regain his starting point, i.e. to show God as coming to himself finally in Hegelianism.

Kant's system of theoretical philosophy was designed to answer the question: how are synthetic *a priori* judgments possible? The comparable underlying question for Hegel's philosophical religion of self would be: how was it possible for God to emerge into full and clear self-consciousness in my mind? The question demanded, in answer, a theory of history as the self-realization of God. Hegel's great 'breakthrough' would be seen in this theory as the event toward which Creation had been moving from the outset. He would regain his starting point, philosophically speaking, by exhibiting it as the culminating moment of the history of the world conceived as the autobiography of a God-in-the-making. This was the purpose of his greatest work, the *Phenomenology of Mind*.* The following exposi-

---

* A. O. Lovejoy discusses the idea of a God-in-the-making or 'evolutionary theology' as a tendency of German thought in the first decade of the nineteenth century. He singles out Schelling and Oken as exponents of this tendency. In 1809, Schelling advocated the idea of a 'humanly suffering God'. In 1810, Oken wrote of the temporal *Realwerden* of God in man. Thus, says Lovejoy, 'God himself was temporalized' (*The Great Chain of Being*, pp. 317, 318, 320–1). Hegel receives no mention in this context. It ought to be pointed out, however, that the *Phenomenology* (1807) was an earlier and also systematically elaborated expression of the 'evolutionary theology'.

tion of Hegelianism is based primarily upon this work, although it draws freely upon Hegel's later writings for clarification or amplification of various points.

A philosophy of God's self-realization in history involves a fundamental recasting of the concept of the Deity as found in the Hebraic-Christian theology. There is no question of the Hebraic-Christian God's actualization of himself, for he is, by definition, fully actualized or perfect being *ab initio*. Accordingly, Hegel rejects the traditional notion of God. He writes in his *Logic*, for example, that it is a great error to view God as eternally complete and perfect being to the exclusion of all 'negation', and to relegate him in this way to 'another world beyond'. Of such a God he remarks acidly: 'Mere light is mere darkness.'[1] To it he opposes a God who has his being *in* the world and must *actualize* himself as God. Only at the end, he says, does the Absolute become fully itself. The history of the world is the process by which God becomes fully God.

Marvellously intricate in its elaboration, this fundamental idea of the Hegelian system is quite simple in its logical structure. By Hegel's definition, God is not fully God until he *knows* himself to be God; self-knowledge or self-consciousness in this specific sense belongs to the nature, essence, or 'concept' of God. At the outset of creation, moreover, he lacks the requisite self-consciousness: God is God, but is not yet conscious of himself as such. Hence, the historical process of God's self-realization is essentially a knowing process. Hegel calls it the 'process of becoming in terms of knowledge'.[2]

Further, the organ of God's slowly growing consciousness of himself as God is the mind of man. God passes from primal unconsciousness in the form of nature to ultimate self-consciousness in the person of historical man. The 'phenomenology of mind', or progress of human knowledge in the course of history, is God's passage to self-knowledge. The self-cognitive journey has its final destination in 'absolute knowledge', which is God's completed consciousness of himself and therefore actualization of himself in the mind of the philosopher. As Hegel summarizes the position: 'God is God only so far as he knows himself; his self-knowledge is, further, his self-consciousness in man, and man's knowledge *of* God, which proceeds to man's self-knowledge in God.'[3]*

* W. T. Stace writes that 'we must not jump to the preposterous conclusion that,

[2]

According to Hegel, God is absolute and infinite being, the whole of reality, the All (*das Ganze*). He is all that ever has been and is, including nature spread out in space and civilization unfolding in historical time. Nature is God in his spatial extension; history is God in his temporal development. Beyond nature and history, nothing is. From the standpoint of the Hebraic-Christian theology, which places God above and beyond nature and history, this would of course have to be qualified as 'atheism'. But Hegel himself does not so view it. He considers it to be the valid philosophical or 'speculative' understanding of the Christian theological position.

For him, God and the world are one. Otherwise expressing it, the world is a divine personality or world-self. Hegel's special term for the world-self is *Weltgeist* or simply *Geist*, which is usually rendered into English as 'spirit' or 'mind'. It must always be borne in mind, however, that what he means by *Geist* is an infinite, all-embracing self or *subjective being* that is motivated by the urge and need to become conscious of itself as a world-self. As he puts it, 'substance is essentially subject'. Alternatively: 'Spirit is alone reality. It is the inner being of the world, that which essentially is and is *per se*.'[4] And he repeatedly points out that he uses the term *Geist* as a synonym for God.

In order for spirit to become conscious of itself, it must express itself, assume various concrete objective forms. It must put itself forth as substance in order to become conscious of this substance as itself: 'Substance, *qua* subject, involves the necessity, at first an *inner* necessity, to set forth in itself what it inherently is, to show itself to be spirit.'[5] Accordingly, Hegel endows the world-self not only with the urge to self-knowledge but also with the capacity for creative self-expression. Thus he speaks of it as 'manifesting, developing and perfecting its powers in every direction which its manifold nature can follow. What powers it inherently possesses, we learn from the variety of products and formations which it originates.'[6]

In effect, Hegel assigns to the world-self the divine creativity

according to Hegel's philosophy, I, this particular human spirit, am the Absolute, nor that the Absolute is any particular spirit, nor that it is humanity in general. Such conclusions would be little short of shocking' (*The Philosophy of Hegel*, p. 118). This might be described as an argument from propriety. It is not clear, however, why we must assume that Hegel could not be 'shocking'.

that the traditional theology assigns to its other-worldly God as the creator of the world. However, there is a serious difference. Whereas the God of traditional theology creates the world out of a selfless overflowing benevolence, the Hegelian world-self's creativity serves its self-centred need to become conscious of itself as a world-self. This is, for Hegel, the explanation for the existence of the world and all that has ever happened in it: 'Itself is its own object of attainment and the sole aim of spirit. This result it is, at which the process of the world's history has been continually aiming; and to which the sacrifices that have ever and anon been laid on the vast altar of the earth, through the long lapses of ages, have been offered.'[7]

Thus, spirit's creativity is a creativity of self-production generated by its need to know itself. It is 'plastic activity' by which spirit objectifies itself, much as an actor might be said to objectify himself in his role or a sculptor in his statue: 'The very essence of spirit is activity; it realizes its potentiality—makes itself its own deed, its own work—and thus it becomes an object to itself; contemplates itself as an objective existence.'[8] The term that Hegel characteristically uses for this productive activity of spirit is 'self-externalization' (*Selbstentäusserung*).

The two spheres of spirit's self-externalization are nature and history. It externalizes itself in space as the world of nature, and in time as the succession of civilizations or culture-worlds that rise and fall by human agency in the long sequence of history. The creative self-externalization of spirit as nature corresponds to the original act of world-creation as represented in the traditional theological system. For Hegel, however, the creativity of man in history is the *continuation* of the original creative act by which nature, together with man, came into being. In the realm of history, spirit's creativity is expressed in the activities by which the successively dominant or 'world-historical' nations—*Völkergeister*—produce their cultures. This too is an activity of world-creation. For each of the great historical civilizations from the ancient Orient to modern Europe represents, in its coherent totality of institutions, way of life and ideas, a particular avenue of expression of the manifold creative potentialities of spirit; it is a *world* of culture.

Nature and man are, therefore, the two different grades of spirit. Nature is externalized spirit that is unconscious of itself as spirit; it is the 'unconscious'. Man, on the other hand, is spirit in the act of becoming conscious of itself as spirit. As a builder of civilizations, a creator of culture-worlds, he is spirit in the historical continuation of its creative, self-externalizing phase. But in his capacity of knower, he is spirit on the path of self-discovery. His mind, and particularly his religious and philosophical mind, is the organ of the world's emergent consciousness of itself as a subjective being. But inasmuch as this long remains an incomplete, limited consciousness, Hegel defines man as 'finite self-conscious spirit'.

In the process of becoming in terms of knowledge, finite self-conscious spirit overcomes its finitude and rises to the plane of absolute self-conscious spirit, or fully actualized God. The urge to self-knowledge, which was the unconscious motivation of the original act of world-creation when spirit externalized itself as nature, becomes in history a conscious desire in the mind of man. As Hegel describes it, moreover, this desire to know is no mere idle curiosity or Platonic wonder but a monstrous and insatiable lust of knowledge. It is a craving in man to pierce the seeming objectivity of the world that confronts him, and grasp it as subjective in nature: 'The aim of knowledge is to divest the objective world that stands opposed to us of its strangeness, and, as the phrase is, to find ourselves at home in it: which means no more than to trace the objective world back to the notion—to our innermost self.'[9]

[3]

If the creative activity of spirit is an activity of self-externalization, by which it takes on objective form, the cognitive activity that goes on in the mind of man is spirit's repossession of itself in consciousness. Knowing is spirit's means of reintegration or 'return to itself' out of the state of self-division that obtains when spirit as conscious subject (man) is confronted with spirit as external object (the world). Hegel calls this state 'self-alienation' or 'self-estrangement'. (*Selbstentfremdung*). The subject-object relation *per se* is one of spirit's self-alienation. In the subject-object relation spirit apprehends itself as 'otherness' (*Anderssein*). According to Hegel, this means that the object is experienced as an alien and hostile being, as something that stands opposed to the conscious subject. Knowing activity, by which the objective world is divested of its strangeness, is the overcoming of alienation.

It is interesting to note the structural analogy between Kant's picture of self-divided man and Hegel's picture of self-alienated spirit. Kantian man, conceiving himself to be in reality a holy being, the personification of moral perfection, experiences his imperfect phenomenal self or human appearance of himself as an offensive stranger, a 'me' who is not the true 'I'. The phenomenal self does not correspond to his idealized image of himself, his conception of the person that he really is. In precisely the same way, Hegel represents spirit as a dual personality in the knowing situation. As object to itself or otherness, spirit does not correspond to its concept of itself. In Hegel's special terminology, which is a direct outgrowth of Kant's, spirit is one thing inherently or 'in itself' (*an sich*) and something else again in its phenomenal appearance to itself or 'for itself' (*für sich*). 'In itself' it is a self, a subjective being; 'for itself', an object, 'other' or nonself.

Thus, the Kantian dichotomy of *homo noumenon* and *homo phenomenon* reappears in Hegelianism writ large as a dichotomy of noumenal world-self and phenomenal world-self. The division of Kantian man against himself in the quest for moral perfection has turned into spirit's division against itself, or self-alienation, in the quest for self-knowledge. And just as Kant pictures the divided man as being at war with himself in the effort to eliminate the discrepancy between the two selves, so Hegel represents self-alienated spirit as locked in conflict with itself: 'Thus spirit is at war with itself; it has to overcome itself as its most formidable obstacle. That development which in the sphere of nature is a peaceful growth, is in that of spirit, a severe, a mighty conflict with itself. What spirit really strives for is the realization of its Ideal being. . . . Its expansion, therefore, does not present the harmless tranquillity of mere growth, as does that of organic life, but a stern reluctant working against itself.'[10] In short, Hegel's world-self is a neurotic personality.

Beyond this point, however, the parallel between Kant and Hegel ceases and the differences begin. Kantian man is bent on the achievement of absolute moral virtue, and the field of the striving is his relations with other men. The self-alienation of Hegelian spirit, on the other hand, has nothing to do with morality in Kant's sense; the pride of virtue has given way to the pride of knowledge. Although it is indeed *in* man that spirit experiences its self-alienation, the conflict is no longer a conflict of man with himself in the understanding of 'himself' that Kant's view exemplifies.

In Hegel's system, the alien phenomenal self has become an alien world. On occasion he calls it a 'perverted world' (*verkehrte Welt*).[11] The image of man against himself has now turned into an image of man against the world. The world-self as conscious subject beholds, in nature and the successive worlds of culture, the world-self as alien object. And spirit's war against itself is expressed in man's ceaseless endeavour to conquer cognitively a world experienced as alien and hostile in its objectivity. Its struggle toward self-realization is a mighty battle of the human mind to re-internalize the world in thought. As Hegel puts it: 'The tendency of all man's endeavours is to understand the world, to appropriate and subdue it to himself; and to this end the positive reality of the world must be as it were crushed and pounded, in other words, idealized.'[12]

Thus, Hegelian knowing means self-discovery, whereby spirit in a given conscious subject comes to recognize itself in what had appeared to be a world apart from it. Knowing is the de-alienation of the external world, which (by Hegel's definition) is a product of spirit's own activity of self-externalization. To spirit become conscious in man, it at first presents the appearance of being simply 'substance', object or non-self. But its substantiality, its apparent otherness or objectivity, is illusory. The consciousness of the given objective world as something other than self is an 'untrue consciousness'.[13] The act of knowing is the piercing of the illusion of otherness. It strips the object of its alien objectivity, and the false consciousness of the object as 'other' gives way to a true consciousness of it as 'self-ish' (*selbstisch*).

Hegel's technical term for this metamorphosis that the object undergoes through the act of knowing is *Aufhebung*, which may be translated as 'transcendence'. He emphasizes that transcendence has the twofold connotation of destruction and preservation. The transcended or *aufgehoben* object has been destroyed *qua* object or 'other' but preserved as mental content. The transcended objective world is, in other words, a de-alienated one. Moreover, the act of knowing is a transcendence of the subject-object relation as one of spirit's self-alienation. It transforms the subject-object relation into a subject-subject relation wherein spirit has only *self* before it in consciousness, having recognized the objective world as externalized spirit.

Spirit is now 'at home with itself in its otherness'. The object has been 'mediated' by the understanding, and spirit has returned to itself out of the state of self-alienation. It has become spirit *for* as well as *in* itself, since the world before it in consciousness is recognized as an externalized self. Spirit has shown itself— or at any rate that part of itself comprised in the given phenomenal world—to be spirit. It now knows that 'What seems to take place outside it, to be an activity directed against it, is its own doing, its own activity; and substance shows that it is in reality subject.'[14] Spirit, however, enters into a new state of self-division and alienation when a new culture-world arises through the next historic act of spirit's self-externalization, and this calls forth a fresh effort of reintegration through knowing. The new historical formation requires to be grasped, recognized as spirit, and thus transcended in thought. History comprises the entire aggregate of such cycles of spirit's externalization, alienation, and transcendence of the alienation by the act of knowing.

[4]

The psychology of Hegelian spirit still remains unclarified in one critically important aspect. Hegel makes out the subject-object relation as such to be a relation of estrangement. But it is not immediately evident why it should be so experienced. It is not clear why man as self-conscious spirit should apprehend the objective world as alien and hostile in its very objectivity. Why does spirit experience 'what seems to take place outside it' as 'an activity directed against it'? The question directs attention to spirit's image of itself, which Hegel calls its 'concept' (*Begriff*). Like Kantian man, the Hegelian knowing subject is an absolute self in his image or idea of himself. The definition of absoluteness has, however, undergone a change. Kantian man's absolute self is a moral absolute; it is the image of the self as a morally perfect being. The absolute self of the Hegelian knower, on the other hand, is an ontological absolute. It is an image of the self as God, and God, as we have seen, is defined by Hegel as absolute and infinite *being*, the whole of reality.

This is the central point for an understanding of Hegel's view of the experience of alienation. It explains why the conscious

subject apprehends the objective world confronting it in consciousness as an alien and hostile world. Hegel points out that
'an object means a something else, a negative confronting me'.[15]
Given the conscious subject's idea of itself as absolute being or
das Ganze, a 'something else' cannot but be experienced as a
'negative' or hostile being, an enemy to be assailed and destroyed.
For it *negates* the absoluteness of the knower. Otherness as such
is an intolerable affront to Hegelian spirit, a mortal challenge
to its idea of itself. The apprehension of a 'something else' is by
implication an apprehension of the self as non-absolute, and
this can only be, in Hegel's famous phrase in the *Phenomenology*,
an 'unhappy consciousness' of self-estrangement. In so far as a
'something else' independently subsists, the world contains
something other than the knowing subject, and the subject is
not the whole, not infinite being—or at any rate is not conscious
of itself as such. This is what makes the object *qua* object a
'negative', and gives it an alien and hostile appearance to
Hegelian spirit.

For Hegel alienation is finitude, and finitude in turn is
bondage. The experience of self-estrangement in the presence
of an apparent objective world is an experience of enslavement.
The logic of this proposition follows from what has already
been said. Spirit, when confronted with an object or 'other', is
ipso facto aware of itself as merely finite being, as embracing
only so much and no more of reality, as extending only so far
and no farther. The object is, therefore, a 'limit' (*Grenze*). And a
limit, since it contradicts spirit's notion of itself as absolute being,
i.e. being-without-limit, is necessarily apprehended as a 'barrier'
or 'fetter' (*Schranke*). It is a barrier to spirit's awareness of itself
as that which it conceives itself truly to be—the whole of reality.
In its confrontation with an apparent object, spirit feels impris-
oned in limitation. It experiences what Hegel calls the 'sorrow
of finitude'.[16]

The transcendence of the object through knowing is spirit's
way of rebelling against finitude and making the break for
freedom. In Hegel's quite unique conception of it, freedom
means the consciousness of self as unbounded; it is the absence of
a limiting object or non-self. As he states in his *Logic*, 'freedom
means that the object with which you deal is a second self. . . .
For freedom it is necessary that we should feel no presence of
something which is not ourselves.'[17] The presence of 'something

which is not ourselves' is imprisonment in finitude. The transformation of it into a 'second self' through the act of knowing,
which divests the object of its illusory objectivity and shows it
to be *selbstisch* in nature, is release from finitude. It yields a consciousness of self as unbounded by any object, hence as infinite
in extent. The knowing self now stands alone with itself in the
universe, unopposed by any alien seeming non-self. This consciousness of 'being alone with self' (*Bei-sich-selbst-sein*)[18] is
precisely what Hegel means by the consciousness of freedom.
And on this basis he speaks of the cognitive enterprise in a
wonderfully vivid metaphor as 'that voyage into the open, where
nothing is below us or above us, and we stand in solitude with
ourselves alone'.[19]

Accordingly, the growth of spirit's self-knowledge in history
is alternatively describable as a progress of the consciousness of
freedom. This is the formula that Hegel uses in his lectures on
the philosophy of history. But it must be understood that
'being alone with self' is his definition of the consciousness of
freedom. Whereas Western philosophers have generally regarded
solipsism, or the state of being the only existent thing, as a predicament to be avoided if possible, a condition from which it is
desirable to extricate oneself at the outset of philosophizing, it
is for Hegel the philosophical goal and ideal. Ultimate freedom
is the awareness of the self as infinite being. This conception of
freedom excludes the possibility that more than one being could
become fully free.

The student of Hegel who fails to grasp this peculiar Hegelian
notion of freedom may wrongly infer from his frequent use of
the term that he is a 'philosopher of freedom' in some one of the
generally accepted meanings of the word. Those who make this
error have often supported it by referring to Hegel's well known
dictum: 'The East knew and to the present day knows that *One*
is free; the Greek and Roman world that *some* are free; the German world knows that *All* are free.'[20] But Hegel proceeds at this
point to explain that monarchy (in the Prussian form) is the
system under which '*All* are free'. The individual subjects are
accorded a merely vicarious experience of freedom in so far as
they consciously merge their being into that of the authoritarian
state, which is the divine substance. They are free only as self-
conscious particles of this substance.

Hegel's conception of freedom is totalitarian in a literal sense of the word. The world-self must experience itself as the totality of being, or in Hegel's own words must elevate itself to 'a self-comprehending *totality*',[21] in order to achieve the consciousness of freedom. Anything short of this spells alienation and the sorrow of finitude. As Hegel writes, 'until and unless spirit inherently completes itself, completes itself as a world spirit, it cannot reach its completion as self-conscious spirit'.[22] Spirit must apprehend itself as absolute being, as *das Ganze*, in order to experience freedom in the consciousness of itself as that which it really is. This is what Hegel means by spirit completing itself as a *Weltgeist*.

The final breakthrough to infinity occurs at the moment of the history of the world when 'absolute knowledge' arises in the mind of the philosopher in the form of 'philosphical science'. On Hegel's postulate, spirit has now exhausted its creative potentialities of self-externalization. It has assumed all the objective world-forms that it has the power to assume, and transcended them all in successive historic acts of knowing. Absolute knowledge, or 'spirit knowing itself as spirit', is the world-self's knowledge of itself as absolute being. And absolute knowledge is embodied in Hegelianism, which comprises the scientific demonstration that the self is absolute being and comes to know itself as such in the history of the world.

This is the point in time at which God becomes fully God. For self-conscious spirit to complete itself as a world spirit is to recognize the whole world as self, and hence to become *absolute* self-conscious spirit. And for spirit thus to realize itself as absolute spirit is to become fully God, for 'God should be defined as absolute spirit'.[23] Only when finite self-conscious spirit completes itself as a world spirit can it be said that God has come to himself. Man is God in his state of self-alienation and in the process of return to himself out of this state. Man confronted with an alien and hostile external world was God in his state of self-alienation; man knowing the world as self (in Hegelianism) is God returned to himself out of alienation. 'Philosophical science' is the final point of consummation of the general godward movement of humanity. In the philosophical awareness of the self as absolute being, man knows himself as God, which means, on Hegel's premises, that God has achieved complete self-knowledge. 'Spirit knowing itself as spirit' is the self-recognition of divinity.

With all this in mind, Hegel struck an apocalyptic note at the conclusion of his lectures at Berlin on the history of philosophy. 'A new epoch has arisen in the world,' he said. 'Finite self-consciousness has ceased to be finite; and in this way absolute self-consciousness has, on the other hand, attained to the reality which it lacked before. This is the whole history of the world up to the present time, and the history of philosophy in particular. . . . For it becomes such only as the result of knowing itself to be absolute spirit, and this it knows in real scientific knowledge. . . . This then is the standpoint of the present day. . . . I bid you a most hearty farewell.'[24]

III

THE DIALECTIC OF
AGGRANDIZEMENT

*For anything to be finite is just to suppress itself and put itself
aside.*   HEGEL

Spirit's self-realization through cognitive activity is for Hegel a
process of the successive transcending of limits. It may therefore
be called a self-infinitizing process. 'Finite self-conscious spirit'
—Hegel's formula for man—is a contradiction in terms, and
meant by him as such. In so far as spirit remains finite, bounded
by the presence of an object, it is not fully itself. In so far as it
becomes fully itself, it has ceased to be finite.

But this is a contradiction which, as Hegel likes to express it,
is always resolving itself. Spirit in history is forever infinitizing
itself. It does this by the act of knowing, through which a given
object or field of phenomenality is recognized as subject or
selbstisch. Once the object is recognized as subject, it no longer
exists as an alien 'something else' outside of spirit, hence no
longer stands in the way of spirit's awareness of itself as the whole
of reality. Spirit has passed a limit, broken a fetter, transcended
itself *qua* finite. It has, momentarily, grown conscious of itself as
being-without-limit, as boundless. This self-infinitizing process, whereby spirit repeatedly resolves the contradiction between its essential nature as infinite and experiential state of
finitude, is dialectical in Hegel's specific understanding of the
term.

The Hegelian dialectic is genuinely intelligible only when
seen in the larger setting of Hegel's theory of history as the
self-realization of God. By dialectic Hegel means the pattern or
mechanism of development through inner conflict. Kant, it
will be recalled, maintained that the moral life of man centres
in an inner conflict or 'natural dialectic' of duty versus inclination. The Hegelian idea of dialectic is a metamorphosis of
Kant's. It remains a concept of inner conflict. But the self having
now become a world-self, its conflict with itself has become a

world conflict. So Hegel asserts, in explaining his dialectical idea, that contradiction is the very moving principle of the *world*.

But the meaning of that proposition turns wholly on the underlying premise that the world is a world-self and that history is the process of its self-actualization in terms of knowledge. The 'contradiction' that furnishes the motive force of the world process is the division of spirit against itself in the knowing situation. It is the contradiction between spirit as implicitly (*an sich*) infinite and explicitly (*für sich*) finite, which it resolves by the act of knowing. Consequently, Hegel speaks of the dialectic as a 'dialectic of the finite, by which the finite, as implicitly other than what it is, is forced beyond its own immediate or natural being to turn suddenly into its opposite'. Again, dialectic is a 'dynamic' whose principle is that 'the finite, being radically self-contradictory, involves its own self-suppression'.[1] The dialectic may therefore be described as the psychodynamics of Hegelian spirit in its quest to know itself as the Absolute. The conception is fundamentally psychological.*

Hegel contends that his dialectic of the finite discloses the secret of the 'genuine infinite', or proper way of understanding the concept of infinity. This he contrasts with the 'wrong infinite', which is the conventional infinite of endless progression. He argues that Kant and Fichte both remained on the ground of the wrong infinite and so failed to transcend the sorrowful standpoint of the 'ought'. That is, they failed to show how that which ought to be actually comes to pass, how the perfect or absolute condition is reached rather than merely endlessly approximated. The reference is to Kant's 'endless progress

---

* It may be of interest to compare this view with the sociological interpretation of the dialectic offered by Herbert Marcuse, who writes: 'It may very well be that the developed antagonisms of modern society impelled philosophy to proclaim contradiction to be the "definite fundamental basis of all activity and self-movement". Such an interpretation is fully supported by the treatment accorded decisive social relationships in Hegel's earlier system. . . . There, the recognition of the contradictory nature of social reality was prior to the elaboration of the general theory of the dialectic' (*Reason and Revolution,* p. 148). In reply to this argument, it may be pointed out that Hegel's earlier system (i.e. the system of 1801–2) was preceded by the *Early Theological Writings,* and that these unsociological writings contain the germ of the dialectic and the whole Hegelian philosophy of history in the idea of religion as man's 'self-elevation from finite to infinite life'. That the Hegelian system represents an elaboration of this idea has, I hope, been shown here. The discovery of dialectic as inner conflict of the self striving to infinitize itself made Hegel sensitively alive to contradiction everywhere, including society.

from the lower to the higher degree of moral perfection'. Fichte, although he went beyond Kant in Hegel's direction, retained the Kantian notion of endless approximation. Thus he saw history as 'a constant progress towards higher perfection in a line that runs out into the Infinite'.[2] Hegel objects that the Kant-Fichte point of view is 'timid and incomplete'[3] in that it fails to provide for a consummation of the self-infinitizing process.

What makes the 'wrong infinite' wrong is that one never gets to it. In effect, a 'dualism' of two realms is set up, with 'the infinite abiding on yonder side and the finite steadfast on this'. 'With such empty and other-worldly stuff', says Hegel, 'philosophy has nothing to do.'[4] The wrong infinite is an expression of the misconception that sets God apart from the world of flux. In contrast, the genuine infinite of Hegelian dialectic is a kind of dynamic monism. It is a process not of endless approximation to a never-to-be-reached state of infinity, but rather of oscillation from finitude to infinity in an ever widening arc, a progress through a series of proximate states of infinity to an ultimate one ('absolute knowledge'). The state of infinity, or being-without-limit, is continually being *reached* through the cognitive act by which the conscious subject destroys the objectivity of the object.

The state of infinity figures in this conception as simply the 'not-finite' or negation of finitude through knowing. Accordingly, the formula for the genuine infinite is 'negation of negation', which Hegel calls the fundamental notion of philosophy. The explanation of it follows from the analysis already given. The limit (object) is a 'negative' of the inherently limitless self, and the self in the state of finitude is a negation of itself. The *Aufhebung* of the object may therefore be described as a negation of negation. Alternatively, it may be said that the knowing subject has by this means suppressed or abolished itself as a limited being, hence has negated itself as a negation of itself. Thus negation of negation is the *schema* of the historical process of spirit's self-aggrandizement to infinity.

Hegel emphasizes that negation of negation is not a 'neutralization' but rather an 'affirmation'.[5] This means that the dialectical process, though immediately destructive in character, is constructive in outcome. Spirit gains positive affirmation of itself as infinite through its successive acts of self-abolition as finite. In an *aufgehoben* external world, it finds itself 'at home with itself in its otherness'. De-alienated through knowing, the world now confirms the knowing self in its essential nature and idea of itself as absolute being, and one more step has been taken in its self-elevation from finite to infinite life. Moreover, it does not return to its previous stage of knowledge, but emerges enriched with new mental possessions that it lacked before. Hence, negation of negation spells affirmation. In the well-known triadic formula, the given world-form or creative self-objectification of spirit is the 'thesis', the world apprehended by the knowing self as an alien and hostile object is the 'antithesis', and the world repossessed by the knowing self as a mental content is the 'synthesis'.

If the dialectical process has its locus for Hegel in 'finite self-conscious spirit' or man, the question arises whether nature is dialectical. It must be said that he is inconsistent on this point. Since dialectical development through inner conflict of the world-self with itself is exemplified in knowing, nature would seem to enter into it only in the sense that the natural world is one of the objects of man's knowledge. This would suggest that the developmental process in nature itself is non-dialectical. Hegel frequently confirms such a view, as in the following passage: 'The spiritual is distinguished from the natural, and more especially from the animal, life, in the circumstance that it does not continue a mere stream of tendency, but sunders itself to self-realization. But this position of severed life has in its turn to be suppressed, and the spirit has by its own act to win its way to concord again.'[6] This implies that the dialectical process of self-infinitizing finds expression only in conscious spirit, and that growth in nature is a non-dialectical 'mere stream of tendency'. However, Hegel in various other places in his writings suggests that nature, or 'unconscious spirit', exhibits a rudimentary dialectic in its developmental processes.

[2]

Hegel's dialectic of the finite is a dynamism of self-aggrandizement. As such it shows a remarkable analogy with a political process known as the 'totalitarian dynamism', which may be described as aggressive expansionism that cannot, if unchecked, stop short of world conquest. The existence of such a parallel is not so surprising as it may seem, for the theory of knowledge and the theory of politics have something basically in common. Hans Kelsen observes: 'The main problem of political theory is the relationship between the subject and the object of domination; the main problem of epistemology is the relationship between the subject and the object of cognition. The process of domination is not so different from that of cognition by which the subject tries to be master of his object . . .'[7]

Hegel's theory of history as a knowing process contains a clear illustration of this parallel. It exhibits what might be called an 'epistemological totalitarianism'. The dialectic is a process of spirit's self-aggrandizement to infinity through the cognitive conquest of the world stage by stage. It is a boundless expansionism on the plane of thought. And the analogy with the corresponding process on the political plane finds further reflection in the character of Hegel's world-conquering *Geist*. He endows it with a monstrous acquisitive urge that expresses, in turn, a will to power over all external things.

Knowing for Hegel is aggrandizement of the self through aggression against the object. The process of transcending limits involves a series of aggressive moves against the limiting not-self. In the act of destroying the object *qua* object or otherness, spirit appropriates it as a self-content, as a subjective possession or, in Hegel's characteristic phrase, as 'property of the ego' (*Eigentum des Ichs*). Hence the process is essentially expansionist, for spirit, having negated the object as object, emerges enlarged, richer in subjective content or 'spiritual substance' (*die geistige Substanz*) than before. This is the point that Hegel has in mind when he emphasizes that *aufheben* has the dual connotation of destroying and preserving. The negated or transcended object has ceased to exist as object or otherness, but is preserved and stored away as spiritual substance.

To illustrate by the parallel political process, an act of armed aggression against another state may mean at once its destruction *qua* sovereign state and the appropriation of the given country by the aggressor. It is an act of aggrandizement via destruction of the other's independence, and in this sense a destructive process has a 'constructive' result. So, for Hegel, knowing means spirit's infinite self-aggrandizement at the expense of the sovereign independence of the objective world. Spirit, by making war upon otherness, aggrandizes itself. It grows richer and richer in spiritual substance as the objective

world becomes poorer and poorer in objectivity. It takes possession of the world as its property. Hegel sums up this aggressive
and expansionist process of the transformation of world-
contents into self-contents under the heading of 'spiritualization'.[8]

The acquisitive theme is strongly accentuated in some of
his descriptions of the process. Finite self-conscious spirit's desire
for knowledge is portrayed as a devouring lust, a greedy urge
to incorporate the entire world within the self. Observing that
'everything which I am to recognize has also the task of becoming
mine and attaining its validity in me', Hegel continues: 'Subjectivity is insatiably greedy to concentrate and drown everything in this single spring of the pure ego.'[9] Not only does he
thus endow spirit with an insatiable voracity. He presents the
growth of knowledge in history as a kind of accumulation of
spiritual capital. 'Spiritualization' is essentially an acquisitive
process whereby an infinite wealth of 'spiritual substance' is
accumulated in the ever expanding treasury of the world-mind.
All the world-forms that spirit's creativity has produced through
the ages are reappropriated by the greedy knowing self as its
private property.

But the devouring lust to appropriate everything as mental
property of the self is for Hegel a manifestation of the will to
power. To gain possession of an object is a means of manifesting one's power over it and so of proving that the self is
absolute:

Thus 'to appropriate' means at bottom only to manifest the pre-
eminence of my will over the thing and to prove that it is not
absolute. . . . The free will, therefore, is the idealism which does not
take things as they are to be absolute, even if they only exist in the
form of finitude. Even an animal has gone beyond this realist
philosophy since it devours things and so proves that they are not
absolutely self-subsistent.[10]

Thus, the will to possession is an expression of the will to power.
The tendency inherent in self-infinitizing spirit is a tendency to
conquer the 'other', to deprive it of all show of autonomous
being, to eliminate it as a reality-in-itself. The image of the
animal that devours things in order to prove that they are not
'absolutely self-subsistent' is vividly illustrative of this point.
Spirit's urge toward absolute knowledge is understood by
Hegel as a kind of cognitive will to power over all things, a drive

for world domination. With this in mind, he observes that dialectic answers to the notion of God's power. It is the 'irresistible power before which nothing can stay, however secure and stable it may deem itself'.[11]

Spirit's 'totalitarian dynamism' has its motivating mainspring in the will to know absolutely everything as *self*, which in turn is an outgrowth of the conception of the self as absolute being. Given this conception, which Hegel posits as the truth, the self is compelled to operate, in its relations with any external object, on the principle: 'If it *is*, then I am not *I*.' It must conquer and absorb everything outside it in order to become, in the full sense, itself. In so far as an 'other' independently subsists, the knowing self is not what it conceives itself to be. The admission of any other thing as a legitimate entity in its own right, as ontologically sovereign, would automatically invalidate spirit's image of itself as absolute being. It must therefore eliminate the 'other' *qua* 'other' in order to gain affirmation of itself *qua* absolute and thus to 'show itself to be spirit'. The conquest is carried out by means of cognition, which shows otherness to be illusory.

This process of affirming the self by conquering and appropriating the object can properly be called 'totalitarian' since it has to go on until self-conscious spirit has absorbed the totality of otherness. It cannot stop until spirit 'completes itself as a world spirit'. This is to become conscious of all reality as self. Like the megalomaniacal world-conqueror, spirit is compulsively driven to extend its dominion to the whole of the world. Only thus can it gain affirmation of itself as the Absolute, as *das Ganze*.

There is no point in the process of aggrandizement at which it can rest and say 'enough'. For so long as something is left over as 'other', this something is necessarily apprehended by spirit as alien and hostile, as a 'negation' of itself, as a contradiction of its own presumed infinity. Each new act of cognitive aggression and aggrandizement must therefore be followed by another until, finally, nothing whatever is left over as 'other', all objectivity has been conquered, and all the world's substance has been appropriated into the receptacle of self as spiritual substance. The end is 'absolute knowledge', comprising spirit's consciousness of itself as omnipotent in the sense of having dominion over everything, as omnipossessive in the sense of

owning the whole of reality as its property, as unified in the
sense that nothing subsists as not-self, and as free in the sense
that all fetters of finitude are broken. And this, according to
Hegel, is the stage now reached.

[3]

His philosophical religion of self involved a radical act of
resignation from the world. Later in life, he emphasized this in
a comment on the nature of philosophy. He remarked that
there are times 'which impel the soul of nobler natures to seek
refuge from the present in ideal regions—in order to find in
them that harmony with itself which it can no longer enjoy in
this discordant real world. . . .'12 His own youthful inner drama
is reflected in this observation. Hegel's soul was the seat of a
deep conflict that grew out of its search for 'harmony with
itself' as divinely omniscient. He attempted to resolve the conflict by withdrawal into a world of imagination. He abandoned
the ground of 'this discordant real world', and soared aloft in
imagination to 'ideal regions'. He gave full rein to a grandiose
fantasy in which the urge of the self-glorifying human self to
be godlike, and its efforts towards this end, are visualized as the
means by which God realizes himself as God. He then took the
still more radical step of drawing the real world up behind him
into the ideal regions. He took the fantasy as the discovery of the
truth, embodied it in a philosophy of history.

In a fragment written shortly after his 'breakthrough' of 1800,
Hegel said that philosophy has to establish 'a new religion in
which the infinite grief and the whole gravity of its discord is
acknowledged, but is at the same time serenely and purely dis-
solved. . . . To embrace the whole energy of the suffering and
discord that has controlled the world and all its forms of culture
for some thousand years, and also to rise above it—this can be
done by philosophy alone.'13 He proceeded to create this 'new
religion' in his own philosophy of history. It was a philosophical
religion of self involving the vicarious experience of world history
as the process of the self's realization. The philosophizing mind
is, as it were, a participant-spectator at the show of existence
conceived as God's own inner drama. It takes part in the drama
through the act of comprehending it. The thinker *qua* thinker is
the principal actor, for the action itself is supremely a process
of thought. Salvation lies in the philosopher's vision of what

is happening, and in his understanding of how it came to pass: 'The consummation of the infinite End consists merely in removing the illusion which makes it seem yet unaccomplished.'[14] As Hegel otherwise expressed it in a statement quoted earlier here, the goal is to participate in the 'redemption' objectively occurring in the history of the world by 'learning to know God as our true and essential self'.

Although the philosopher is the principal actor, his mind being the organ of God's growing self-consciousness, the men who compose the non-philosophizing mass of humanity also have their large or humble parts to play in the historical drama. Hegel ingeniously explains their role in a doctrine of the 'cunning of reason'. It holds that the doers of history, the world-historical individuals and nations, are unwitting 'agents' of the realization of the Absolute Idea or God. The heroes of history and the nations they lead achieve results that transcend their immediate conscious ends-in-view. They are not aware, or not fully aware, of the significance of their own empire-building exploits and other great deeds in the total plan of history. Their conscious goals are private and self-seeking, having in view only the glory of the individual or the nation. Driven compulsively by the 'passions' for fame or power, they expend and finally destroy themselves. Thus Hegel says of the world-historical individuals: 'They attained no calm enjoyment; their whole life was labour and trouble; their whole nature was nought else but their master-passion. When their object is attained they fall off like empty hulls from the kernel. They die early, like Alexander; they are murdered, like Caesar; transported to St Helena, like Napoleon.'[15]

But the self-sacrifice of men and nations in the search for glory yields spirit the knowledge of itself that it seeks. Individual and collective labours of culture-creation are performed in the service of the self-regarding passions. These labours objectify the manifold potentialities of spirit, and furnish spirit as personified in the contemplative knower with the requisite materials for its self-knowledge. 'The special interest of passion is thus inseparable from the actualization of the universal', writes Hegel. 'It is not the general Idea that involves itself in opposition and combat and exposes itself to danger; it remains in the background, untouched and uninjured. This may be called the *cunning of reason*—that it sets the passions to work for itself, while that through which it develops itself pays the penalty and suffers the loss.'[16] The Idea does not have to do any work to gain actualization; self-glorifying man does all the work, and destroys himself in the process. The Idea—meaning concretely the idea that the self is God—merely ignites the passion for self-aggrandizement in individuals and nations, and they themselves do the work, put forth great bursts of historical energy, use themselves up destructively, and finally perish in exhaustion. It is very clever of the Idea—runs Hegel's argument—to be able to exploit men's capacities and energies in this way, to evoke so much labour and sacrifice and suffering without, so to speak, lifting a finger on its own part. There emerges the picture of a diabolically cunning deity who gains realization at the expense of man's self-destruction as man. This has stimulated one of Hegel's commentators to remark that the Hegelian philosophy of history may be seen not as the Theodicy that Hegel claimed it to be, but as a demonodicy or justification of the ways of the devil.[17]*

However, the most accurate formula for it would seem to be: an *apologia* for pride. Hegel gives us a picture of a self-glorifying humanity striving compulsively, and at the end successfully, to rise to divinity. If man as knower is inspired by the Faustian urge towards omniscience, man as historical doer pursues the absolute in more mundane ways. The generic tendency of man is megalomania. Hegel clearly sees and stresses that he becomes its victim. The demonic force in man that leads him to reach out for the absolute and unlimited in his own person or nation is one that also divides him against himself, deprives him of happiness, and ultimately encompasses his ruin. Hence Hegel's self-deifying humanity is likewise a suffering humanity. The path it traverses through time is a 'highway of despair'. History is the 'slaughter-bench' at which the happiness of peoples is sacrificed. Again, 'The history of the world is not

---

* Hegel was at one time an interested reader of Adam Smith, and the influence of Smith is probably to be seen in the doctrine of the cunning of reason. Smith wrote that economic **man** 'is led by an invisible hand to promote an end which was no part of his intention' (*The Wealth of Nations*, p. 423). The idea was that the pursuit of egoistic self-interest in the economic realm promotes a beneficent ulterior consequence (the wealth of nations) that is not the end-in-view of the individual agents concerned. Hegel's cunning of reason may be viewed as an adaptation of Smith's invisible hand. In his version, the egoistic 'passions' for fame or power impel men to fulfil a supra-individual purpose (the realization of the Absolute Idea) that does not figure in their separate individual intentions.

the theatre of happiness. Periods of happiness are blank pages in it, for they are periods of harmony—periods when the antithesis is in abeyance.'[18]

Happy is he who is in harmony with himself, remarks Hegel. Pride, by destroying this harmony, by setting man against himself, deprives him of happiness. Afflicted with the sorrow of finitude, the despairing consciousness of a discrepancy between the absolute self that he would be and the merely finite self that he empirically is, man ceaselessly strives to find a way out of the conflict through more and more self-aggrandizement. He seeks to infinitize himself. But no matter how much he obtains of whatever it is that he is driven to seek—power, wealth, fame, knowledge—it is never enough to satisfy the insatiable absolute self. Consequently, he is compelled, on pain of defeat in the war of the self, to aggrandize himself still further. The process absorbs his creative energies, exhausts his resources, and finally takes the toll of life itself. It is his ruination.

In the light of all this, it would seem that a philosophy of self-realization must condemn pride as the deadly enemy. How could a force that ravages and destroys man be a force for his self-realization? The self-aggrandizement resulting from pride is comparable to the organic aggrandizement resulting from cancer; in both instances, the human vehicle of the process is destroyed. Yet Hegel's philosophy is founded on the moral affirmation of the destructive force. The logic of this affirmation turns on the fact that he has historicized the process of self-realization. No longer, as with Kant, is the struggle toward actualization of the absolute self enclosed as a merely personal drama within the confines of each individual's life. It is a cumulative process, a kind of relay race in which the whole procession of human generations takes part, the achievements of each one contributing in some measure to the ultimate outcome.

Hegel is not concerned with what happens to the individual *qua* individual or the nation *qua* nation; he is concerned with the final result. Pride may indeed bring its human vehicles to ruin, but meanwhile it drives them to accomplish colossal projects, deeds of universal scope. The world-historical acts performed in its service, the prodigies of activity and achievement that it elicits from man, make for the eventual actualization of the absolute self as the end-result of the history of the world. The destructive process has a constructive outcome. This is the master-theme of Hegel's *apologia* for pride, just as it is the crux of the Hegelian dialectical idea.

History takes on, in Hegel's mind, the aspect of an unbroken sequence of tragedies, mitigated and redeemed by the triumph that occurs at the end when man *does* become God. The notion that the story has this happy ending is the key to his statement that the philosophical religion must both accept the suffering and discord and 'rise above it'. History becomes a kind of spiritual ascent of Everest in which all the climbers save one have to drop off along the way in order that this one, the last in time, may clamber to the very summit and plant there the flag of victory on which is inscribed: 'The self is God.'

[4]

Hegel's *apologia* seeks to justify not only what man does to himself through his pride, but also what he does to other men. Consequently, a radical transvaluation of moral values takes place in the transition from Kant to Hegel. Although Kant paved the way to Hegelianism with his conception of the real self as a being of godlike perfection, he saw this perfection as moral virtue, a holiness of character that would find its proper outward expression in rectitude in the dealings between man and man. For Kant the content of this rectitude was given in the conventional norms of personal morality handed down in the Hebraic-Christian tradition. Hegel preserves a modest and subordinate place for this morality in his system (under the heading of *Moralität*), but expressly exempts the actions that contribute to the movement of world history from evaluation on the basis of its norms.

He holds that the 'litany of the private virtues' must not be raised against world-historical acts and agents. One must not approach the spectacle of world history in the spirit of 'moral reflections' or allegiance to a 'formal rectitude'. This is to indulge in 'sentimentalities'. 'For the history of the world occupies a higher ground than that on which morality has properly its position, which is personal character. . . .'[19] To make his meaning perfectly clear, Hegel refers here to 'those whose crimes have been turned into the means—under the direction of a superior principle—of realizing the purposes of that principle'. Of world-historical individuals obsessed with the passion for glory, he writes that 'such men may treat other great and even

sacred interests inconsiderately—a conduct which indeed subjects them to moral reprehension. But so mighty a figure must
trample down many an innocent flower, crush to pieces many an
object in its path.'[20] He explains that the egoistic passions, such
as the 'morbid craving' for fame and conquest, are the 'most
effective springs of action'. Their historicity is bound up with
their immorality. Their very power to make history lies in the
fact that 'they respect none of the limitations which justice and
morality would impose upon them; and that these natural impulses have a more direct influence over man than the artificial
and tedious discipline that tends to order and self-restraint, law
and morality'.[21]

Thus the *apologia* for pride embraces a doctrine of the historical
beneficence of moral evil. Moreover, Hegel verges on the complete and explicit 'transvaluation of values' that Nietzsche later
carried through. He argues that those who would morally condemn the great man's 'master-passion' as a vice are mean-
minded souls consumed, like Homer's Thersites, with envy and
resentment. They are 'psychological valets', exponents of 'Ther-
sitism'.[22] This suggests a *morality* of pride, which does not simply
justify it by its historical fruits but glorifies it for its intrinsic
beauty and goodness. Nietzsche drew this radical conclusion
when he propounded his 'morality of self-glorification' based on
'pride in oneself, a radical enmity and irony toward "selfless-
ness" '.[23] Out of it emerges the well known Nietzschean antithesis between 'master-morality' and 'slave-morality'. The
former is the morality of pride. The latter, which is said to
have its source in envy and resentment, is Hegel's servile Ther-
sitism broadened to include the whole of the Hebraic-Christian
moral tradition. If Nietzsche's condemnation of that tradition
was thus implicit already in Hegel, this only reinforces the view
that Hegel never really abandoned the ground of his early
attack upon Christianity. Instead, he built a theology upon it.

PART II

FROM HEGEL TO MARX

IV

PHILOSOPHY REVOLTS AGAINST
THE WORLD

*I went on from idealism—which, by the way, I equated with
Kantian and Fichtean idealism, since I drew it from that source—
to search for the Idea in reality itself. If previously the gods
dwelt above the earth, now they were the centre of it.*

MARX (letter to his father, 1837)

The influence of Hegel's philosophy reached its peak in Germany
during the decade following his death in 1831. The Hegelians
split into conservative and radical camps. For the radicals or
so-called Young Hegelians, among whom Karl Marx and
Friedrich Engels were numbered, there was no 'secret of Hegel'.
Hegelianism was an open book, and an indescribably exciting
one. The message that they found in it was stated very simply by
Engels in an early article: 'Hitherto the question has always
stood: What is God?—and German philosophy has resolved it
as follows: God is man.' Having grasped this truth, he continued, man must now 'arrange the world in a truly human way,
according to the demands of his nature—and then the riddle of
our time will be resolved by him'.[1] The Young Hegelians found
in Hegelianism a revolutionary gospel of the apotheosis of man.

Accordingly, the Young Hegelian movement of thought began
in the field of theology. Its starting point was the 'criticism of
religion'. This meant a critical attack upon the dualism of God
and man that lay at the foundation of the Hebraic-Christian
religious tradition. The attack started in 1835 with the publication of David Strauss' *Life of Jesus,* and culminated six years later
in Ludwig Feuerbach's *Essence of Christianity.* The fundamental
theme around which the movement of thought revolved was
formulated by Strauss as the idea of the unity of the divine and
human natures. This idea was, of course, Hegelian in inspiration. It was implicit in Hegel's dynamic monism of God and
man. Even the Young Hegelian watchword 'criticism', of which
Bruno Bauer was the principal author, derived easily from

73

Hegel's picture of the advancement of knowledge as a progressive puncturing of illusions. Bauer interpreted this to mean the evolution of critical consciousness via the progressive exposure of dogmas, and saw it as the present task of the critical consciousness to expose the God-illusion and show man to be the real Deity.

The extremists among the Young Hegelians, including Marx, proclaimed 'atheism' as the motto of the movement. This term, however, had a very special connotation for them. It meant the recognition of man as the sole divinity. 'Atheism' was a belligerent way of saying 'God is man'. Marx formulated this position in the preface of his doctoral dissertation: 'Philosophy makes no secret of it. The confession of Prometheus: "In one word, I hate all the gods", is its very own confession, its own sentence against all heavenly and earthly gods who refuse to recognize human self-consciousness as the supreme divinity—by the side of which none other shall be held.'[2] Man, in other words, shall have no other gods beside himself. He shall worship himself as the Supreme Being.

Marx entered the University of Berlin in 1836 at the age of eighteen. He soon steeped himself in Hegelianism and became a leading figure in the circle of Young Hegelians at the University. Keen of mind and mordant of temper, he quickly mastered the intricacies of the dialectic. But it was by no means purely an intellectual impulse that drew him to Hegel's teaching. What made Hegelianism irresistibly compelling to young Marx was the theme of man's soaring into the unlimited. His own darkly proud and boundlessly ambitious nature, in which his worried father Heinrich discerned what he called a 'Faust-like spirit', was the key to this response. Otto Rühle, a Marxist biographer of Marx, writes of Karl's student period: 'The urge to be godlike forms his plans in life and guides all his activities.'[3] It is small wonder, then, that he succumbed to the spell of a philosophical system in which the 'urge to be godlike' receives the highest metaphysical sanction and is pictured as the motive force of the history of the world.

Marx found Hegel superior to Kant and Fichte because of his seeming success in disposing of the dichotomy of 'is' and 'ought' that remained unresolved in the systems of his two predecessors. In a letter to his father in 1837, when he was beginning to steep himself in philosophy, he described the opposition between that which is and that which ought to be as the distinguishing feature of idealism, which in turn he equated with the philosophies of Kant and Fichte. What especially attracted him to Hegel was this philosopher's surmounting of the characteristic difficulty of idealism. Among some verses written by young Marx that year, there is an epigram in which Hegel says: 'Kant and Fichte were fond of flying off into the upper air, seeking there a distant land; I only try valiantly to understand what I find on the roadway.'[4]

Marx became a passionate disciple of Hegelianism, and distinguished himself among the Young Hegelians at Berlin by the fierceness of his loyalty and attachment to the master. In one of the notes to his doctoral dissertation, for example, he reproached those among the radicals who presumed to stand in judgment over Hegel for the philosopher's 'accommodation' to the authorities. It is unscrupulous, wrote Marx, to make such criticisms of a teacher 'for whom science was not something received ready-made but was just being created, so that the spiritual blood of his very heart pulsated to its farthest periphery'.[5]

The electrifying message that he found in Hegel was the idea that man is God. Hegelianism was the 'philosophy' whose very own confession was that of Prometheus. Its epochal significance lay in the revelation of 'human self-consciousness' as the supreme divinity by the side of which none other should be held. Marx was so carried away with this idea that he propounded among his Young Hegelian friends in Berlin the argument that Hegel himself should be regarded as an 'atheist' in their sense. One of these friends, Bruno Bauer, embodied this argument in a pamphlet that was published anonymously in 1841 under the title, *The Trumpet of the Last Judgment Over Hegel the Atheist and Antichrist*. Whether Marx directly collaborated with Bauer in the writing of this pamphlet is not certain, but it undoubtedly reflected his views and his inspiration. Affecting the standpoint of a devout Lutheran dismayed by the official approbation of Hegelianism, it presented a series of quotations from Hegel designed to show that he was not at all a pious conservative but a dangerous radical and atheist. In other words, Hegel himself was portrayed as a Young Hegelian.

It must be acknowledged that the Young Hegelians had a strong claim to the Hegelian inheritance. Their 'criticism of religion' was a logical outgrowth of Hegel's philosophical religion of self. For the idea of the dialectical unity of the divine and human natures was indeed, as we have seen, the axis of Hegelianism. Hegel rejected in no uncertain terms the traditional dualism of God and man. He presented history as the story of man's self-elevation from finite to infinite life, as God's own self-realization in the person of man. It may be argued that Marx's 'atheist' interpretation of Hegel simply drew the radical conclusion implicit in this idea.

On the other hand, it is rather obvious that Hegel himself would have disowned his ardent young champion. He was not a Young Hegelian. In order to explain this paradox, we must recall the peculiar personal experience in which the Hegelian philosophical religion of self centred for its founder. He had started from a position similar to that of the Young Hegelians, i.e. by denying the transmundane God of Christianity. Then, however, he *identified* himself with this God, and recast the concept of God accordingly. The quietism and conservatism of his later outlook, and his claim to have assimilated the truth of Christianity into his own system of philosophy, rested on this act of self-identification. Naturally, one who conceives himself as the man in whom God has come to clear and full self-knowledge does not proclaim himself an atheist.

The relation between Hegel and the Young Hegelian movement must be understood against this background. After breaking through the too confining walls of traditional religion in order to lift his head to infinity, Hegel constructed, in his philosophical system, a tower of pride that purported to envelop the broken temple walls. He practised therein a private religion whose ritual consisted essentially in Hegelian philosophizing, the apprehension and demonstration that the self is God. The Young Hegelians, on the other hand, were not practitioners of the religion, but only devotees of the idea. They experienced in themselves, as in the case of Marx, at most an 'urge to be godlike'—something different from the experience of oneself as God come to full self-consciousness. They worked with Hegelianism in detachment from the special personal experience that enabled Hegel to argue that all was right with the world since God was realized. For him, the private religion was a solution, a way of life, redemption, and his outlook, accordingly, was quietistic. For them, Hegelianism was not a solution but a programme.

What they derived from Hegel was the *idea* of the unity of the human and the divine. Their outlook, therefore, was radical. The great system was a map on which one could trace the road to man's destination—divinity. But man had yet to arrive at the destination. His divinity was something yet to be existentially realized. Hence the Young Hegelian slogan, which was at once the outcome of Hegelianism and quite un-Hegelian: 'Realization of philosophy!'

The detachment of the Hegelian idea from the setting of the private religion as practised by Hegel was explosive in its consequences. As Engels put it, German philosophy's discovery that 'God is man' called for a rearrangement of the world that would make it possible for man to experience himself in it as a godlike being. This world-revolutionary inference from Hegelianism was Marx's first premise too, and started him off on the path to the creation of Marxism as a doctrine of world revolution.

[2]

Marx elaborated the concept of the realization of philosophy before coming into serious contact with contemporary doctrines of socialism and communism. He did so in a series of notes for his doctoral dissertation, which was written between 1839 and 1841.* In the notes Marx sketches what he calls the *curriculum vitae* of philosophy. He says that there are certain 'key points' in its development at which spiritual existence becomes free and enriched to universality, and an integral new thought-world is born in the mind of the philosopher. Such key points are the great world philosophies, the Aristotelian in antiquity and the Hegelian in modern times. In the historical aftermaths, philosophy assumes a practical attitude toward the world, appears on the scene as an 'actor'. In antiquity, it 'takes on canine appearance as the Cynic, dons the cloak of a seer as the Alexandrian, or fresh spring apparel as the Epicurean'. But the essence of the situation at such a time is that philosophy, as 'subjective consciousness', comes into collision with the existing world, revolts against reality.

* The substance of the work, entitled *On the Difference between the Democritean and Epicurean Philosophies of Nature,* is of little interest. The choice of topic reflected Marx's idea that the present post-Hegelian period was historically analogous to the post-Aristotelian period in antiquity. Hegel was the Aristotle of modern thought. Hence a study of the post-Aristotelian period might contribute to a clarification of the present situation.

The inner self-satisfaction is broken, says Marx, and 'That which was an inner light becomes a consuming flame, turned outward.' The 'spiritual monad', ideally formed in all respects, cannot accept existing reality: 'It is a psychological law that the theoretical spirit, having become free within itself, is transformed into practical energy and, appearing as *will* from Amenthes' shadowy realm, turns against the earthly reality existing apart from it.' Thus, the Hegelian philosophical idea is transformed in Hegel's disciples into a will to revolt against a world not yet shaped in the image of that idea: 'Just as Prometheus, having stolen fire from heaven, begins to build houses and establish himself on earth, so philosophy, having embraced the whole world, revolts against the world of phenomena. So now with the Hegelian philosophy.'[6]

The workings of the 'psychological law' behind philosophy's revolt against the world are explained by Marx as follows. The relation of a philosophical system to the existing world is one of 'reflection'. That is, the system's 'spiritual bearers' aspire to 'make the world philosophical', to bring reality into harmony with the idealized image of a world which philosophy has brought forth in thought. They want to liberate the 'earthly reality' from its present 'unphilosophical condition'. In fact, they are driven to do so, for only in this way can they liberate themselves: 'By liberating the world from the unphilosophical condition, they at the same time liberate themselves from philosophy, which, in the form of a definite system, has held them in fetters.' Thus, the realization of philosophy is, at the same time, its loss. That is to say, the translation of philosophy into earthly reality, the transformation of the 'world of phenomena' in the image of philosophy, will spell the end of philosophy's existence *qua* philosophy or thought-world. 'Thus it transpires that in the degree to which the world becomes philosophical, philosophy becomes worldly, that its realization is simultaneously its loss.'[7]

Finally, Marx permits himself some reflections on the character of the impending period of history. One should not be dismayed, he says, by the storm which follows upon a great world philosophy. The lines are drawn now for battle. The world is a 'split world'. It is rent by a mighty 'inner discord'. On one side stands the integral thought-world of Hegelian philosophy; on the other, the unphilosophical earthly reality or world of phenomena. Humanity is now on the verge of an 'iron epoch' comparable to the Roman era of the ancient world. The iron epoch will be a happy one if it is marked by a 'titanic struggle'. What this situation calls for is not 'half-way minds' but rather 'integral commanders' who will never accept a 'peace treaty with real needs'.[8]

This declaration of unlimited war against the existing world on behalf of the 'realization of philosophy' was the initial major step that Marx took along the road leading to the creation of Marxism. Although he was still very far from the Materialist Conception of History, he had already arrived at a general idea of world revolution. And he had done so as a disciple of Hegel. The image of spirit in hostile confrontation with an alien world, and of the revolutionary transformation of this world by spirit, was an integral part of the Hegelian philosophy. This has undergone a metamorphosis and become, in Marx's mind, the image of 'philosophy' in hostile confrontation with an alien world. In its original form, the Marxian revolutionary imperative was a demand to 'make the world philosophical'. It expressed a sweeping indictment and rejection of earthly reality on the ground of its 'unphilosophical condition'.

It is often said that Marx began his intellectual career as an Hegelian idealist and that he abandoned the Hegelian starting point in the course of the later evolution of his thought to Marxism. The materials just reviewed show that this point of view is not quite accurate. Marx indeed began as a disciple of Hegelianism, but his relation to the Hegelian system was from the start a very peculiar one. If being an Hegelian means accepting Hegelianism as true, then Marx was never at any time an Hegelian. The original impulse of his thought was expressed in the watchword of 'realization of philosophy', which in turn implied that Hegelianism was *not* true but ought to be. Marx from the beginning 'believed' in Hegelianism not as a true account of reality but only as a programme. He was an Hegelian in this sense alone; and in this sense he always remained one.

As he saw it at the time he wrote the notes to the dissertation, Hegelianism was a grand fantasy, a fantasy of man's historical self-realization as God. Hegel was a philosophical Moses who had led mankind to the promised land *in thought*. He had constructed a universe in imagination, a thought-world in which man, in the course of history, comes to know himself as God. However, the existing world was not 'philosophical'. It was not a

world in which man had come to experience himself as a godlike
being. The idea of making the world philosophical arose in
Marx's mind as the idea of acting out Hegelianism in real history,
of making it come true, of translating Hegel's beautiful philosophical dream into reality.

The motto of the Young Hegelian movement was 'criticism',
and Marx in his first period looked to criticism as the means by
which the world might be made philosophical. He and others
enlarged upon the notion of criticism of religion. Typically, he
went farther than anyone else. In a letter to his friend Arnold
Ruge in 1843, he called for '*a merciless criticism of everything
existing*, merciless in two senses: this criticism must not take
fright at its own conclusions and must not shrink from a collision
with the powers that be'.[9] And in an essay published the
following year under the title of 'Introduction to the Criticism
of the Hegelian Philosophy of Right', he explained further that
criticism 'is not an anatomic knife but a weapon. Its object is its
enemy, which it wants not to refute but to destroy. . . . Criticism
concerned with this object is *hand-to-hand* criticism. . . . The real
oppression must be made still more oppressive by joining it to
the consciousness of oppression; the shame more shameful by
publicizing it. . . . The people must be made to *take fright* at
itself as a means of breathing valour into it.'[10] At this time,
however, he added that the weapon of criticism would have to
be supplemented with 'criticism by weapons', and announced
that philosophy had found its 'material weapon' in the proletariat.

[3]

Marx completed his dissertation in March 1841. Some months
later Feuerbach's *Essence of Christianity* was published. This was
the most important philosophical event in Germany since the
death of Hegel. It marked both a culmination of the Young
Hegelian trend and at the same time a reaction against Hegel
from within the movement. In the following year Feuerbach
published his *Preliminary Theses on the Reform of Philosophy*, and in
1843 another important work, *Fundamental Tenets of the Philosophy
of the Future*. These writings caused a tremendous stir within the
world of the Hegelian philosophical self-consciousness.

Marx was ecstatic, as can be seen from his following reaction
to the first of them: 'I advise you speculative theologians and

philosophers to rid yourselves of the notions and preconceptions of the old speculative philosophy if you want to get to things as they are in reality, i.e. to the truth. And there is no other road to truth and freedom for you than the road through the "brook of fire" (*Feuer-bach*). Feuerbach is the *purgatory* of our time.'[11] In later years he was to alter his attitude toward Feuerbach very considerably. The deep Hegelian affiliation of his thought re-asserted itself. For example, he remarked to Engels in a letter of 1868, commenting acidly on Dühring and others in Germany who thought Hegel's dialectic a 'dead horse', that 'Feuerbach has much to answer for in this respect'.[12] Nevertheless, the influence of Feuerbach upon the development of Marx's thought was a decisively important one, so important that Marxism might perhaps be epitomized as Hegelianism mediated by Feuerbach's critique of Hegel.

In the pamphlet on Feuerbach that he wrote late in life, Engels recalled the enormously 'liberating effect' of his *Essence of Christianity*, and explained it by saying that Feuerbach here 'placed materialism on the throne again'. He assessed the book's message and impact as follows: 'Nature exists independently of all philosophy. It is the foundation upon which we human beings, ourselves products of nature, have grown up. Nothing exists outside nature and man, and the higher beings our religious fantasies have created are only the fantastic reflection of our own essence. The spell was broken; the "system" was exploded and cast aside. . . . Enthusiasm was general; we all became at once Feuerbachians.'[13] Marx, in 1845, had expressed a similar evaluation: 'Only Feuerbach consummates and criticizes Hegel, proceeding from the Hegelian viewpoint. Reducing the metaphysical absolute spirit to "real man on the foundation of nature", Feuerbach brought to a culmination the criticism of religion and at the same time masterfully drew the main lines of a critique of the Hegelian system and thereby of any metaphysic.'[14]

As these statements suggest, Feuerbach's book exerted a kind of shock effect upon the Young Hegelians. He did not tortuously argue his way out of the labyrinth of Hegelianism. He simply took his stand outside it. He proclaimed 'real man on the founda-tion of nature' as the proper starting point for thought. He opted for what he called the 'real material world'. Styling himself 'a natural philosopher in the domain of mind', he announced that the first principle of his philosophy was neither the God of Christian theology nor any one of the various surrogates for this God that 'speculative theology' (philosophy) had created, such as Hegel's Absolute, but rather 'a *real* being, the true *Ens realissimum*—man'.[15] Reading his book, Marx, Engels and others seem to have experienced a sense of breakthrough to reality. They awoke to discover themselves—in Marx's words written in 1844—as 'actual, corporeal man, standing on firm and well rounded earth, inhaling and exhaling all the natural forces'.[16]

This, however, is by no means a full explanation of the significance of Feuerbach as the fulcrum of Marx's transition from Hegelianism to Marxism. In order to clarify the matter further, it is necessary to look more closely into Feuerbach's position, and especially into his relation to Hegel. Superficially he has made a break with 'the system'. Ostensibly he has departed the universe of Hegelian philosophy, and taken his stand on naturalistic *terra firma*. But the ghost of Hegel haunts Feuerbach's 'real material world'. It is, in its way, a world of *naturalized Hegelianism*. And this is the crucial point for an understanding of the role of Feuerbach's thought in the rise of Marxism.

The relation of Feuerbach to Hegel can best be explained by reference to the distinction between 'manifest' and 'latent' meaning-contents that Freudian thought has made familiar to us. The 'manifest' content is the surface meaning of the material, that which it seems to be saying. The 'latent' content is its underlying or symbolic meaning, that which it indirectly reveals. Feuerbach distinguishes between the manifest and the latent Hegelianism. Manifest Hegelianism is the system *qua* system, and this Feuerbach rejects as 'speculative theology'. On the other hand, he construes Hegelianism to have a latent, underlying, or in his own words 'esoteric' content, and this he accepts an an epochal revelation of the truth about real man. As he states the point in his *Preliminary Theses*, 'Metaphysics is esoteric psychology.'[17] The Hegelian metaphysics of spirit, in other words, is a recondite revelation of psychological or 'anthropological' truth. It is a reflection of processes actually going on in man; it has an existential bearing.

According to Feuerbach, Hegel's speculative theology is a philosophical extension of ordinary theology and as such clarifies certain hidden implications of the latter. Hegelianism is a revelation of the truth about religion as a phenomenon of man's self-deification and resulting self-alienation (*Selbstentfremdung*). The subject of Feuerbach's book is Christianity, which he takes to be the prototype of all religion. But he builds his interpretation of Christianity upon the concept of alienation that lies, as we have seen, at the foundation of Hegelianism. He holds that man has so far in history lived primarily a life of religion, and that the essence of religion (or 'essence of Christianity') is man's estrangement from himself. The actual psychological fact reflected darkly in the Hegelian metaphysics of self-alienated spirit is the fact of *man's* self-alienation in the religious consciousness of himself as God. This is the way in which Feuerbach naturalized Hegelianism. His 'real man on the foundation of nature' is an alienated religious man. His 'real material world' is peopled with a species of self-alienated humanity.

As all this indicates, Feuerbach's view of the relation between Hegelianism and Christianity differs fundamentally from the position of Bauer and Marx as expressed in *The Trumpet of the Last Judgment*. They had presented an 'atheist' Hegel in opposition to the Christian theology. Feuerbach agrees that Hegel is no ordinary Christian theologian, that the traditional theological concept of God is a far cry from Hegel's 'contradiction-torn atheistic God' who has to 'win his divinity'.[18] However, he holds that Hegelianism is in fundamental harmony with the Christian position. In the final analysis, he says, the antithesis between them is superficial only. Hegel's doctrine contradicts religion 'only in the same way as, in general, a developed, consequent process of thought contradicts an undeveloped, unconsequent, but nevertheless radically identical conception'.[19]

For Feuerbach, Hegelianism is the traditional Christian theology spelt by dialectic. Hegel's picture of a self-alienated God simply brings into focus what was always present in the religious consciousness, and in traditional theology as its theoretical transcript. Feuerbach argues on this basis that Hegelianism is to be viewed as 'rational mysticism' and 'the last rational support of theology'. 'The philosophy of Hegel', he writes, 'is the last grandiose attempt to restore lost, ruined Christianity with the aid of philosophy.' From this it follows that 'he who does not renounce the philosophy of Hegel does not renounce theology'.[20]

So the Young Hegelian criticism of religion culminated in a criticism of its own inspirer, and Hegel himself fell victim to the critical fire he had lit in the minds of his radical disciples. However, the vital substance of his philosophy was incorporated into the new doctrine of self-alienated religious man, which Feuerbach called 'anthropology'.

V

METAPHYSICS AS ESOTERIC
PSYCHOLOGY

*Religion is the dream of the human mind. But even in dreams we
do not find ourselves in emptiness or in heaven, but on earth, in
the realm of reality; we see only real things in the entrancing
splendour of imagination and caprice, instead of in the simple
daylight of reality and necessity.* FEUERBACH

Feuerbach's *Essence of Christianity* would have been more
accurately entitled *Essence of Hegelianism,* although it could
hardly have been written at all had the author understood this
fact. His 'Christianizing' of Hegel went along with, and in fact
stemmed from, an interpretation of Christianity itself in
Hegelian terms. Hegel's philosophy seemed to provide a clue to
the real meaning of the Christian religion, which in turn
Feuerbach regarded as the prototype and highest form of religion
in general. The clue was contained in Hegel's conception of the
underlying unity of man and God.

Hegel, as we have seen, represents man as God in his state of
self-alienation and return to himself. This, says Feuerbach,
expresses the truth about religion in a 'mystified' form. The true
statement is just the reverse: God is man in his state of self-
alienation, i.e. man in his religious life is alienated from himself.
The Hegelian God who experiences alienation in the consciousness of himself as finite man is a representation in reverse
of the actual fact that Christian or, more generally, religious
man experiences alienation in the consciousness of himself as
almighty God. So Hegelian metaphysics is esoteric psychology,
or more accurately psychopathology. Instead of saying with
Hegel that man is God in his self-alienation, one must turn the
proposition on its head and say: God is man in his self-alienation.
The Hegelian idea of God's or the Absolute's self-alienation
reflects the actuality of man's.

To arrive at the truth, therefore, one has only to turn Hegel's
key propositions upside down or right way up. This process of

inversion, which Feuerbach calls 'transformational criticism', extracts the esoteric psychology from Hegelian metaphysics. It clarifies the latent truth-content of Hegelianism: 'It suffices to put the predicate in place of the subject everywhere, i.e. *to turn speculative philosophy upside down,* and we arrive at the truth in its unconcealed, pure, manifest form.'[1] Hegelian theology turned upside down equals the truth about man in his religious condition of self-alienation. This is the constitutive formula of Feuerbach's philosophy of religion as elaborated in his *Essence of Christianity.* Thus it was not Marx but Feuerbach who originally turned Hegel 'upside down'. Marx was Feuerbach's follower in this pivotal operation.

The reasoning process involved in it is revealed most clearly in the chapter of the book dealing with Hegel's doctrine of God. First Feuerbach formulates the 'manifest' position of Hegel: 'Man is the revealed God; in man the divine essence first realizes itself and unfolds itself. In the creation of nature, God goes outside of himself, he has relation to what is other than himself, but in man he returns into himself:—man knows God, because in him God finds and knows himself, feels himself as God.'[2] This, Feuerbach continues, is the truth in reverse. It has to be turned upside down if we are to see things in the simple daylight of reality.

The actual fact reflected upside down in Hegel's proposition that man is the 'revealed God' is that God is the revealed man:

But if it is only in human feelings and wants that the divine 'nothing' becomes something, obtains qualities, then the being of man is alone the real being of God—man is the real God. And if in the consciousness which man has of God first arises the self-consciousness of God, then the human consciousness is, *per se,* the divine consciousness. Why then dost thou alienate man's consciousness from him, and make it the self-consciousness of a being distinct from him? Why dost thou vindicate being to God, to man only the consciousness of that being? . . . The true statement is this: man's knowledge of God is man's knowledge of himself, of his own nature. . . . Where the consciousness of God is, there is the being of God—in man, therefore; in the being of God it is only thy own being which is an object to thee, and what presents itself *before* thy consciousness is simply what lies *behind* it.[3]

Thus, by the method of 'transformational criticism' Hegel's proposition that man is the revealed God is transformed into

Feuerbach's proposition that God is the revealed man. The image of man as manifestation of the divine substance gives way to the image of God as manifestation of the human substance.

Hegel, on this view, furnished the key to unlock the mystery of religion. He did so by portraying man as the 'revealed God', thus bringing the concepts of God and man into indissoluble connection. His error lay solely in the mystified inverted manner in which he described the connection. He formulated it theologically instead of anthropologically. He made man's being an emanation of God conceived as a thought-process, instead of showing the divine thought-process to be an emanation of man's own being in the material world. In a generalized restatement of this argument, which Marx later took over intact, Feuerbach asserted: 'The real relation of thought to being is as follows: '*Being is subject, thought is predicate*. Thought proceeds from being, not being from thought.'[4] The reference is to the God-man relation as presented by Hegel. The contention is that man is not, as Hegel would have it, the expression or attribute ('predicate') of the divine thought-process. On the contrary, God is an expression of the thought-process of man. Man is the being; God, the thought. Man is the subject; God, the predicate. 'Where the consciousness of God is, there is the being of God—in man. . . .'

Thus, Hegel's self-alienated God becomes Feuerbach's self-alienated man, and history as the process of God's attaining to full self-consciousness through man turns into history as a process of man's attaining to full self-consciousness through God. Instead of man being conceived as the self of the Absolute, we have the Absolute represented as the self of man projected into objectivity. Instead of God being divided against himself in the Hegelian knowing situation, we have man ('real man') divided against himself in the Feuerbachian religious situation. A conscious subject contemplates its externalized being as an object or 'other'. The subject, however, is now redefined as man, and the object before it in consciousness is God: 'Man—this is the mystery of religion—projects his being into objectivity, and then makes himself an object to this projected image of himself thus converted into a subject. . . . Thus in God man has only his own activity as an object. . . . God is, *per se*, his relinquished self.'[5] The 'activity' of self-externalization here referred to is activity of the human imagination.

[2]

Feuerbach typically employs the word 'man' in a generic or collective sense. His human subject is the human race, the species (*Gattung*). The species is the real being, and individual man is simply a particular instance of the life of the species. God, or the absolute self, is an idealized image of the positive attributes of the species: 'God as the epitome of all realities or perfections is nothing other than a compendious summary devised for the benefit of the limited individual, an epitome of the generic human qualities distributed among men, in the self-realization of the species in the course of world history.'[6] This idealized generic man, or absolute self representing the sum of perfections of the species, is projected as God and entertained by individual man as his object of worship. Hence religion is human self-worship.

The result, according to Feuerbach, is man's estrangement from himself. He dualizes himself through his self-externalization as God. He becomes a divided being, a dual personality, two selves: the idealized generic self that he worships as God, and the limited and imperfect empirical human self that he sees when he turns back upon himself from the standpoint of God. What he sees when he thus looks down upon himself from the divine heights of his own imagination is a poor, inferior, contemptible and in sum *alien* being. Having invested all the riches of human nature in the image of himself as God, he feels worthless and abased in his merely human capacity: 'To enrich God, man must become poor; that God may be all, man must become nothing.'[7] All that is highest and best in man has been incorporated in the divine *alter ego:*

Religion is the disuniting of man from himself; he sets God before him as the antithesis of himself. God is not what man is—man is not what God is. God is the infinite, man the finite being; God is perfect, man imperfect; God eternal, man temporal; God almighty, man weak; God holy, man sinful. God and man are extremes: God is the absolutely positive, the sum of all realities; man the absolutely negative, comprehending all negations.[8]

Bereft of all the ideal attributes that are conceived to belong not to him but to God, man has nothing of value left in himself. This is the suffering consciousness of human self-alienation as portrayed by Feuerbach. His alienated religious man is a suffering man.

If God is the standard by which religious man measures himself and finds himself worthless, the inference can only be that he apprehends in God the self that he himself *ought* to be. While projecting God as a being outside himself, man must, at the same time, somehow identify this being as his own true self. This alone would explain why the awareness of a vast discrepancy between God and himself should be a suffering consciousness of self-alienation. Feuerbach quite clearly makes this inference. 'If God is really a different being from myself', he inquires, 'why should his perfection trouble me?' Elsewhere he is still more explicit: 'God is nothing other than the prototype and ideal of man: as God is, so man *should* be and *desires* to be, or at least hopes to become sometime.'[9] Again, in discussing the conception of God as the morally perfect being, he remarks that this 'is no merely theoretical, inert conception, but a practical one, calling me to action, to imitation, throwing me into strife, into disunion with myself; for while it proclaims to me what I ought to be, it also tells me to my face, without any flattery, what I am not'.[10]*

Although he here presents the God-ideal as a call to action that man issues to himself, Feuerbach elsewhere pictures the self-worshipping religious man as a passive being given over to the 'life of theory'.[11] Instead of realizing his human potentialities, he consoles himself with a purely imaginary and therefore pseudo-realization of himself in the dream about God. Living a life of fantasy, absorbed in the beautiful vision of himself as God, man lets real life pass him by unlived. The imaginary realization of himself in the contemplation of God as fully actualized being is a 'compensation for the poverty of life' and 'substitute for the lost world'. And the poorer his life outside the religious dream, the richer the dream life and its object must themselves become: 'The more empty life is, the fuller, the more concrete is God. The impoverishing of the real world and the enriching of God is one act.'[12]

One of Feuerbach's illustrations of this general thesis merits special mention here because of its important role in the rise of Marxism. He argues that man is inherently a creative being who derives joy from productive activity willingly performed:

* Significantly, he refers here to the authority of Kant, citing the statement in Kant's *Critique of Practical Reason:* 'That which, in our own judgment, derogates from our self-conceit, humiliates us. Thus the moral law inevitably humiliates every man when he compares it with the sensual tendency of his own nature' (*Essence of Christianity*, p. 47).

The idea of activity, of making, of creation, is in itself a divine idea; it is therefore unhesitatingly applied to God. In activity man feels himself free, unlimited, happy; in passivity, limited, oppressed, unhappy. Activity is the positive sense of one's personality. . . . And the happiest, the most blissful activity is that which is productive. To read is delightful, reading is passive activity; but to produce what is worthy to be read is more delightful still. . . . Hence this attribute of the species—productive activity—is assigned to God; that is, realized and made objective as divine activity.[13]

Man realizes his creativity in the imagination by projecting God as the supremely creative being. Consequently—runs Feuerbach's argument—he fails to fulfil himself in this properly human capacity. Instead of *being* productive, he experiences a merely theoretical productivity. Engrossed in the image of himself as Producer of the world, he forgoes actual productive living.

This, in brief, is Feuerbach's theory of human self-alienation in the religious life. It follows from the theory that the emancipation of man from religion is the only possible path of escape from alienation, the only means by which man can actualize himself as a human being. This means renunciation of the God-illusion. Once he has awakened from the religious dream in which he contemplates himself as God, man will be delivered from the 'hellish torments of contradiction'.[14] He will cease being divided against himself in the despairing, suffering consciousness of his distance from the divine absolute self. Above all, he will cease living a life of fantasy and accepting the shadow of self-realization for the substance. He will attend to his actual self, develop his latent potentialities, seek fullness of life in the real material world, and generally *be* human instead of merely dreaming about being God.

Post-religious man is to reconcile himself with his humanity in the persons of other men. This Feuerbach offers as the positive content of the 'humanism' or 'realized Christianity' that is to take the place of historic religion. Instead of fixing his gaze upon God as his object of adoration, man is to lavish his love upon man. By the love of man is to be understood not love of self but love of the *other* man: 'The true dialectic is not a monologue of a lone thinker with himself, but a dialogue between the I and the Thou.'[15] Feuerbach's underlying idea here is that religious man, and his spokesmen the theologian and speculative philosopher, are fundamentally self-centered, concerned with the self in the form of the divine *alter ego*, whereas what man should have before him is not an illusory 'other' in God but a real and living 'other' in the other human being. So Feuerbach writes: 'The being of man is given only in communion, in the unity of man with man, a unity resting on the reality of the distinction between the I and the Thou. . . . Man for himself is man in the ordinary sense; man in communion with man, the unity of the I and Thou, is God.'[16] On one of the occasions when he touched upon this theme, Feuerbach announced that his philosophical principle was 'communal man, *communist*'.[17] Thus, self-divided religious man, once awakened from the dream, would recover his lost unity in the 'communism' of the I-Thou relation, in the unity of man with man.

[3]

Feuerbach conceived it to be the mission of his own 'criticism of religion' to effect the liberation of humanity from religion. He would free man from religion by demonstrating to him that the religious life is a life of his self-estrangement. His purpose was to expose the illusion that God is a being other than man, or to bring about man's recognition that the supra-human being is none other than *himself* projected by the imagination into objectivity. The act of recognition would signify the retrieving by man of his externalized being, the recovery of the 'relinquished self'. In terms of the Hegelian parallel, this is the phase of *Aufhebung* or transcendence of the object and of the alienation inherent in the subject-object situation. Feuerbachian criticism of religion corresponds, then, to Hegelian knowing. Just as the latter means the transcendence of the knowing situation in which the subject has itself before it in the guise of an alien and illusory 'other', so the former means the transcendence of the religious situation in which man is afflicted with a false consciousness of himself as God. In both instances, alienation is surmounted by a cognitive act that brings recognition of the object as an externalized self.

Implicit in Feuerbach's position is an 'anthropological' restatement of the Hegelian philosophy of history. History remains an epic of self-realization, and the process shows the familiar Hegelian three-phase pattern of externalization, resulting alienation, and final transcendence of the alienation by an act of knowing. In the Feuerbachian anthropological version, however, the being that realizes itself in history is the human species or *Gattung*, and the whole of history resolves itself into a single great episode of the three-phase process. The original human act of self-externalization as God marks the beginning of a phase of human alienation in religion that extends all the way to the present time, to the criticism of religion. Feuerbach concerned himself mainly with the details of this criticism, and merely adumbrated the anthropological metamorphosis of the Hegelian philosophy of history. It was left to Marx to elaborate the restatement of Hegel in a systematic manner in his philosophical original Marxism. However, the structure of the latter was already prefigured in Feuerbach's thought.

Feuerbach's scheme, growing out of the inversion of Hegel's, naturally shows a broad structural resemblance to the parent-system. At the same time, a deeply significant change of moral perspective takes place in this transition. Feuerbach, as it were, changes sides in the war of the self. His image of suffering humanity goes back to Hegel's own philosophy of history. Hegel, as we have noted, pictures history as a record of human suffering caused by man's ceaseless striving to actualize the Absolute in himself. He justifies the suffering on the ground that the striving eventually reaches its goal. Feuerbach, identifying the Hegelian Absolute with Christianity's God, takes the picture of unhappy humanity as literally true—and revolts against 'religion'. He sees no justification for the suffering. He sees only that man is oppressing himself. Morally speaking, Feuerbach turns against the Absolute and takes the part of suffering man. He rebels against the misery that self-deifying man inflicts upon himself. He wants to deliver him from the 'hellish torments of contradiction' arising out of this self-deification. His philosophy is, therefore, imbued with a profound compassion, perhaps one might even say a Christian compassion, for man conceived as a being historically divided against himself in 'religion'.

All this reflects a deep change in the diagnosis of alienation. If Hegel's God was alienated from himself in the degree to which man still fell short of becoming the Absolute, Feuerbach's man is alienated from himself *as a consequence* of projecting himself as the Absolute. If Hegel's self-deifying man finally becomes God, Feuerbach's remains incompletely human so long as he lives in the illusory consciousness of himself as God. For Feuerbach, therefore, man's self-deification is both the cause of his alienation and the obstacle to his realization of himself as human. The hand that inflicts the wound is no longer, as for Hegel, the hand that heals it. And this change in the diagnosis of alienation is accompanied by a corresponding change in the definition of the goal of history. For Hegel it is the self-realization of God in man; for Feuerbach, the self-realization of man *qua* man after he has ceased to project himself as God. In the Feuerbachian reformulation of Hegelianism, the goal of history is simply for man to become fully human. This is what Feuerbach means by 'humanism'.

In conclusion, it may be suggested that he was confused in his understanding of the nature of religion. The misunderstanding was implicit in his 'Hegelianizing' of Christianity. He took the Hegelian religion of the self as God to be the key to the meaning of Christianity as the prototype of religion in general. But it was a mistake on his part to do this. The phenomenon with which he deals in his *Essence of Christianity* is a reality of human experience, but is not properly described as 'Christianity' or 'religion'. It is the neurotic phenomenon of human self-glorification or pride, and the estrangement from the self that results from it. As suggested earlier, this phenomenon is indeed religious in a sense, but not in the Hebraic-Christian sense. Feuerbach errs in *equating* religion with human pride, in identifying the worship of God with the worship of the human self as God. In effect, he finds the essence of Christianity in that which it regards as the essence of evil. As a consequence, he misreads the meaning of the religious experience. What he has disclosed is not the 'mystery of religion' but the secret of Hegel. He has taken the peculiar Hegelian form of religious experience, which is pride become theological, as the paradigm of all religion. His criticism of religion is predicated upon this fundamental error.

But precisely because he has thus 'Hegelianized' the religious life, Feuerbach's opposition to religion is more anti-Hegelian than genuinely anti-Christian. Morally speaking, it expresses a revulsion against the supreme form of human pride. Regarding the matter in this light, I believe it fair to say that Feuerbach the self-proclaimed atheist is far less distant from the basic Hebraic-Christian outlook on life than is Hegel the theologian of self. For Hegelianism is a philosophical and religious affirmation of pride, whereas Feuerbach's philosophy, although it dispenses with the notion of a transmundane God and sets up the human race as the Supreme Being, nevertheless contains elements of a critique of pride.

He moves in a new direction. He recasts the absolute self as the alien one, and gropes toward a solution for the dilemma of divided man along the line of undoing self-alienation. He adumbrates the idea of stopping the war of the self as distinguished from winning it, and of removing the conflict in man at its source. He senses that there is something radically wrong with self-alienated man, and that one way, and in fact the right way, for man to be at one with himself again is simply to cease hostilities against himself, which requires that he first renounce illusions about himself. Gravitating from the standpoint of pride to that of love, Feuerbach points toward a peace of man's reconciliation with his humanity as opposed to an Hegelian peace of his conquest of it. In this sense and to this degree, he moves back into a positive relation to the religious tradition against which German philosophy from Kant to Hegel had been in unwitting rebellion. Marxism was to reflect to some extent the influence of this deeply meaningful change of moral perspective.

VI

MARX AND FEUERBACH

*Feuerbach is the only one who has a serious, critical attitude
to the Hegelian dialectic, and who has made genuine discoveries
in this field. He is in fact the true conqueror of the old philosophy.*

MARX (1844)

The enthusiastic reception that Marx accorded Feuerbach's
Essence of Christianity and subsequent writings of 1842–3 has been
noted. Feuerbach was the 'brook of fire' through which all
speculative philosophers and theologians must go if they wanted
to reach things as they are in reality. Many similar comments by
Marx during the years between 1842 and 1845 attest to the
enormous impact that Feuerbach's thought had upon him. In
his Paris manuscripts of 1844, for example, he stated that
Feuerbach's chief writings were the only ones since Hegel's
Phenomenology and *Logic* that contained 'a real theoretical
revolution'.[1] The question is what, precisely, he meant by this.
What was Feuerbach's message to him?

Judging by Marx's own statements of the period, some
typical examples of which have been cited, he saw in Feuerbach
the anti-Hegel who had accomplished single-handedly the
revolutionary overthrow of 'the system'. In the doctoral dissertation Marx had referred to Hegel's disciples as captives of the
system, minds held fast in its fetters. Feuerbach is pictured in
various subsequent statements as a liberator. He has delivered
the disciples from bondage, shown them the way out of the
wilderness of Hegelian idealism to real man in the material
world. Significantly, the new Marx no longer speaks of the
teacher in the worshipful tones he had previously sounded. His
references to Hegel and Hegelianism are no longer those of a
grateful disciple, but rather of a thinker who looks back upon
Hegel's philosophy as a traversed stage in the evolution of
thought. In *The German Ideology,* for example, he casually dismisses the *Weltgeist* as a 'metaphysical spectre', and describes
the post-Hegelian period in German intellectual life as the time
of the 'putrescence of the absolute spirit'.[2] Clearly, the spell of

Hegelianism upon Marx's mind had in some sense been broken, and Feuerbach was instrumental in breaking it.

All this, however, is only a part, and not yet the decisive part, of the story of Feuerbach's role in the rise of Marxism. To say that it lay in the overthrow of Hegelianism is, in one sense, deceptive. For the 'conqueror of the old philosophy', as Marx describes Feuerbach, had been seduced by the very system that he conquered. If in one sense he overthrew Hegelianism, in another he enthroned it. He grounded it in the human psyche. This was the implication of his contention that 'Metaphysics is esoteric psychology'. What Hegel represents as taking place in the imaginary world of *Geist,* it said in effect, is actually taking place in the real world of *Mensch.* Hegel's self-alienated God is a mystified portrait of religious man—real man suffering estrangement from himself on the foundation of nature.

This was Feuerbach's 'real theoretical revolution'. His immensely exciting message to Marx was that *Hegelianism has truth-value.* If one has only to turn speculative philosophy 'upside down' in order to reach the truth in its 'unconcealed, pure, manifest form', it follows that Hegelianism is the truth, albeit in concealed, inverted or mystified form. Here, indeed, was a revolutionary idea for Marx, quite dazzling in its implications. We have outlined earlier his starting point. Two worlds stand in hostile opposition, he had reasoned. On the one hand, there is the grand fantasy, the subjective thought-world of the Hegelian philosophical consciousness, in which the self comes to know itself as God. On the other hand, there is the decidedly unphilosophical 'earthly reality' or 'world of phenomena', which needs to be transformed in the image of philosophy. Now Feuerbach was arguing that the 'earthly reality' *is* philosophical in the sense that processes imputed by Hegel to spirit are actually operative in man. He was saying in effect that the Hegelian philosophical fantasy is not simply a fantasy, but a fantastic reflection of reality, the reality of man's self-alienation in religion.

Feuerbach persuaded Marx that there are not two worlds, after all, but only one: the real material world, where man stands on firm and well rounded earth, inhaling and exhaling all the natural forces. The world of the Hegelian philosophical consciousness, in which spirit is alienated from itself and striving to transcend its alienation, is nothing but a fantasy-reflection, a mystical representation, of the condition of man in the real world. The fantasy corresponds to something quite real. The hard, empirical, objective fact of life in earthly reality is the fact of man's estrangement from himself. Hegelianism, if you only invert it and substitute 'man' for 'God' or 'spirit', gives you the truth. It is a revelation of truth by way of a code that the method of transformational criticism enables us to decipher.

Considering the immensity of this message, it is no wonder that Marx called Feuerbach 'the purgatory of our time'. There can be no doubt that Feuerbach played a momentous part in Marx's mental evolution. His 'naturalization' of Hegelianism, through which all humanity was projected as self-alienated in the sense of Hegelian philosophy, was a *sine qua non* of the rise of Marxism; for the main subject of Marx's first system is just this self-alienation of man. Hence Feuerbach was truly the fulcrum of the movement of thought from Hegelianism to Marxism. Paradoxically, he 'cured' Marx of his Hegelianism by giving him a life-long case of the disease. He freed Marx's mind from its bondage to the system *qua* system, but he did so by persuading him of the system's factuality, by suggesting that it was an inverted representation of human reality, a reflection in the philosopher's mind of the existential condition of man in the natural world. Consequently, the new 'anti-Hegelian' Marx, who dismisses the *Weltgeist* as a metaphysical spectre, is, in a decisive sense, more Hegelian than ever; it is a Marx whose processes of thought about the natural world are infected through and through with Hegelianism.

Significantly, Marx no sooner assimilated Feuerbach's message than he turned back to Hegel, devoting himself in 1843 to a textual commentary on the *Philosophy of Right* in which he applied the method of transformational criticism. In other words, the immediate result of his baptism in the 'brook of fire' was to convince him of the topicality of Hegel. Far from carrying him away from Hegelianism, it carried him back into it. Hegelianism, as he now saw it, was a true reading of human existence, but expressed in a confused manner; and Feuerbach had made the point clear. This, I believe, is the underlying sense of a statement that Marx made long afterward, in a letter written in 1865: 'Compared with Hegel, Feuerbach is very poor. All the same he was epoch-making *after* Hegel, because he laid stress on certain points which were disagreeable to the Christian

consciousness but important for the progress of criticism, and
which Hegel had left in mystic semi-obscurity.'³ The 'certain
points' refer to Feuerbach's presentation of religion as the self-
alienation of man. Marx is saying, in effect, that Hegel was the
giant of thought who had penetrated to the truth, and that
Feuerbach, a small thinker by comparison, contributed a
clarification of Hegel's latent meaning and thus rendered his
doctrine usable.

In the commentary on Hegel to which he turned in 1843, we
see Marx caught up in the heady rhythm of transformational
criticism as practised by Feuerbach. He says that the fundamental defect of the Hegelian way of thought is the 'mystification'. It is expressed in this: 'In Hegel a mystical substance
becomes the real subject, and the real subject is pictured as
something else, as an attribute of the mystical substance.' The
activity of the real subject—man—becomes in Hegel the
'imaginary inner activity of the Idea', and thus, 'in speculative
thinking everything is turned onto its head'. 'For in reality the
development takes place on the exoteric side.'⁴ In *The Holy
Family*, written in 1835, Marx returns to this theme: 'Instead of
making self-consciousness the *self-consciousness of man*—real man,
i.e. man living in the real, objective world and conditioned by it,
Hegel makes man the *man of self-consciousness*. He turns the world
on its head, and for this reason can transcend all the barriers in
his own head, which, of course, in no way keeps them from
continuing to exist for *real* man in wretched *experience*.'⁵

Man is not the 'man of self-consciousness', i.e. expression of
God; rather the Hegelian self-consciousness is the self-consciousness of 'real man'. Here is Marx engaged in the mental process
of turning Hegel upside down in accordance with Feuerbach's
prescription. And, as he himself makes plain in the same text,
the humanization of Hegel involves the Hegelianization of man:
'Hegel very often presents, within the speculative description, a
real description, one that grasps the *matter itself*' (*die Sache selbst*).⁶
Or as Marx puts it in his Paris manuscripts, the thinker who
would get to reality must abstract from the Hegelian abstraction
and substitute for self-consciousness the self-consciousness of man,
since 'Hegel posits man as self-consciousness'.⁷

[2]

Feuerbach's criticism of religion persuaded Marx of the

existential relevance of the Hegelian philosophy. Feuerbach had shown—or so it seemed to Marx—that the 'world of phenomena' was actually 'philosophical' in the sense of Hegelianism. Not, however, fully so. It was not yet a world in which philosophy had been wholly realized. It was 'philosophical' in the sense that the fundamental category of Hegelianism—self-alienation— applied to it; it was a world of *human* alienation. Therefore, the 'realization of philosophy' would mean, in concrete terms, the transcending of human alienation. To make the world philosophical would mean making it a world in which man is no longer estranged from himself, a world of human *self-realization*.

Thus Marx followed Feuerbach's lead and redefined the goal of history in terms of 'humanism'. Man's ultimate end is simply to become fully human, which he cannot be so long as he remains alienated from himself in religious fantasies of self-realization. This is a principal theme of the article that Marx wrote at the end of 1843 as an introduction to his critical commentary on Hegel's *Philosophy of Right*.* The criticism of religion, he declared in it, is the beginning of all criticism. It culminates in the precept that man is the supreme being for man. By exposing the God-illusion, it frees man to revolve around himself as his real sun: 'Religion is only the illusory sun that revolves around man so long as he has not yet begun to revolve around himself.'[8]

What would it mean for man to revolve around himself? It would mean, says Marx, that he insists upon actualizing himself *qua* man, becoming what he essentially is, instead of losing himself in the religious dream of self-actualization. The fantasy-life of religion is a pseudo-self-realization. Man does not become himself; he merely dreams about it. 'It is the *fantastic realization* of the human being, since the *human being* possesses no true reality.'[9] So the life of man in religion is an acceptance of the shadow of self-realization in lieu of the substance, the seeming in lieu of the being. Moreover, the seeming becomes for man a compensation for the non-being. And this Feuerbachian thought is the one that underlies Marx's statement here that 'Religion is the opium of the people'. He is simply restating the argument that Feuerbach, as we have seen, developed in his *Essence of*

* The article's title is 'Introduction to the Criticism of the Hegelian Philosophy of Right'. It was published in early 1844 in the *Deutsch-Französische Jahrbücher,* a journal published in Paris under the joint editorship of Marx and Arnold Ruge. The first issue of the journal proved also to be the last. For the sake of brevity Marx's article will be referred to here simply as the 'Introduction'.

Christianity. He does not mean simply that religion is a consolation for man's poverty, but that it is a consolation for his non-humanity, a surrogate for *being* man.

Further, the criticism of religion, which informs man that the imaginary being that he has projected as God is only an idealized image of himself, opens his eyes finally to what he could be and should be, and fires him with the desire to become it: 'Man, who sought a superman (*Übermensch*) in the fantastic reality of heaven but found there only a *reflection* of himself, will no longer wish to find merely an *appearance* of himself, only a non-man (*Unmensch*), in the realm where he seeks and must seek his true reality.'[10] The 'realm where he seeks and must seek his true reality' is, of course, the existing world. The argument is that man, as he now exists in the world, lacks reality as man. The complaint is not that he has failed to become God, but that he has failed to become human, that he exists as *Unmensch,* save in the religious imagination wherein he is an *Übermensch*. The goal for man is to realize his humanity, his human nature. And this, says Marx, carries the 'categorical imperative to overthrow all relations in which man is a debased, enslaved, helpless, contemptible creature—relations that can best be characterized by a Frenchman's exclamation concerning a projected dog tax: "Poor dogs! They want to treat you like people!" '[11]

This was the tendency of Marx's thought under the impact of Feuerbach's. He immediately and exultantly accepted Feuerbach's reading of the human situation as the true one, but proceeded to interpret it in his own way and to draw his own conclusions. The direction in which he proceeded was the direction in which he had started. He had begun with the programme of changing the world into a world of realized 'philosophy'. Never for a moment did he abandon his first premise concerning the need for world-change. However, this revolutionary imperative underwent a metamorphosis after he assimilated Feuerbach's 'de-mystification' of Hegelianism. The world of phenomena having been shown to be a world of human alienation, the Marxian revolutionary imperative took shape as a call to end human alienation by changing the world. It now said that a world in which man is everywhere estranged from himself and exists only as 'non-man' ought to be transformed into a new world of humanism in which alienation would be overcome and man would realize his nature as man. This was

the core of the reasoning process underlying Marx's eleventh
thesis on Feuerbach: 'The philosophers have only *interpreted* the
world, in various ways; the point is, to *change* it.'

Against this background it is understandable why Marx,
after assimilating Feuerbach's criticism of religion, very soon
embarked upon the criticism of Feuerbach. His world-revolutionary prescription for the cure of alienation was strikingly at
variance with the practical conclusion that Feuerbach himself
had drawn from the criticism of religion. What Feuerbach called
for, as has been noted, was first and foremost a reorientation of
thinking. The liberation of man from alienation required
essentially no more than a critical cognitive act on the scale of all
humanity. Men's attitude to themselves and one another would
change of itself once they had freed themselves from the religious
illusion. To this Marx rejoined that Feuerbach 'knows no other
"human relationships" "of man to man" than love and friend-
ship, and idealized at that'.[12] Thus, man is not to awaken from
the religious dream merely to engage in dialogues between the
I and the Thou. But Marx's main reproach is that Feuerbach
'accepts' reality, that he only wants to 'establish a correct
consciousness'.[13]

This is to turn inward in search of a solution for self-
alienation, whereas the need is to turn outward *against* the
world. 'The demand to renounce illusions about one's situation',
Marx declares, 'is a demand to renounce a situation that
requires illusions.'[14] The responsibility for man's self-alienation
rests with his life-situation in the existing state and society, with
the 'world of man' (*Menschenwelt*). Accordingly, the life-situation
will have to be radically altered in order for human nature to be
realized, for *Unmensch* to become *Mensch*. This is the burden of
the fourth of Marx's 'Theses on Feuerbach':

Feuerbach starts out from the fact of religious self-alienation, the
duplication of the world into a religious and a worldly one. His work
consists in dissolving the religious world into the worldly foundation.
But the fact that the worldly foundation raises itself above itself and
establishes itself as an independent realm in the clouds can only be
explained by the self-discord and self-contradictions within it. It
must itself, therefore, be understood in its contradiction and
revolutionized in practice. For example, after the earthly family is
seen to be the secret of the holy family, one must proceed to destroy
the former both in theory and practice.[15]

And so Marx is led to his position, enunciated in the eighth thesis,* that the solution of all problems, 'theoretical' ones included, lies in 'praxis'. Since all problems are at bottom problems of alienation, and since alienation is rooted in the life-situation of man in the world, practical action to change this situation is the key to a total solution. There is no way of ending alienation short of revolutionizing the world in which man finds himself existing in an inhuman condition.

Thus, Marx came to envisage the entire 'world of man' as a field of alienation. In this he was true to Hegel, who had described the objective world confronting spirit in consciousness as an alien, 'perverted world'. Marx employs this very term in arguing that Feuerbach's position is incomplete. He writes in the 'Introduction' that religion is merely the 'theoretical' form of alienation, behind or beneath which there are diverse 'practical' forms. If it is a 'perverted world-consciousness', they are constitutive aspects of the 'perverted world' itself. Hence the task at present is to proceed to the criticism of the practical forms: 'Now that the *holy form* of human self-alienation has been exposed, the next task for a philosophy in the service of history is to expose self-alienation in its *unholy forms*. The criticism of heaven thus turns into the criticism of earth, the *criticism* of religion into the *criticism of law*, the *criticism of theology* into the *criticism of politics*.'[16]

As this statement implies, Marx was extending and enlarging the concept of man's self-alienation. Feuerbach had concentrated upon the religious life as the sphere of human self-externalization and estrangement. Marx, together with others in the Young Hegelian circle, saw alienation as a phenomenon not confined to the religious life. Typically, he carried the idea to its farthest extreme. He came to see alienation everywhere. It was a phenomenon pervading every single sphere of human life in the existing world—religion, the state, law, the family, morality and, last but not least, the economic life.

[3]

Summering in Kreuznach in 1843, after his short and stormy career as editor of the *Rheinische Zeitung* had ended, Marx began the criticism of earth. His decision to write a critical commentary

---

* 'All social life is essentially *practical*. All the mysteries which urge theory into mysticism find their rational solution in human practice and in the comprehension of this practice' (*The German Ideology*, p. 199).

on Hegel's *Philosophy of Right* was motivated not only by the urge to apply the epochal new method of transformational criticism that Feuerbach had discovered. He was also interested in exposing the state, the political sphere of life, as one of the 'unholy forms' of human self-alienation.

As a student of Feuerbach, he took it for granted that the way to accomplish this was not to gather empirical data on politics but to subject the Hegelian philosophy of politics to transformational criticism. Since man's estrangement in the religious life was expressed theoretically in theology, to which Hegel's speculative theology had provided Feuerbach an interpretative key, it seemed to Marx that man's estrangement in the political life must be reflected, albeit in a mystified form, in Hegel's philosophy of the state. Accordingly, he examined the *Philosophy of Right* in search of an understanding of the state as a sphere of alienated human living. He did not complete the commentary, but summarized and extended his conclusions in two published articles written later in 1843, the 'Introduction' and an article entitled 'On the Jewish Question'.

According to Hegel's political philosophy, the state is the supreme form of human association and partakes of divinity. It is God on earth, the divine substance, the highest form of objectification of *Geist*. The state is the supreme social being, of which the family on the one hand and 'civil society' (*die bürgerliche Gesellschaft*) on the other are only incomplete expressions. In terms of the triadic formula, the family is the thesis, civil society is the antithesis, and the state is the higher synthesis in which both lower forms of association are transcended and perfected. In his concept of civil society, it should be added, Hegel drew upon the work of Adam Smith and other eighteenth-century thinkers who had formed a picture of society as a universe of 'economic men' each pursuing his own material self-interest. In the *Philosophy of Right*, for example, he describes civil society as a 'battlefield where everybody's individual private interest meets everyone else's'. 'In civil society each member is his own end, everything else is nothing to him. But except in contact with others he cannot attain the whole compass of his ends and therefore these others are means to the end of the particular member.'[17] Civil society, in Hegel's conception, is an economic sphere of universal egoism.

Applying Feuerbach's formula, Marx begins by turning

Hegel's political philosophy 'upside down'. For Hegel society is a manifestation of the state. This, says Marx, is a mystification. The true statement is precisely the reverse: the state is a manifestation, an outgrowth, of civil society. Calling the inverted position 'democracy', Marx writes in the commentary: 'Hegel proceeds from the state and turns man into a subjectified state. Democracy proceeds from man and turns the state into an objectified man. Just as religion does not create man but man religion—so the political system does not create the people but rather the people create the political system.'[18]

Thus, collective man ('the people') is not to be regarded as an attribute of the divine substance externalized in the state. Rather the state, the system of political institutions, is to be seen as an externalization of collective man in the form of political power, an embodiment in a separate sphere of the power of the human species. The real being that evolves in history is collective man or society. Instead of society being an expression of the state-in-the-making (Hegel's view), the state is an expression of society-in-the-making. It is externalized man in practical political form, just as God is externalized man in an imaginary or theoretical form. It is an earthly sphere of man's alienation corresponding to the heavenly sphere or religion: 'The political system has so far been the religious sphere, the religion of popular life. . . . Monarchy is the finished expression of this alienation. The republic is its negation within its own sphere.'[19]

This conception of political alienation follows the Feuerbachian model in further respects. According to Feuerbach, alienated man is a divided being leading two lives—one in the glorious fantasy world of the religious consciousness where he is God, and the other in the real world where he is a miserable and contemptible creature. The same, says Marx, applies to the practical side. As a citizen of the state, on the one hand, man is a 'communal being' (*Gemeinwesen*) or 'species being' (*Gattungswesen*); he participates in the communal life of the species. But civil society is prior to the state. The primary sphere of human existence is the 'sphere of egoism' or economic 'war of all against all', where man, especially in the modern world, feels and acts as an 'egoistic man' and not at all as a communal being.[20] Man, therefore, is dualized. His self-realization as a member of the political community is a spurious, empty, purely formal self-realization, just as in the religious fantasy he obtains at most a pseudo-realization of himself: 'Where the political state achieves fully developed form, man not only in thoughts, in consciousness, but in *reality*, in *life*, leads a double life, heavenly and earthly, a life in the *political community* in which he recognizes himself as a *communal being*, and a life in *civil society*, in which he acts as a *private person*, treats others as means, reduces himself to the role of a means, and becomes the plaything of alien forces.'[21]

This one-sentence summary of the concept of political aliena-tion is taken from Marx's essay 'On the Jewish Question'. In the same essay he indicates his solution for political alienation. It too follows the Hegel-Feuerbach *schema*. The cure for political alienation is the transcendence of the state, which means the repossession by man of the social power that has been external-ized in political institutions: 'Only when real individual man takes back into himself the abstract citizen of the state and, as individual man, in his empirical life, in his individual labour, in his individual relations, becomes a *species being*; only when man recognizes and organizes his *"forces propres"* as *social* forces and so ceases to separate social power from himself in the form of *political* power—only then will human emancipation take place.'[22] But Marx concludes that the liberation of man from alienation in the state, unlike his liberation from religion, will require a real social revolution.

VII

THE RISE OF PHILOSOPHICAL
COMMUNISM

Just as philosophy finds in the proletariat its material *weapon,
the proletariat finds in philosophy its* spiritual *weapon . . .*

MARX (1844)

The quest for elucidation of the 'unholy forms' of alienation
brought Marx to the economic studies that were to occupy him
the rest of his days. His analysis of the state as an unholy form of
the phenomenon was merely a transitional episode on the way
to his rendezvous with another unholy form that he soon began
to call 'material' or 'political-economic alienation'. Already in
the essay 'On the Jewish Question' he touched upon this theme.
He called the economic life in civil society 'the *extreme practical*
expression of human self-alienation'.[1] It should be noted that he
had barely begun at this time the study of political economy.
And when, in early 1844, he did begin this study in earnest, he
did so in search of proof of the proposition just cited. He sought
in the science of economics a theoretical idiom of expression of
man's estrangement from himself in the life of production.

Marx made no mention of this, however, in the brief account
of the history of his opinions that he offered many years later in
the preface to his *Critique of Political Economy* (1859). Referring to
his unpublished commentary of 1843 on the Hegelian political
philosophy, he wrote here: 'My investigation led to the result
that legal relations as well as forms of the state are to be grasped
neither from themselves nor from the so-called general development of the human mind, but rather have their roots in the
material conditions of life, the sum total of which Hegel,
following the example of the Englishmen and Frenchmen of
the eighteenth century, combines under the name of "civil
society", that, however, the anatomy of civil society is to be
sought in political economy.'[2] This statement invited the inference that Marx had proceeded directly from his discovery of
civil society in Hegel to the construction of Marxism in the form

made public in the later 1840's. And very many students of Marxism have drawn this inference.

But it is an erroneous one. Marx's account of the history of his opinions was extremely misleading because of what it omitted. He correctly indicated that his critique of Hegel's political philosophy had been a milestone on the road to Marxism. For it brought him to the premise that economic life in civil society is the basis of human existence, and this, of course, is a central notion of the Materialist Conception of History as formulated in mature Marxism. However, Marx was not ready at the end of 1843 to come forward with mature Marxism. He had to go through a critically important preparatory stage not mentioned in his famous preface of 1859. This was the stage of his creation of the unpublished early philosophical version of Marxism, which revolves around the idea of human self-alienation in the economic life.

He was preceded in this direction, and deeply influenced as well, by an older Young Hegelian, Moses Hess, who became known in the circle as the 'communist rabbi'. Hess was the originator of the German philosophical communism that Engels described in an article of 1843* as the inevitable outcome of the modern movement of German philosophy from Kant to Hegel and beyond. Engels' article expressly acknowledged that Hess was the first of their group to reach communism by the 'philosophical path'. Having done so, moreover, Hess was instrumental in the conversion of both Marx and Engels, who were not yet associates at the time, to the gospel of philosophical communism. They both became acquainted with him in 1842 through the *Rheinische Zeitung,* of which Marx was editor and Hess a correspondent. In long conversations in the offices of the paper at Cologne, Hess proselytized the two younger men. A single long session was sufficient to convert Engels.† Marx was slower to respond. His conversion took place only after he became convinced in 1843 that the economic life in civil society is the prime locus of human self-alienation.

Hess was an enthusiastic disciple of Feuerbach, and constructed the doctrine of philosophical communism as an ex-

* See above, pp. 26-7.

† As Hess later described it, 'We talked of questions of the day. Engels, who was a revolutionary to the core when he met me, left as a passionate communist' (Gustav Mayer, *Friedrich Engels,* p. 30).

tension of Feuerbach's 'humanism'. As noted earlier, Feuerbach wrote in his *Essence of Christianity* that 'productive activity' is an attribute of the human species projected by theology as divine creativity. Hess enlarged upon this theme. He postulated that productive activity is the essential attribute of the species. The life of the human species, he argued, is ideally a life of co-operative producing activity through which men objectify their productive power (*Produktivkraft*) in a variety of useful material objects. But man in the modern world lives in a state of egoism. Instead of producing cooperatively and for the welfare of the species as a whole, egoistic men appropriate the productive power of the species in the form of money or private property. The modern 'commercial state' is, therefore, a 'perverted world' in which the productive power of mankind becomes the wealth of money-worshipping egoistic individuals. Hess presented this argument in an essay with the Feuerbachian title 'On the Essence of Money' ('*Über das Geldwesen*'), which he submitted to Marx and Ruge, probably at the close of 1843, for publication in their *Deutsch-Französische Jahrbücher*.*

Earlier Hess had steeped himself in the contemporary litera-ture on socialism and communism, of which France in those days was the fountainhead. A French book that particularly im-pressed him was Proudhon's *What Is Property?* Published in 1840, this work eventually became famous in Europe because the author answered the title question with the sensational statement that 'Property is theft'. The statement, it must be added, was somewhat less radical than it appeared. For Proudhon defined 'property' or 'private property' in a very special way. He distinguished it from the individual right of possession and use of goods, including capital goods; of such 'possession' he heartily approved. 'Property' was specifically the right of the owner of capital goods to employ the labour of others to augment his own wealth. It was 'theft' in the sense that their labour contributed to his enrichment. Proudhon anticipated Marx in calling this capital-labour relation an exploitation of man by man: 'From the right of the strongest springs the exploitation of man by man, or bondage.'[3]

---

* Inasmuch as the journal was suppressed after its first issue came out in early 1844, Hess' article was first published more than a year later in the *Rheinische Jahrbücher zur Gesellschaftlichen Reform*. It has been reprinted in *Sozialistische Aufsätze 1841–1847*, a collection of Hess' essays edited by R. Zlocisti.

Proudhon once remarked that the three main influences in his life were Hegel, Adam Smith and the Bible. He sketched in his book an economically oriented philosophy of history with an Hegelian structure of thesis, antithesis and higher synthesis. History he pictured as a three-phase affair proceeding from primitive communism through the intermediate long stage of private property to a final and future stage called 'liberty'. He condemned communism, or community ownership of goods and persons, as a system that denies individuality, places mediocrity on a par with excellence, and means exploitation of the strong (i.e. the gifted few) by the multitude of the weak. 'Communism is oppression and slavery', he wrote. 'The greatest danger to which society is exposed today is that of another shipwreck on this rock.'[4]

Proudhon's prescription for solving the social problem was: 'Suppress property while maintaining possession . . .' The result of such action would be the third form of society, or 'liberty'. It would be a synthesis of the historical thesis (communism) and the historical antithesis (property), excluding the negative features of both—communal ownership on the one hand and the exploitation of man by man on the other. The existing order of private property would thus be replaced with a system of cooperative production by individual small proprietors secure in their right of individual possession of the means and fruits of their labour. This would be the 'true form of human association'.[5]

To Hess, and subsequently to both Engels and Marx, Proudhon's book appeared the 'most philosophical' of all the French communist writings.* One reason for their enthusiasm was that Proudhon had adumbrated the idea of incorporating socialism or communism into an Hegelian philosophy of history. Hess, for his part, was prepared to accept Proudhon's 'true form of human association' as a fair description of the economic arrangements under socialism or communism itself (these two terms being used more or less interchangeably at that time). More important, he assimilated Proudhon's concept of private property into his own Feuerbachian theory of alienation in the

* In *The Holy Family*, written in 1845, Marx hailed it as 'a scientific manifesto of the French proletariat', comparable in historical significance to Sieyes' revolutionary pamphlet *What Is the Third Estate?* (*MEGA*, III, pp. 201, 211). He continued to profess high admiration for the work even after his subsequent break with Proudhon.

economic life. He identified the perverted commercial world, where man externalizes his substance in the form of money, as a world of private property in Proudhon's special sense of 'theft', i.e. as a world in which egoistic man exploits the labour of working man in order to amass money. He viewed the exploitative relation of the two men as one of their mutual estrangement. Accordingly, 'money is the product of mutually alienated men; *it is externalized man*'.[6] Under the future system of socialism or communism, meaning free cooperative production in the service of the species, the mutually alienated men would cease to be alienated and would enter into truly human I-Thou relations in their lives as producers. Hence communism would be the positive content of humanism.

In presenting this doctrine of philosophical communism, Hess made much of an analogy between the religious life in Feuerbach's image of it and the acquisitive life in the commercial state. He compared Christianity ('the theory, the logic of egoism') and the pursuit of money as the theoretical and practical expressions of one and the same basic religious phenomenon: self-worship. Money, he argued, has become the practical object of worship 'for our Christian merchants and Jewish Christians'.[7] Hence the 'essence of money' is the materialistic counterpart of the 'essence of Christianity'. If in the one case egoistic man externalizes himself mentally in God, in the other he externalizes himself materially in money. Hess put it as follows: 'The essence of the modern world of exchange, of money, is the realized essence of Christianity. The commercial state . . . is the promised kingdom of heaven, as, conversely, God is only idealized capital and heaven only the theoretical commercial world.' From this it followed that 'National economy is the science of the earthly, as theology is the science of the heavenly, acquisition of goods'.[8] That is, the new science of political economy, which deals with the accumulation of capital, must disclose the practical alienation of man in the economic life just as theology disclosed to Feuerbach his theoretical alienation in Christianity.

[2]

Marx, as has been indicated, addressed himself to economic alienation in his essay 'On the Jewish Question'. The formal aim of this essay was to criticize the views on the Jewish question that

Bruno Bauer had expressed in two articles published earlier in 1843. In reply to Bauer's contention that the social emancipation of the Jews was dependent upon their religious emancipation, Marx argued that the real emancipation of the Jews was necessarily connected with the general emancipation of humanity from the state. This thesis was presented in the broad frame of the doctrine of political alienation summarized above.

The theme of economic alienation was broached in a separate concluding section of the article.* Here he offered a trenchant formulation of the idea that the economic life in the 'state of egoism' is a practical religion of money-worship. He gave the religious analogy a special new twist and emphasis by calling the practical religion 'Judaism'. This may have been prompted by Hess' reference to the 'Christian merchants and Jewish Christians'. It capitalized upon the fact that the German term 'Judaism' (*Judentum*) had the secondary connotation of 'commerce'. So Marx describes Judaism or commerce as a religion in which money is the god: 'What is the worldly cult of the Jew? *Huckstering*. Who is his worldly god? *Money*.' And further: 'Money is the jealous one God of Israel, beside which no other God may stand. Money dethrones all the gods of man and turns them into a commodity. Money is the universal, independently constituted value of all things. It has, therefore, deprived the whole world, both the world of man and nature, of its own value. Money is the alienated essence of man's work and his being. This alien being rules over him and he worships it.'[9]

Following Hess, Marx conceives the practical religion as a material form of self-alienation corresponding to the spiritual form as analyzed by Feuerbach: 'Selling is the praxis of externalization. Just as man, so long as he is engrossed in religion, can only objectify his nature by turning it into an *alien* creature of the fantasy, so, under the domination of egoistic need, he can act in a practical way, create objects practically, only by subordinating these products as well as his activity to the power of an alien being and bestowing upon them the signifi-

---

* This section has the appearance of a postscript, for it follows the natural conclusion of the essay and raises a new question. It may have been written as late as January, 1844. Marx wrote the bulk of the article shortly after his move to Paris at the end of October, 1843. Whether he had received the manuscript of Hess' 'On the Essence of Money' by the time of writing of the concluding section is not certain but seems quite probable. In any event, he was quite familiar with Hess' position from personal conversations.

cance of an alien being—money.'[10] On this basis Marx argues
that the modern commercial world, where man is universally
dominated by egoistic need, is practically speaking a world of
Judaism: 'The Christian was from the beginning the theorizing
Jew; the Jew therefore the practical Christian, and the practical
Christian has once more become Jew. . . . Christianity is the
sublime thought of Judaism; Judaism is the lowly application of
Christianity, but this application could only become universal
after Christianity, as fully developed religion, had *theoretically*
completed the alienation of man from himself and from nature.'[11]
The reasoning turns wholly on Hess' thesis, summarized above,
that Christianity and commerce are respectively the theoretical
and practical forms of egoistic man's self-alienation. It brings
Marx to the conclusion that the emancipation of Jew and non-
Jew alike depends upon the 'emancipation of humanity from
Judaism'. This, he writes, would mean the organization of
society in such a way as to eliminate the possibility of
'huckstering'.[12]*

An acceptance of the idea of socialism or communism was
implicit in this formulation. It may be noted that Marx had been
slow in his conversion to a communist position. A year or so
earlier, as editor of the *Rheinische Zeitung*, he declared editorially
that communist ideas in their present form did not appear to
have even theoretical validity, adding, however, that he knew
very little about them. Not until the closing months of 1842 did
he embark upon a systematic perusal of the contemporary
French literature on socialism and communism. With the
notable exception of Proudhon, the writers on this subject
occupied themselves with the designing of blueprints of a future
communist organization of society. Marx reacted quite negative-
ly to this. In a letter to Ruge in September 1843, he dismissed
the communist 'systems' or utopias, along with the whole notion
of 'designing the future', as a 'dogmatic abstraction', adding

* An English translation of Marx's article has recently been published under the
highly misleading title *A World Without Jews* (Philosophical Library, New York,
1959). An introduction by the publisher and translator, Mr Dagobert D. Runes,
makes out the article to be a doctrine of anti-semitism and a forerunner of the anti-
semitic policies of certain modern states, which 'bring to reality the sanguinary
dream of Karl Marx—a world without Jews' (p. xi). This reflects, at best, a gross
misconception of the article. Although Marx did at times express anti-Jewish
feelings, his article was in no sense a plea to rid the world of Jews. It was a plea to
rid the world of 'Judaism', by which he meant a practical religion of money-
worship. What he here called 'Judaism' he later renamed 'capitalism'.

that a new world could be discovered through a merciless criticism of everything existing.[13] By this time, however, he was prepared to accept the idea of communism in the framework of the German philosophical communism evolved by Hess. But he was moving toward a different and characteristically Marxian version of philosophical communism. He was, in particular, incorporating into it an idea wholly absent from Hess' version—the idea of the proletariat.

[3]

Marx's image of the proletariat was not of empirical origin. He did not come by it, for example, by observation of contemporary factory conditions, by direct contact with industrial workers and work, or even by the study of political economy. His earliest meetings with working-class people appear to have taken place after he moved to Paris in the late autumn of 1843. By then, however, the idea of the proletariat was already formed in his mind. The path by which he reached it was the philosophical path traced in the preceding pages. He assimilated the concept of the proletariat into the doctrine of human self-alienation that he had developed under the primary influence of Hegel, Feuerbach, and Hess. Briefly, in Marx's mind *man became proletariat*.

He came to see in the proletariat, defined by property-lessness, the prototype and visible manifestation of man in his state of self-alienation in the existing world. The image of self-alienated humanity turned into an image of the proletariat as the living, breathing, suffering expression of self-alienated humanity, and also its *rebellious* expression—alienated man in revolt against his condition. This momentous metamorphosis is reflected in Marx's 'Introduction to the Criticism of the Hegelian Philosophy of Right', written also at the end of 1843. It is the first of his writings in which he speaks of the proletariat.

At the outset of the article he expounds his idea that human nature possesses no true reality, that man exists in this world as *Unmensch*. At the close of it he proclaims that 'philosophy finds in the proletariat its *material* weapon'. He explains that revolution requires a 'material foundation', meaning an element of society tending toward 'practical-critical activity'. 'It is not enough for thought to strive toward realization; reality itself must drive toward thought.'[14] The element of contemporary 'reality' that is driving, albeit unconsciously, toward 'thought' is the proletariat. It is a class with 'radical aims', a class that is no mere class but the dissolution of all classes, that is universal because of the universality of its sufferings, that claims no special right because it is the victim of no special wrong but of wrong in general, that cannot emancipate itself without emancipating at the same time all other spheres of society. In sum, the proletariat is a class that 'represents the *complete loss of man* and can only regain itself, therefore, by the *complete resurrection of man*'.[15] 'Complete loss of man' means, of course, totally alienated man.

How did Marx arrive at this singular philosophical conception of the proletariat? First of all, from what source did he derive the term 'proletariat'? According to Sidney Hook, the term came into currency among the German intellectuals after the dissemination of French socialist ideas among them in the 1830's. 'In their most advanced phase', writes Hook, 'they spoke in the name of the proletariat, but the only proletarians they knew were the ones talked about by the French socialist writers.' Some even began to proclaim that '*Das Proletariat ist die Menschheit*'.[16] Marx was one of these German intellectuals, and it must be said of him too that the only proletarians he knew were the ones he read about in books. Moreover, the book that particularly influenced his thinking in regard to the proletariat was a German book published in Leipzig in 1842, *Der Socialismus und Communismus des heutigen Frankreichs*. Its author was Lorenz von Stein, a conservative Hegelian and staunch monarchist.

In 1840 Stein was commissioned by the Prussian Government to make an on-the-spot study of the disturbing new French doctrines of socialism and communism, and while in Paris to observe and report on any communist connections of migratory German workers. The resulting book was a history of fifty years of French radical thought, presented in a framework of Hegelian theorizing about society. It treated French communism and socialism, originating with Baboeuf in the late eighteenth century, as ideologies expressing the interest of the proletariat, an entirely new class that had entered the stage of history during the great French Revolution when the workers of Paris took events into their own hands. This propertyless mass, so far most evident in France and England but showing signs of emergence elsewhere in Europe as well, was imbued with an imperious tendency to generalize its condition by creating a 'community of goods' (*Gütergemeinschaft*). Consequently, it bore within itself the seeds of the total overthrow and dissolution of historic European society founded on the principles of personality and property. It was the fate of this revolutionary new class that the anti-property doctrines of socialism and communism had in view. Wittingly or unwittingly the theorists of socialism and communism were elaborating a *Weltanschauung* for the proletariat in its 'battle of labour-power with capital'.[17] Here in Stein's book we see perhaps the first significant formulation of the thesis that has since become familiar under the heading 'revolt of the masses'.

In his *Philosophy of Right* Hegel said that modern civil society shows a dangerous tendency to the 'concentration of disproportionate wealth in a few hands' at one pole and the 'creation of a rabble of paupers' at the other. In a note he explained that poverty in itself does not make a rabble, for 'a rabble is created only when there is joined to poverty a disposition of mind, an inner indignation against the rich, against society, against the government, etc.'[18] In his first chapter, entitled 'The Proletariat and Society', Stein pictured the modern proletariat as a pauperized rabble in Hegel's sense. He insisted that one must sharply distinguish between the notions of 'proletarian' and 'poor'. There had always been poor people in society, but proletarians were something new. They were not simply destitute people, but a mass of proud and defiant poor, rebellious against the society that had given birth to them as a class. They possessed neither property nor education, but were unreconciled to their lot. Accordingly, this was a class 'which may very properly be called a dangerous element; dangerous in respect of its numbers and its often tested courage; dangerous in respect of its consciousness of unity; dangerous in respect of its feeling that only through revolution can its aims be reached, its plans accomplished'.[19]

Marx's writings of the middle forties show a minute textual familiarity with Stein's book. Although he never explicitly acknowledged his debt to the conservative Hegelian and one-time Prussian police agent for the germ of his own concept of the proletariat, the fact of the debt is not seriously in doubt. If Marxist circles have never been willing to admit this, it is doubtless in part because of their desire to believe that Marx discovered the proletariat in much the same way as Newton discovered gravity, i.e. by a direct insight into the reality. However, the circumstantial evidence for the view that he actually 'discovered' the proletariat in Lorenz von Stein's book is compelling. His concept of the proletariat, as developed in the 'Introduction', endows this class with the attributes Stein has seen in it. It is proud, resentful and defiant, possessing that 'revolutionary valour which hurls in the face of the adversary the insolent challenge: "I am nothing, but I have to be everything".' It carries within itself the seeds of a mighty revolutionary up- heaval that will destroy the existing order of society: 'In an- nouncing the *dissolution of the existing world order,* the proletariat merely reveals the secret of its own being, for it *is the factual* dissolution of this world order. In demanding the *negation of private property,* the proletariat merely elevates into a *principle of society* that which society has made into *its* principle.'[20] All this is straight out of Stein.*

There was, of course, a serious difference of evaluation between Stein and Marx. If the rise of the proletariat betokened the coming fall of historic European society, one could logically react in either of two opposite ways depending on one's attitude toward existing society. The conservative Stein deplored the dangerous new historical phenomenon; the revolutionary Marx greeted it with great rejoicing, seeing in it the material weapon of philosophy.

Marx's response to the thesis of Stein that communism is the class ideology of the proletariat was the opposite of Hess'. Hess and his coterie completely rejected the idea. They accused Stein of maligning socialism or communism by seeing in it nothing but the relation to the proletariat. To link these doctrines with a single class, with the material interests of the proletariat, with the 'needs of the stomach', was to miss the whole point of 'true socialism'. It was to obscure the fact that socialism or com- munism is concerned with mankind as a whole, and that man's

---

* Arguing the other side of the case, Sidney Hook writes: 'As far as the mooted question of Stein's influence on Marx is concerned, it is sufficient to point out that Stein prophesied that the existing proletariat would not develop in Germany. Responsibility for the existence of the proletariat is laid at the door of the *Weltgeist*' (*From Hegel to Marx*, p. 199). However, Stein's prophecy regarding Germany in no way prevented Marx from accepting his concept of the proletariat minus that prophecy. And the linking of the proletariat with the *Weltgeist* (or general move- ment of world history) would not have been likely to diminish Marx's interest in Stein's theory of the proletariat or stand in the way of his assimilation of it into his own developing position.

self-alienation rather than crass material want is the problem to which it offers the solution.* Marx fully accepted the latter two points, but did not take Stein's thesis regarding the proletariat to be inconsistent with them. For he saw something more in the proletariat than either Stein or Hess did. In the proletariat, with its revolutionary tendency to abolish itself as a proletariat by the socialization of private property, Marx saw a mighty manifestation of human self-alienation and the urge to transcend it.

He had not for a moment abandoned the tenets of philosophical communism. He fused the ideas of alienated man and the proletariat into the new and original idea that the modern proletariat is the supreme expression of alienated man. As he saw it, the proletariat is a special class, to be sure, but a class into which all mankind is slowly sinking. This dissolution of society as a special class represents, as Marx put it in *The Holy Family*, 'a dehumanization (*Entmenschung*) that is conscious of its dehumanization and therefore seeks to cancel itself'. Its state of dispossession (*Nichthaben*) is to be grasped as a spiritual as well as material condition: 'Dispossession is the most desperate *spiritualism*, total unreality of man, total reality of non-man.'[21]

The argument behind these statements will be examined at length in the following chapters and may be summarized briefly here: if man externalizes his being or human essence in the material things that he produces, then working man made propertyless by 'theft', i.e. proletarian man, is self-alienated man *par excellence*. And if, further, society is now generating in the proletariat a rebellious propertyless mass, this is proof that self-alienated man is striving to overcome his alienation and recover his human nature by overthrowing the world order that has made him an alienated being. Consequently, communism, although it is the class ideology of the proletariat, is destined to serve not alone the material interest of this own class but the universal spiritual need of man to end his self-estrangement.

The discovery of the proletariat did not, therefore, shake the

* Hess developed these points in a review of Stein's book, published under the title '*Socialismus und Communismus*' in the collection *Einundzwanzig Bogen aus der Schweiz* in 1843. The essay is reprinted in the Zlocisti collection. As an outcome of this controversy, Hess and his immediate adherents became known as the 'true socialists'. Marx and Engels later devoted the third part of their *German Ideology* to a polemic against the 'true socialists' and their refusal to see the connection between socialism and the revolutionary proletariat. The disagreement was real and highly important, but should not obscure the important part that Hess played in the rise of Marxism.

hold of philosophical communism upon the mind of Marx. It had the opposite effect; it persuaded him of both the validity and the burning topicality of the whole conception. He was now all the more deeply convinced that alienation was no mere figment of Hegel's philosophical imagination, but a massive fact of real life throughout modern society. There were, in particular, masses of alienated men in every centre of industry where wretched proletarians slaved from dawn till dark, sacrificing themselves on the altar of the worldly god. The visible signs of their unrest, of the proletariat's incipient rebellion against its conditions, were merely the surface symptoms of dehumanized man's revolt against his dehumanization. So Marx concluded his 'Introduction' with the following proclamation: 'Philosophy cannot realize itself without the abolition of the proletariat; the proletariat cannot abolish itself without the realization of philosophy.'[22]

[4]

This was the point he had reached in early 1844, when the suppression of the *Deutsch-Französische Jahrbücher* left him jobless in Paris. He was on the threshold of Marxism. He had all the essential ingredients of Marxism save one—the generative idea, the organizing insight that causes all the separate components to fall into place in a single systematic structure. Every original and powerful system of thought presupposes such a creative act; it is something decisively more than the sum of the component ideas that its author has taken from others or forged for himself. With Hegel, as we have seen, the generative idea was the formula for religion as man's self-elevation from finite to infinite life; with Feuerbach, it was the proposition that metaphysics is esoteric psychology. Marx had not yet conceived his generative idea. He had presented his major 'components' in two short articles in the *Jahrbücher*. On the strength of these alone his name would have rated scarcely more than a footnote in a history of the Young Hegelian movement. There was still no Marxian system.

He knew this, and set to work during 1844 to develop a system, i.e. to write a full-length book. As he had said in the 'Introduction', the next task for a philosophy in the service of history was to expose human self-alienation in its 'unholy forms'. He had already worked on the political form and had come to the conclusion that there was a still more fundamental form—economic alienation. Hess had suggested that political economy might furnish the materials for an exposure of alienation in the economic life comparable to Feuerbach's exposure of religious alienation via theology. A criticism of political economy was, then, the next business on the agenda of philosophy. The practicability of such an enterprise had been shown already by Hess' convert Engels, who in January 1844 sent Marx and Ruge, for publication in the *Jahrbücher*, an essay entitled 'Outlines of the Criticism of Political Economy'. Marx liked the essay immensely. This led to a meeting with Engels in August 1844 in Paris, which in turn was the beginning of their working partnership.

So Marx set out on his life-long path of 'criticism of political economy'. By way of preparation he began to read and make extracts from some of the standard writings on economics, such as Smith's *Wealth of Nations* and Say's *Treatise on Political Economy*. This was his first serious application to the literature of political economy, and it is worth noting that it occurred only some weeks or months before he created the economic interpretation of history. He embodied many of the extracts into his own manuscript. As he explained in the draft preface, the work at hand was to be a criticism of political economy as one part of a larger systematic enterprise—a criticism of every single sphere of present human existence under the aspect of estrangement. Criticisms of law, ethics, politics, etc., would be issued in a series of pamphlets to follow.

Marx worked for some time without making any progress toward the desired systematic organization of the material. In the background of his mind at this time was the concept of 'economic alienation'. The alienation of things is the praxis of human self-externalization, he had written in the article 'On the Jewish Question'. Man externalizes his being in material objects that assume the form of money. Now all this was quite Hegelian in a sense. It conceived of man the economic producer on the analogy of Hegelian spirit, which externalizes itself and then seeks, through knowing, to re-appropriate the alien objective world as its property. Marx was brooding along these lines when, one day in the late spring or early summer of 1844, he suddenly had what struck him as a colossal insight. It must have hit him with the force of a lightning bolt out of the blue. And no wonder, for it was the truly astonishing thought that

Hegelianism is fundamentally about economics. In Marx's own words, 'Hegel has the point of view of modern political economy.'[23]

Metaphysics is esoteric psychology, Feuerbach had reasoned. It is not that alone, Marx now added; it is also *esoteric economics*. The latent referent of the Hegelian philosophy of spirit is man's life as an economic producer. Accordingly, Hegelianism provides the necessary clue to a criticism of political economy! With this thought Marxism was conceived. In the ensuing weeks Marx amplified it in a series of papers now known as the *Economic and Philosophic Manuscripts of 1844*.

PART III

ORIGINAL MARXISM

VIII

WORKING MAN AS WORLD CREATOR

> *The object of labour is, therefore, the* objectification of man's
> species-life; *for he duplicates himself not only, as in conscious-
> ness, intellectually, but also actively, in reality, and therefore
> he looks at himself in a world that he has created.* MARX (1844)

Marx founded Marxism in an outburst of Hegelizing. He
considered himself to be engaged in no more than a momentous
act of translation of the already discovered truth about the
world from the language of idealism into that of materialism.
He was only restating in a clear scientific form what Hegel had
said before him in a confused philosophical form. Hegelianism
itself was latently or esoterically an economic interpretation of
history. It treated history as a 'history of production' (*Produktionsgeschichte*), in which spirit externalizes itself in thought-
objects. But this was simply a mystified representation of *man*
externalizing himself in *material* objects. Consequently, what
Hegel was really talking about in his philosophy, in so far as his
philosophy itself was real, was the economic life, the human
labour process. Such was Marx's generative idea.

If the analysis of Hegelianism presented earlier in this book
is a valid one, we may infer that he was mistaken. Although it
covers the economic aspect of life along with all others, the
Hegelian philosophy of history as the self-realization of spirit
was not a sublimated economic interpretation of history, and
Marx created his own system on the basis of a misreading of
Hegel. This judgment will stand, I believe, in the face of the
recent effort by George Lukacs, the foremost Marx scholar in
the Communist world, to substantiate Marx's position. In his
Der Junge Hegel und die Probleme der Kapitalistischen Gesellschaft
(1948), Lukacs attempts to find in the youthful Hegel's reading
in Adam Smith the central source of inspiration for his later
philosophical system. But this interpretation of Hegelianism
appears untenable. Although Hegel, as has been indicated, was
indeed influenced by Smith at certain points in his thinking,
these were not the central points. Above all, the Hegelian dia-

lectic, associated with the idea of spirit's self-externalization and
self-alienation in the cognitive quest for the Absolute, was not
economic in meaning but psychological.*

Nevertheless, Marx viewed it all as esoteric economics. And
looking back over the whole strange Odyssey of German
thought that preceded and prepared this step, we can see a
certain inevitableness in it. Feuerbach had established to his
followers' satisfaction that Hegelianism, though theological
in manifest content, was latently anthropological. Hegel's concept of the self-alienated God was an inverted representation of
man alienated from himself in religion. With this key Feuerbach
attempted to unlock all the mysteries of the Christian theology,
which now became for him an open book telling the story of
self-estranged humanity in mystical terms of self-estranged
divinity. Hess then took the next step of postulating that Feuerbach's 'Christianity' had a materialistic counterpart in the commercial life, and that the special theology of this practical religion of money-worship ought to be found in the science of
political economy. Marx's was simply the logical final step of
supposing that the theology of the worldly god must, like the
other theology, have its open sesame in Hegelianism. Had not
Hegel, after all, made constant use of such terms as 'production', 'appropriation' and 'property'? Was this not indicative of
an underlying 'point of view of modern political economy'?
Such was Marx's position, and he never abandoned it.

It presupposed the distinction that Feuerbach had made
between the manifest and latent content of Hegelianism, together
with the notion that the latter can be extracted by the method of
transformational criticism or inversion. Marx clearly recognizes
his great debt to Feuerbach. He speaks of Feuerbach's 'discover-

---

* It would seem that a faithful follower of Marx must concur with Lukacs in
his 'economic interpretation' of Hegelianism. For if Marx misread Hegel, he very
probably misread reality as a consequence. If, to be more specific, Hegelianism was
not latently a true representation of the human labour process, then Marx's
deciphered Hegelianism is scarcely likely to be economically real. It is interesting
in this connection that a Soviet Marxist, E. I. Solov'ev, has recently disputed
Lukacs' position. 'G. Lukacs' inference concerning a direct continuity between
Smith and Hegel in economic theory is erroneous'. Further, Hegel must not be
seen 'as a thinker who already performed part of the work that in reality lay wholly
on the shoulders of Marxism' (*'Razdelial li Gegel' trudovuiu teoriiu stoimosti?'* ['Did
Hegel Share the Labour Theory of Value?'], *Voprosy filosofii*, 1959, no. 3, pp. 114,
124). Solov'ev does not seem to realize that in rejecting Lukacs' attempt at an
economic interpretation of Hegel, he is implicitly rejecting the idea around which
Marx constructed Marxism.

ies about the nature of philosophy', and says that 'positive criticism as a whole—and therefore also German positive criticism of political economy—owes its true foundation to the discoveries of *Feuerbach*. . . .'[1] At the same time, he criticizes Feuerbach for confining himself to 'theological criticism'. He believes, in other words that Feuerbach did not fulfill the promise of his own 'discoveries' about the nature of philosophy. He saw in Hegelianism only a representation of the alienation of man in the theoretical life of religion. He did not grasp it as esoteric economics. He failed to take Marx's own further step of assuming that Hegelianism turned 'upside down' in the Feuerbachian manner gives you a valid picture of man's alienation in the practical life of religion, the economic processes of labour under the 'money-system'.

Consequently, Marx declares in his preface that German thought still faces 'the *necessary* task of settling accounts between *criticism* and its point of origin—the Hegelian *dialectic* and German philosophy as a whole'.[2] He promises to provide this final critical settling of accounts with Hegel in his concluding chapter. The draft of the concluding chapter, entitled by the editor 'Criticism of the Hegelian Dialectic and Philosophy as a Whole', has survived among Marx's manuscripts.

[2]

This crucial document shows, in the first place, that when Marx speaks of Hegelianism he has in mind primarily the philosophy of history set forth by Hegel in his *Phenomenology of Mind*. The point needs stressing because it has often been assumed that the work of Hegel's from which Marx took his departure in the creation of his own system was the *Philosophy of Right*. Such an inference is understandable in the light of Marx's own mention of the latter work in the short account of the history of his opinions that he gave in the preface of the *Critique of Political Economy*.* It is a reasonable one, moreover, considering that this is the book in which Hegel deals most directly with social and political questions, and that mature Marxism purports to be above all a theory of society. However, Marx's manuscripts, and particularly his 'Criticism of the Hegelian Dialectic and Philosophy as a Whole', make it unmistakeably plain that the inference is erroneous, and that

* See above, p. 106.

Hegel's *Phenomenology* is the work with which Marxism is immediately affiliated.

Having asserted that criticism must now settle accounts with 'its mother, the Hegelian dialectic', Marx writes further: 'Let us take a look at the Hegelian system. One must begin with Hegel's *Phenomenology*, the true birthplace and secret of the Hegelian philosophy.'[3] He then writes out the whole table of contents of this book, analyzes it, and extols it. He contrasts its 'critical' character with 'the uncritical positivism and equally uncritical idealism of the later Hegelian works'.[4] But most important of all, Marx takes the philosophy of history developed by Hegel here as his model in the construction of his own system, which becomes therefore a kind of phenomenology of man centering in the idea of man's self-alienation in the labour process. This he takes to be what Hegel, underneath it all, was really driving at. Hegel's phenomenology of *Geist* was, in unconscious intent, a phenomenology of *Mensch*: 'Briefly, within an abstract framework, he grasps labour as the self-productive act of man, the relation to himself as an alien being, and his manifestation *qua* alien being as the developing consciousness and life of the species.' 'The *Phenomenology*', maintains Marx, 'is criticism in a concealed, un-self-clarified and mystifying form. However, in so far as it firmly grasps the alienation of man (*Entfremdung des Menschen*), even if man appears only in the form of spirit, *all* the elements of criticism lie hidden in it and are often prefigured and worked out in a manner far transcending the Hegelian standpoint.'[5]

Thus Marx undertakes to invert the *Phenomenology*. He construes it as a revelation of the truth about man in a 'concealed, un-self-clarified and mystifying form'. But unlike Feuerbach, who saw here only a mystified picture of the truth about *religious* man and hence only the foundation of a criticism of religion, Marx sees in Hegel's self-alienated God an upside-down portrait of man as an *economic producer*. He believes, therefore, that the criticism hidden and prefigured in the *Phenomenology* was a 'criticism of political economy'. Spirit producing itself as spirit and finding itself confronted with an alien world was man producing himself as man and finding himself so confronted. The secret of Hegelianism was the human labour process: 'The greatness of the Hegelian *Phenomenology* and of its end-result—the dialectic of negativity as the moving and generative principle—

lies, firstly, in the fact that Hegel grasps the self-production of man as a process, objectification as de-objectification, as externalization and transcendence of this externalization; that he therefore grasps the essence of *labour* and conceives objective man, true man because real man, as the result of his *own labour*.'[6]

Feuerbach considered Hegel's philosophy a vehicle of truth in so far as the criticism of religion was latently present in it, but rejected the manifest Hegelianism as a philosophical extension of theology. Marx reasons in precisely similar fashion in his critical settling of accounts with Hegel. On the one hand, he regards the *Phenomenology* as a gigantic vehicle of truth in that the criticism of political economy was implicit already in its theory of self-alienated spirit. When 'man' is substituted for 'spirit', this theory shows man's economic life to be a life of alienated labour (*entfremdete Arbeit*). And here is the key to a criticism of political economy, for 'political economy has merely formulated the laws of alienated labour'[7], as, for example, in its iron law of wages. To this extent, then, Marx considered himself to be involved in a salvaging operation upon the Hegelian philosophy. He is salvaging from it, by the method of inversion, that which is of enduring scientific value.

On the other hand, he also assails Hegel. He rejects the manifest Hegelianism as a mystification, an idealistic misrepresentation of the human labour process. The latter is a 'material' process in that it comprises the production of material objects. For Hegel, however, the process of production as expounded in the *Phenomenology* is a process of thought-production only. It yields only objects of thought. 'The only labour that Hegel knew and acknowledged was the abstractly spiritual.'[8] That is, he considered all productive activity, and activity of reappropriation, as an expression of the divine thought-process. As a consequence, 'he has only discovered the abstract, logical and speculative expression for the movement of history, but not yet the *real* history of man as a presupposed subject'. For as Marx later explains, 'thinking cannot be conceived as the mode of assertion of man's being as a human and natural subject with eyes, ears, etc., in society and the world and nature'.[9]

This is Marx's negative criticism of Hegel. According to the manifest Hegelianism, 'only the spirit is the true essence of man, and the true form of spirit is the thinking spirit, the logical speculative spirit. The humanity of nature and of the nature produced by history, the products of man, appear in it as products of abstract spirit and so as *spiritual* elements, thought-beings.'[10] Moreover, the alienated subject-object relation appears here only as a relation within thought between man as self-consciousness and his object as 'abstract consciousness'. Production is thought-production, externalization is externalization of consciousness only, and the reappropriation of the object 'is only an appropriation that proceeds in consciousness, in *pure thought*, i.e. in abstraction'.[11] All the movements involved in the historical process are merely *Gedankenbewegungen*.

The outcome is that the transcendence of self-alienation is also for Hegel merely an affair of thinking. It is merely an appropriation of the object—man's alienated being—in thought. Hegel, who has inverted the actual relation between thought and being, does not see that the consciousness of alienation is an 'expression in thought and knowing of the *real* alienation of man's being',[12] its alienation in the labour process, and that this cannot be transcended by a mere act of cognition. Hegel executes the transcendence of alienation by a philosophical sleight-of-hand movement; he makes it a question simply of recognizing things to be what they actually are. Thus it turns out that 'Man, once he has recognized that in law, politics, etc., he is leading an externalized life, pursues in this externalized life as such his true human life'. The overcoming of externalization becomes 'confirmation of externalization', and this is the root of Hegel's false positivism or 'only apparently critical position'. A transcendence of alienation through thinking is no real transcendence. It leaves the alien real world just as alien as ever. That is why Hegel could accommodate himself to religion, the state, property, and so on, and be a conservative. And yet, says Marx loyally, 'this lie is the lie of his progress'.[13]

Summing up the criticism, Marx maintains that Hegel has reversed everything. Man is not spirit in its activity of thought-production. On the contrary, the Hegelian thinking spirit is a mental efflux, a reflection in Hegel's own mind, of man in his real activity of material production. Hegel makes out man's real alienation in the labour process to be an outward manifestation of the alienation of thinking spirit or the 'Idea', whereas in fact the alienated Hegelian Idea is only a philosophical reflex of man's real alienation in the economic life. All this was presupposed by Marx when, nearly thirty years after, he epitomized his relation to Hegel in a single enigmatic proposition that has baffled the critics and commentators to this day. In 1873 he included in the preface to the second edition of *Capital* a passage saying: 'For Hegel, the thought process (which he actually transforms into an independent subject, giving to it the name of 'Idea') is the demiurge of the real; and for him the real is only the outward manifestation of the Idea. In my view, on the other hand, the ideal is nothing other than the material when it has been transposed and translated inside the human head.' Here Marx abruptly cut short the explanation, adding mysteriously: 'Nearly thirty years ago, when Hegelianism was still fashionable, I criticized the mystifying aspect of the Hegelian dialectic.'[14] This was a reference to his then unpublished manuscript of 1844 on the Hegelian dialectic and philosophy as a whole, whose very existence still remained unknown to the world. It is only in the context of this manuscript that the meaning of his famous statement about his inversion of Hegel becomes clear. When he says that the 'ideal' is nothing other than the 'material' translated inside the human head, he means that the self-productive Hegelian thinking spirit, or alienated Idea, was the reflection in Hegel's head of real human history as a process of material production and alienated labour.

[3]

Marx, then, sees the real history of man as the latent content of Hegel's philosophy of history. In his manuscripts he elaborates the conception of the self-productive process of man. He sketches his own version of the phenomenology of man adumbrated, as he sees it, in Hegelianism. In so doing he develops a philosophy which, while it revolves within the Hegelian orbit of thought, is novel and un-Hegelian at points and generally bears the distinctive imprint of Marx.

Its subject is the history of the world viewed as a process by which man makes himself fully man. Marx says that man is a natural being and must, like any other natural being, undergo a developmental process or act of becoming. This self-developmental process of man is the 'act of world history'. By 'man', moreover, Marx, following Feuerbach, means mankind or the human species. The act of world history is the self-realization of man in this collective or generic sense. Marx, of course, does not overlook (any more than Hegel did) the existence of individuals as parts of and participants in the collective life of the species. But the self-developing being of whom he speaks in his system is man writ large in the species. 'The individual life and species-life of man are not distinct', he says, for 'the determinate individual is only a *determinate* species being'.[15] The life of the individual is a microcosm of the life of man on the generic scale. Accordingly, the 'man' of whom Marx speaks in his manuscripts is understood as man in general.

Marx transfers to generic man the creativity that Hegel earlier had transferred from the Christian God to the world-self. He sees man as fundamentally a productive being, a creator. The life of the species is 'productive living' in various different forms. Material production is the basic form, but man is a producer too in all the non-material realms of life. Marx mentions religion, the family, the state, law, art and science as so many different 'modes of production' (*Weisen der Produktion*). Thus man is universally a being who produces things—material things in the economic life, children in the family, the image of himself as a divine being in religion, and so forth. He is endowed with a multitude of creative capacities, faculties and drives (*Triebe*) that seek outlet in productive activity. These are his 'powers' or 'forces' as a species. Marx variously calls them 'essential powers', 'vital powers' and 'species powers' (*Wesenkräfte, Lebenskräfte, Gattungskräfte*). Somewhat later he began to call them simply the 'productive powers' or 'productive forces' (*Produktivkräfte*).

Marx says in this connection that industry must be seen in relation to the essence of man and not, as has hitherto been the case, merely in terms of external relations of utility. In industry we must see a complex of already materialized productive powers of generic man. The history of industry is 'the open book of human essential powers, human psychology sensuously considered'. It is 'the *exoteric* unfolding of human essential powers', and when it is so understood 'the human essence of nature and the natural essence of man are also understood'.[16] Marx means that industry is an essentially subjective phenomenon in relation to man writ large in the species. Machines, factories, etc., are materialized faculties of generic man's self-expression in productive activity. They are physical extensions and enlargements of the hands, ears, eyes and brains of the species.*

* G. D. H. Cole points out that Marx in his later writings is ambiguous in his use

Taking his cue from Hegel, Marx says that the history of production is an *Entäusserungsgeschichte*, a history of man's own self-externalization. For Hegel, as we have seen, spirit is a world-creating force. The world of nature and the successive worlds of culture are objectifications of its creative activity. All this reappears in Marx's image of man, save that now the world-creating productive activity is seen as material production primarily and the prime product is the world of 'anthropological nature'. According to Marx, the objects that man produces are concrete external embodiments of the species powers expended in the activity of producing them. 'The object of labour is the objectification (*Vergegenständlichung*) of the species-life of man.'[17] These objects form, in their vast accumulative aggregate over the ages, a man-made enviroment or 'nature produced by history'. It is superimposed over the primeval nature or 'sensuous external world' (*sinnliche Aussenwelt*), which for Marx is simply the 'stuff' out of which man produces his own objective world in the course of history. Thus, Marx's equation of man's history with world history is intended with the utmost philosophical seriousness. Man is a world-creator, and his history is an activity of production of the world of created objects that now surrounds him. As Marx states it, 'the whole so-called world-history is nothing other than the production of man through human labour, nothing other than the becoming of nature for man'. 'The nature that develops in human history . . . is the *real* nature of man, so that nature as it develops in industry, even if in alienated form, is true anthropological nature.'[18]

This conception of anthropological nature as the self-externalization of man lies at the core of Marx's thought. As will be shown later, it is by no means a youthful vagary that he abandoned when he went on from original Marxism to reformulate his system in its mature expression. The world is the

of the key term 'productive powers'. He asks: '. . . are not the "powers of production" thought of sometimes as coal and iron, steam and water, and other things external to man, and at other times, without open or conscious transition of meaning, as man's power over coal and iron, steam and water, and the other things which he manipulates for his ends?' (*Socialist Thought: The Forerunners*, p. 273). That the ambiguity was intentional is shown by Marx's exposition in the manuscripts. The productive powers are, on the one hand, the creative faculties and energies *in* man (later known in Marxism as his labour power). Secondly, they comprise such material productive facilities as machines and factories. These are man's externalized productive powers, for industry is 'human psychology sensuously considered'.

objectification of generic man's productive powers; nature is human nature in external material form. It is an ever evolving result of the human historical process, growing over time as generation after generation of working men add their material creations to the aggregate human product. And this production of a world by man is man's own way of actualizing himself; it is the method by which he makes himself fully human in the total sweep of history. In Marx's words, 'The practical production of an *objective world*, the working-up of inorganic nature, is the expression of man as a conscious species being. . . . It is in the working-up of an objective world, therefore, that man first really proves himself as a *species being*. This production is his practical species-life. Through it nature appears as *his* work and his reality.'[19]

Marx takes all this to have been implicit in Hegel's *Phenomenology*. The conception of history as a world-creating process of material production by man, which he later began to call the 'materialist' conception, is only, in his view, a scientific restatement of Hegel's position. Furthermore, it is the theoretical setting in which one may come to terms critically with the concepts of political economy as developed by Adam Smith and the other classical economists. The classical political economy is based upon the labour theory of value, according to which the value of any commodity is equivalent to the amount of human labour invested in its production. From the political economist's standpoint, the commodity is so much materialized labour. In Marx's terms, this means that man the world-creator objectifies his species-powers in material objects of production that become commodities, and that the objective world is a world of commodities, a world of private property. Marx calls Adam Smith the 'Luther' of political economy because Smith's labour theory of value implies the subjectivizing, so to speak, of the notion of private property: 'When one speaks of private property, he believes that he has only to do with a fact outside man. When one speaks of labour, he has to do directly with man. This new posing of the question already includes its solution.'[20] By 'speaking of labour', Smith had brought the whole of political economy within the purview of the de-mystified Hegelian theory of history.

[4]

The act of world history is man's becoming as man only when

taken as a whole. For an ultimate revolution is required, according to Marx, in order to consummate it. Regarded at any prior point, the process presents itself under the aspect of estrangement. The history of externalization is an *Entfremdungsgeschichte,* a history of man's self-alienation. Man in history reifies himself in an objective world of material things (*Sachenwelt*). He becomes object to himself in this way, and 'looks at himself in a world that he has created'. When he does so, the objects into which he has externalized himself confront him as 'alien beings', and what he sees when he looks at himself in the vast aggregate of these objects is 'an alien and hostile world standing over against him'.[21] Just as in the Hegelian system, moreover, the experience of the objective world as alien and hostile is an experience of bondage or, as Marx prefers to phrase it, 'object-bondage' (*Knechtschaft des Gegenstandes*).[22] What working man sees in the world that he has created is a gigantic fetter upon him.

In his manuscript on 'Alienated Labour', Marx addresses himself to the question as to why the produced objective world appears alien and hostile to man the producer. His explanation is not the same as Hegel's although the two conceptions coincide in a formal sense. In the Hegelian system, as shown earlier, the alien character of the phenomenal world is a function of its objectivity, which constitutes it a limit and fetter for spirit as a knowing subject seeking to become conscious of itself as unlimited being. The subject-object relation *per se* is a relation of spirit's self-alienation. Marx rejects this idea. He says that man, as a natural being, naturally lives in transaction with his external surroundings, with things outside him that answer to his needs and gratify his senses: 'A being that does not have its nature outside itself is no *natural* being. . . . A being that has no object outside itself is no objective being. . . . An unobjective being is an un-being' (*Unwesen*).[23]

What makes the man-created world alien and hostile is not its objectivity, but rather the fact that man, in the act of producing it, objectifies himself 'inhumanly, in opposition to himself'. Marx argues that alienation has its source 'within the producing activity itself', of which the objective world is, he says, only a 'résumé'. 'How could the worker experience the product of his activity as something alien standing opposed to him if he himself were not alienated from himself in the very act of production? The product is only a résumé of the activity, the producing. . . . The alienation of the object of labour merely epitomizes the alienation, the externalization, in the activity of labour itself.'[24] The alien character of the product of labour, and of the *Sachenwelt* in general as the collective product, is, therefore, a reflection of the self-alienation of man in the labour process. The alien object is a mirror for man, a reminder as it were, of his own experience of alienation in the activity of producing it. The world becomes an alienated world (*entfremdete Welt*) because man's world-creating productive activity is alienated labour.

By 'labour' or 'alienated labour'—terms that he employs interchangeably—Marx means productive activity performed by man in the state of alienation from himself. He declares that all human activity up to now has been labour. Each of the realms of productive living, beginning with that of material production, has been a realm of alienated labour. All that mankind has produced in history in every mode of production has been produced by alienated men. Consequently, man has never been fully himself in his creative activity. This activity has never been 'self-activity' (*Selbstbetätigung*), by which Marx means free creativity in which a person feels thoroughly at home with himself, enjoys a sense of voluntary self-determination to action, and experiences his energies as his own.

This notion of man as a being whose natural and healthy condition is one of self-activity reflects the deep influence upon Marx of Feuerbach, who enunciated in his *Essence of Christianity* the view that free, unconstrained productive activity is an essential attribute of the human species mistakenly assigned by theology to God. 'The whole character of a species, its species-character, lies in the character of its life-activity', writes Marx, 'and free conscious activity is the species-character of man.'[25] The lower animals also produce, he observes, but only under the spur of immediate physical need, whereas man produces even when free from physical need and he only genuinely produces when he *is* free from it. Spontaneous, voluntary producing activity is his element, and in such activity he expresses himself as an artist. Man for Marx is essentially an artistic being who 'knows how to apply everywhere the inherent standard of the object' and 'forms things in accordance with the laws of beauty'.[26] That, at any rate, is what he would do if his productive activity were genuine self-activity instead of alienated labour.

The latter, as Marx portrays it, is the very antithesis of the free, spontaneous creativity in which man realizes his nature as man. Self-activity would be activity in which he experiences the productive powers latent in him as his own. In the labour process, on the other hand, productive activity is experienced not as one's own but 'as activity for another, and as activity of another, life as sacrifice of living, production of the object as loss of the object to an alien power, to an alien man'. Man's relationship to himself in the labour process is an alienated one: 'This relation is a relation of the worker to his own activity as an alien activity not belonging to him; activity as suffering, strength as weakness, begetting as emasculating, the worker's *own* physical and spiritual energy, his personal life—for what is life but activity?—as an activity turned against himself, independent of him, not belonging to him.'[27] And whereas self-activity would be spontaneous and free, the essence of labour is compulsiveness. Labour, says Marx, is *'nicht freiwillig'*. It is 'servitude'. It is by its very nature 'forced labour' (*Zwangsarbeit*), hence 'labour of self-sacrifice, of mortification'. Alienated man is enslaved man enduring torment in his productive activity: 'He develops no free physical and spiritual energy but mortifies his body and ruins his spirit.'[28] Accordingly, concludes Marx, labour does not belong to man's essence; it contradicts his species-character.

But on what foundation does he believe that all of man's productive activities in history have been alienated labour? How does he explain man's alleged universal alienation from himself? It must be said that Marx does not make his position on this cardinal question fully explicit. However, a definite explanation is contained in his manuscripts, and our task in what follows is to clarify it.

IX

ALIENATION AND MONEY-WORSHIP

. . . all is under the sway of an inhuman *force.*

MARX (1844)

It is Marx's postulate that human productive activity in every
sphere of life, and not alone in the economic sphere, has been
alienated labour. He considers material production, however,
to be the fundamental sphere of man's productive living. And
alienated labour here is the production of material objects that
become commodities or private property. This suggests the
hypothesis that alienated labour has its ground and source in
the institution of private property. Marx himself considers this
hypothesis, but only to discard it. Speaking of the notion of
private property, he writes: 'But on analysis of this concept it
becomes clear that though private property appears to be the
source, the cause, of alienated labour, it is really its consequence,
just as the gods *in the beginning* are not the cause but the effect of
man's mental aberration.'[1] Private property is the function of
alienated labour, not *vice versa*. Far from being the source and
cause of alienated productive living, the institution of private
property is its outgrowth and consequence. Alienated labour is
itself the prior fact; it is a form of living that generates private
property as its product. It too, like the gods, must be grounded
in man's 'aberration'.

An alternative hypothesis half suggested by some of Marx's
statements in the manuscripts and his later writings as well is
that alienation is rooted in the despotism of physical need. He
says that man differs from the lower animals in that he is a free
conscious producer who would create things and arrange them
according to the laws of beauty even if there were no pressure
upon him to produce in order to survive. May it not be that the
stern necessity to produce the means of subsistence deprives man
of self-activity, accounts for the compulsiveness of labour, and
makes him an alienated being? One might easily draw this
inference from such statements of Marx as the following:
'Labour is not the satisfaction of a need but only the means of

satisfying needs outside it.' 'Alienated labour, by degrading spontaneous activity, free activity, to a means, makes man's species-life a means to his physical existence.'[2]

On closer analysis, however, it turns out that the compulsion to produce in order to live is not, for Marx, the source and cause of alienated labour but rather an *expression* of it. And given his own underlying premise about the inherently creative nature of man, it could hardly be otherwise. A being who spontaneously tends to be productive might well experience self-activity in work that he performs for a living. Thus, a carpenter might derive creative satisfaction and a personal sense of fulfillment from the carpentry by which he lives. Certainly the need to work in order to live could not in itself explain the alienated condition, the trance-like state of compulsiveness, in which Marx's working man produces. There is no *necessary* connection between self-alienation and the need to work for a living. Nor does Marx himself, as becomes plain when we probe more deeply into his thinking, really believe that there is. When he says that alienated labour is only the means to satisfy 'needs outside it', the reference is primarily to needs other than the simple need to survive.

His explanation of alienated labour is the one already briefly stated in the essay 'On the Jewish Question', where he wrote: 'Money is the alienated essence of man's work and his being. This alien being rules over him and he worships it. . . . Just as man, so long as he is engrossed in religion, can only objectify his nature by turning it into an *alien* creature of the fantasy, so, under the domination of egoistic need, he can act in a practical way, create objects practically, only by subordinating these products as well as his activity to the power of an alien being and bestowing upon them the significance of an alien being—money.' Having undertaken the systematic criticism of political economy in his manuscripts, Marx still considers that his subject-matter is religious in essence, that political economy is the theology of a worldly religion. He is still speaking of money as the 'alien being' and of the worship of this 'worldly god' as the force that alienates man from himself in his productive activity.

Marx's alienated man is a man who produces 'under the domination of egoistic need'. This is the need 'outside' the labour process to which the process is subordinated. The compulsion that transforms free creative self-activity into alienated labour is the compulsion to amass wealth. Marx portrays it in his manuscripts as a maniacal obsession with the accumulation of capital, a veritable fanaticism of appropriation of the world of created things, a lust for money. He entitles it 'greed' (*Habsucht*), and ascribes the concept of it to political economy: 'The only wheels that political economy sets in motion are *greed* and the war between the greedy—competition.'[3] But this is a motive force qualitatively different from the earthy calculating self-interest with which Smith and the other classical economists endowed their 'economic man'. Although he imputes the notion to Anglo-French political economy, Marx thinks and writes as a German philosopher of the Hegelian school for which passion is the moving force in human life.

Thus he describes greed as a kind of acquisitive mania that sees in money the means of exercising power over everything. Man worships money as the 'externalized potentiality of mankind' and 'almighty being' that confers unlimited power upon its possessor. Money is the 'divine power' (*göttliche Kraft*) that overturns all things and 'transforms fidelity into infidelity, love into hate, hate into love, virtue into vice, vice into virtue, servant into master, master into servant, idiocy into intelligence and intelligence into idiocy'.[4] Marx refers to Goethe and Shakespeare as his authorities on this point. He quotes, for example, some passages from *Timon of Athens* in which 'Yellow, glittering precious gold' is apostrophized as 'Thou visible God!' and the poet says: 'Thus much of this will make black white, foul fair, wrong right, base noble, old young, coward valiant.'

Marx says that the drive to amass wealth *ad infinitum* is the 'ethic' implicit in political economy, whose foremost representative has declared in *The Wealth of Nations* that capital is 'a certain command over all the labour, or over all the produce of labour, which is then in the market'. The key word for Marx is 'command'. Money is the means of exercising command over all that the hand and mind of man have ever produced or will produce. The moral message of political economy is, therefore, the following:

The less you eat, drink and read books; the less you go to the theatre, the dance hall, the public-house; the less you think, love, theorize, sing, paint, fence, etc., the more you *save*—the *greater* becomes your treasure which neither moths nor dust will devour—your *capital*. The less you *are*, the more you *have*; the less you express your own life, the greater is your *externalized* life—the greater is the store of your alienated being. Everything that the political economist takes from you in life and in humanity, he replaces for you in *money* and in *wealth;* and all the things that you cannot do, your money can do. It can eat and drink, go to the dance hall and the theatre; it can travel, it can appropriate art, learning, the treasures of the past, political power—all this it *can* appropriate for you—it can buy all this for you; it is the true *endowment.* Yet being all this, it is *inclined* to do nothing but create itself, buy itself; for everything else is after all its servant. And when I have the master I have the servant and do not need his servant. All passions and all activity must therefore be submerged in greed.[5]

This all-embracing passion of greed is seen by Marx as an 'utterly alien power' or 'inhuman force' (*unmenschliche Macht*) that holds sway over the whole of human existence.[6] It has been the motive force of the historical process up to now. Man has created his objective world under its iron compulsion. Marx calls it 'alien' and 'inhuman' because he sees in it the force that alienates man from himself, deprives him of freedom, and dehumanizes him. Under the despotism of the acquisitive passion he 'develops no free physical and spiritual energy but mortifies his body and ruins his spirit'. His producing activity grows '*nicht freiwillig*' and is experienced by him as 'an activity turned against himself, independent of him, not belonging to him'. He objectifies himself 'in an inhuman manner' and the objects into which the alienated activity is materialized confront him as alien beings, reminders of the torment endured in producing them.

In drawing this picture of man alienated from himself in servitude and sacrifice to the worldly god, Marx constantly keeps before his mind's eye the Feuerbachian analysis of religion. Feuerbach had argued that God is only the externalized mental activity of self-worshipping religious man, but apprehended as the activity of another being separate from man. It is just the same, says Marx, in the practical religious sphere: 'Just as in religion the self-activity of the human imagination, of the human brain and human heart, operates independently of the individual, i.e. as an alien, divine or diabolical activity, so the activity of the worker is not his self-activity. It belongs to another; it is the loss of himself.'[7] The worker, in other words, experiences his own productive activity as though it belonged not to himself but to his externalized being, his own creation—capital.

Further, Feuerbach had argued that religious man invests all the wealth of generic human nature in the image of himself as God, and impoverishes his merely human empirical self as a result: 'To enrich God, man must become poor; that God may be all, man must be nothing.' Marx reasons that the religion of money-worship is the practical and material counterpart of this. Enslaved by the acquisitive mania, the human species pours the whole wealth of its species powers into the worldly god, and impoverishes itself in the process. The inner world of working man is progressively devalued as the *Sachenwelt* expands in value: 'It is clear that the more the worker exerts himself, the more powerful becomes the alien objective world that he creates, the poorer he himself, his inner world, becomes; the less belongs to himself. The same applies to religion. The more man attributes to God, the less he retains in himself.'[8]

Hence Marx's correlative of Feuerbach's formula reads: to enrich the worldly god, man must become poor; that capital may be all, man must be nothing. In place of Feuerbach's God, the mental objectification of self-worshipping religious man, we have the 'alien objective world' as the material *alter ego* of a working man alienated by the inhuman force of money-worship. The realization of labour, its objectification in goods, appears as the de-realization (*Entwirklichung*) of him, the expropriation of his life-energies, the loss of himself. And the world of products that arises out of the labour process takes on the character of the power that dominates man. It too becomes 'alien and hostile'. It stares back at man the producer, and he sees there the hideous lineaments of the diabolic force that holds him fast in its grip. He beholds the entire man-created world in the possession of this force, as its 'private property'. This, according to Marx, is what *man in general* sees when he 'looks at himself in a world that he has created'. Here is the image of reality that was in Marx's mind when he wrote of the world that 'the point is, to *change* it'. The world that he condemned to capital punishment in the name of the *Vehmgericht* of history was one that appeared to him in the shape of a monster.

[2]

It goes without saying that Marx drew inspiration from the inner depths of his own being in portraying the 'inhuman force'. A person who had not experienced this urge to self-aggrandizement within himself, in one or another of its many expressions, could never have produced such powerful images of it as Marx did in his manuscripts and his later writings.* It is equally plain, however, that the conceptual source lies in the Hegelian philosophy, which presided over his mind at the birth-time of Marxism. From Adam Smith and the other political economists came the terms 'capital' and 'labour', together with the notion that capital is 'command over labour'. Postulating that Hegelianism provides the key with which one can unlock the secrets of political economy, Marx proceeded to infuse these terms with an Hegelian idea-content. 'Labour' became 'alienated labour', and 'capital' assumed the aspect of the infinite self aggrandizing movement that Hegel, in his *Phenomenology*, had ascribed to spirit. As we have seen, Marx steeped himself anew in the *Phenomenology* during the period of his work on the manuscripts. His notion of the 'inhuman force' in man must be understood against this background.

In Hegel's system, it will be recalled, spirit performs its world-creating productive activity under compulsion of the drive to become conscious of itself as *das Ganze*. The dialectic of finitude is a dynamism of its self-aggrandizement to infinity. If spirit is, on the one hand, a force and principle of creativity, it is also, on the other hand, a force or will to limitless aggrandizement. Its only motive for producing itself as a world is to grasp and behold the world as itself. The cognitive process is a movement of appropriation of the created world as 'property of the ego' or 'spiritual substance'. Spirit is 'insatiably greedy' to incorporate the seemingly substantial objective world within the receptacle of self, and the self-infinitizing movement whereby it destroys

* Rühle, who has been quoted above as saying that the urge to be godlike was a dominating force in Marx, fills in the character sketch as follows: 'Throughout life, Marx remains the young student, who is afraid of disappointing others through the inadequacy of his achievement, and therefore sets himself aim upon aim, piles task upon task. He cannot escape the voices calling after him: "You must show what you can do! Must climb! Must have a brilliant career! Must do something extra-ordinary! Must be the first!" This will-to-conquest and this urge-to-superiority dominate all phases of his existence as worker and fighter. . . . Unquestionably Marx was a neurotic. For everyone familiar with neurotic symptoms, the neurotic traits in his clinical history are unmistakeable. . . . Yet he never, mentally speaking, surrendered wholly and permanently to neurosis—and this is the decisive matter. . . . He had to be whipped on by overweening ambition, blinded by intolerable selfishness, goaded day and night by a torturing sense of inferiority—that he might be equipped for his formidable achievements' (*Karl Marx: His Life and Work*, pp. 379, 388–9, 397).

the object *qua* object is an appropriation of everything as its private property. Hegel presents it as an acquisitive movement, a process of enrichment, an accumulation of 'spiritual substance'. He conceives it, of course, as something 'inner', something taking place in thought.

But Marx is completely convinced that the referent is something 'outer', that Hegelianism is esoteric economics and requires to be translated into materialistic economic terms. Hegel's logic, as he puts it, is 'the money of the spirit'.[9] Consequently, the dialectic of the finite reappears in his reconstructed Hegelianism as a dynamism of infinite self-aggrandizement *in material terms*. The drive of Hegelian spirit to aggrandize itself to infinity in terms of knowledge becomes a drive of Marxian man to aggrandize himself to infinity in terms of money. The insatiable greed of Hegelian spirit turns into the 'egoistic need' that dominates Marxian man in his activity of material production. The accumulation of spiritual substance in history becomes the accumulation of capital. Only in *Capital* itself does this decisive aspect of the Hegel-Marx relation receive full systematic expression.

However, Marx already had the basic idea squarely in mind in 1844. In the manuscripts, as we have seen, he views the act of world history as a process of human self-objectification motivated by a drive for absolute enrichment. Not only does historical man reify himself in an objective world as does spirit in Hegel's system. His self-productive act is similarly performed under compulsion of a self-infinitizing acquisitive drive. Like Hegelian spirit, he produces a world only in order to appropriate it as private property. Thus, what has been said here concerning the dual aspect of Hegelian spirit applies equally to Marxian man as man in history. If he is, on the one hand, an inherently creative being, whose productive powers crave outward expression in productive activity, he is also, on the other hand, an infinitely acquisitive being imbued with an urge to become *das Ganze* in a material sense. Here the absolute self is no longer simply a splendid vision of the self as an absolute being. It has become an autonomous, dynamic force within man, an 'inhuman force' in Marx's phrase. As such, it exerts a tyrannical sway over him, usurping his life-energies and exploiting his productive powers.

Hegel construes the acquisitive movement as something taking place in the mind and terminating in 'absolute knowledge', whereas Marx treats it as a practical appropriation of the world in the drive toward absolute material enrichment. But this is not the crucial difference between the two systems. More important in many ways is the change that has occurred from Hegel to Marx in the conception and evaluation of the acquisitive drive. For Hegel the appropriation of the world cognitively as property of the ego is the way in which spirit's self-alienation is overcome and freedom is achieved. For Marx it is just the reverse. The acquisitive striving is the force that turns man's creative activity into compulsive alienated labour and depersonalizes him. It is the ground and source of his alienation from himself. Instead of freeing him, it enslaves him; instead of restoring him to himself, it causes him to lose himself; instead of humanizing him, it degrades him to the level of *Unmensch*. Accordingly, that which Hegel affirms as good, Marx condemns as evil, as an utterly alien power. The acquisitive movement that Hegel sees as a process of spirit's growing consciousness of freedom, Marx sees as one of man's growing consciousness of bondage. The shift of moral perspective is profound, and must be clearly grasped by all who would comprehend Marxism and its influence in the world.

Behind it lies not only the inner tendency of Marx's own nature but also the influence of Feuerbach's thought upon him. As we have noted, Feuerbach turned against the Absolute as the alien self, and took the side of suffering finite man whom he saw as the victim of the historical movement of actualization of the 'Idea'. Marx proceeds in the same direction. He too recasts the Absolute, or rather the dynamism of aggrandizement, as the villain of the piece, and ranges himself on the side of suffering humanity. He pronounces 'inhuman' and 'alien' the force that compels man to absolutize himself in terms of money; he sees the real self of man as his enslaved powers of creativity. He desires the 'emancipation of labour' (to borrow a later Marxian phrase) from bondage to the passion of greed. The whole theory of alienated labour outlined above rests on this position.

Marx's repudiation of the 'alien power' finds reflection and embodiment in the image of proletarian man in which Marxism itself centres. Here man the producer is in revolt against the inhuman force that holds both him and his world in its greedy grasp. The working man is a 'dehumanization' conscious of himself as a dehumanization and striving to abolish himself as such. If Hegelian man was the willing tool and victim of the quest for the Absolute, Marxian man is a tool and victim aware of himself as such, conscious of the despotic force that rules over him as a despotism, and rebelling against his situation. If Hegelian man was divided against himself in the striving to break all fetters of finitude, Marxian man is at war with himself to break the fetter of the self-infinitizing tendency and repossess his alienated productive powers. It is a war between the *Unmensch* and the *unmenschliche Macht*. And Marx, in his manuscript on 'Alienated Labour', performs upon this species-man at war with himself a portentous operation: he divides him into two men.

[3]

'Alienation' is an ancient psychiatric term meaning loss of personal identity or the feeling of personal identity. Marx quite accurately applies it to the man depicted in his manuscripts. The phenomenon that he describes as a 'self-alienation process' (*Selbstentfremdungsprozess*) is precisely that. It is a recognizable psychological phenomenon.

The self-alienated working man is a being who has lost himself. Devoid of all spontaneity, all sense of self-determination in action, and all joy in living, he has grown quite depersonalized. To such an extent has he become a stranger to himself that his own energies and activity seem to him to belong not to himself but to an alien power that holds sway over him, and all that he does he does at the bidding of this power. All the activity is alienated labour. Yet his estrangement from himself is not yet total. For he resents the state to which he has come. He recognizes it as wrong, evil, unnatural, a dehumanized condition. He wants to emancipate himself from it, to repossess his energies and activity, to regain himself.

This description of an alienated man is clinically accurate. It coincides in all important respects with descriptions by psychiatrists of the symptoms of alienation as experienced by persons in the advanced stages of the neurotic process. From the psychiatrist we learn, for example, that a neurotic person at first finds a feeling of identity in the idealized image of himself as a godlike being and experiences only his imperfect empirical self as a stranger. But later on, when the drive to actualize the godlike self has evolved into an autonomous dynamic force within him and exerts a tyrannical power over him, he gradually comes to experience a far more pervasive sense of alienation. He grows depersonalized, 'removed from himself'. He no longer experiences his energies as his own. All his activities are performed compulsively as though at the bidding of another (the absolute self) and with the feeling: 'I am driven instead of being the driver.' 'He has the feeling of not being a moving force in his own life.'[10] These and other statements by Dr Horney on the symptoms of severe alienation in neurotic persons parallel point for point the descriptions of alienated man that Marx offers in his manuscripts.

But of course he does not consider himself to be dealing with a psychiatric phenomenon. He regards himself as engaged in a criticism of political economy and believes that he has grasped and analysed a fact of the economic life *per se*. Having set forth the symptoms of alienation in the labour process, he declares: 'We have proceeded from a fact of political economy—the alienation of the worker and his production. We have formulated the concept of this fact, the concept of *alienated, externalized* labour. We have analysed this concept—hence have merely analysed a fact of political economy.'[11]

And at this point he proceeds to ask himself the fateful question: to whom does the alien activity belong? 'If my own activity does not belong to me, and is an alien compulsive activity, to whom does it belong?' 'To a being *other* than myself', he replies, and then inquires further: 'Who is this being?' To this his answer is: 'The alien being to whom the labour and the product of labour belong, in whose service and for whose enjoyment the labour is performed, can only be man himself (*kann nur der Mensch selbst sein*). . . . Not the gods, not nature, but only man himself can be this alien power over man (*nur der Mensch selbst kann diese fremde Macht über den Menschen sein*).'[12] Thus, the alien being in whose service alienated man labours can be no other than *himself*. However, adds Marx in the same breath, himself apprehended as *another man outside himself*:

If he experiences the product of his labour, his objectified labour, as an alien, hostile, powerful object independent of him, he experiences it in such a way that another alien, hostile, powerful man, independent of him, is the master of this object. If he experiences his own activity as an unfree activity, he experiences it as activity in the service, under the domination, compulsion and yoke of another man *(so verhält er sich zu ihn als der Tätigkeit im Dienst, unter der Herrschaft, dem Zwang und dem Joch eines andern Menschen).*[13]

What Marx says is psychologically quite true. A person who has become alienated from himself in the neurotic process may indeed experience his own activity as activity 'in the service, under the domination, compulsion and yoke of another man' (i.e. the alien absolute self). But Marx, as we know, does not consider that the truth of his diagnosis of alienation is a psychological truth. He believes that he has 'merely analysed a fact of political economy', i.e., a social fact.

He changes the 'as though' into an 'is'. Having said that the man *experiences* his own activity as activity in the service and under the domination of another, alien, hostile, powerful man, independent of him, he declares that there *is* such a man. He posits the actual existence of an alien, hostile, powerful man, outside the worker to whom the worker and his activity belong. He identifies this other man as the capitalist, whom he proceeds to describe as the 'non-worker' (*Nicht-Arbeiter*). Instead of one being—working man alienated from himself in the labour process—there are now two. Man as such has vanished, and in his place two personalities, the worker and the capitalist, stand in hostile confrontation. Neither is fully human. The worker is a non-man, a dehumanization, a proletarian devoid of every human attribute save the essential one—creativity. On the other side, the insatiable acquisitive urge, the alien power within man that transforms his productive activity into alienated labour, has been detached and housed in 'another man outside the worker'. It has assumed flesh and blood, semi-human form, in the capital*ist*.

Thus, the discordant alienated self has become, in the full sense, a split personality. Self-alienated man at war with himself and rebelling against the tyrannical drive to infinite aggrandizement has broken apart, in Marx's mind, into warring 'worker' and 'capitalist', the one embodying his rebellious productive powers and the other embodying the inhuman force. But this self-alienated producing man was conceived by Marx as mankind or the human species. Hence the splitting of his personality means the splitting of humanity into warring *classes* of workers and capitalists. The war of self-alienated Marxian man with himself has become a class war across the battlefield of society. If the proletariat is for Marx the collective incarnation of

Unmensch, the capitalist class is the collective incarnation of the *unmenschliche Macht.* As he sees it, mankind has split apart between these two forces, and the scene of history is set for the ultimate battle.

What Marx has done here will bear comparison with the dissociation of the self imagined by Robert Louis Stevenson in his classic tale, *Dr Jekyll and Mr Hyde.* The theme of the story is the separation of the conflicting constructive and destructive forces in man. Recognizing how irreconcilable is the antagonism of good and evil within himself, Dr Jekyll says: 'From an early date . . . I had learned to dwell with pleasure, as a beloved daydream, on the thought of the separation of these elements. If each, I told myself, could be housed in separate identities, life would be relieved of all that was unbearable.' In Stevenson's fantasy, the destructive forces in Dr Jekyll are separated from him and personified in another man outside him, Mr Hyde. In Marx's manuscripts of 1844, a similar operation is performed upon a self-alienated *man in general.*

In a deadly serious way Marx performs on the discordant self of German philosophy the act of dissociation that Stevenson performs in a purely fictional way in his story of Dr Jekyll and Mr Hyde. The boundlessly aggrandizing, exploiting, enslaving, oppressing part, which is also for Marx the alien and hostile part, takes shape in his mind as the 'capitalist' and collectively as the capitalist class, while the productive part remains with the collective worker. The conflicting forces in the self-divided species-man have been housed in separate collective identities. Marx felt he had weighty scientific authorities behind him in what he was doing. Hegelianism was his chief guide, and he appears to have had in mind at this moment the section of the *Phenomenology* in which Hegel treats of the dualization of spirit into 'Master and Bondsman' (*'Herr und Knecht'*). Thus, the manuscripts not only refer to labour as a state of *Knechtschaft,* but also to the capitalist and worker as *Herr* and *Knecht* respectively. But there was also the authority of Feuerbach, whose 'great feat', says Marx, lay partly in 'making the social relation "of man to man" likewise a basic principle of theory'.[14] He is thinking of Feuerbach's argument that man is only fully real when he is in relation with another man.

Still, he realizes that he is doing something questionable in transforming man's alienated relationship to himself into a

social relationship 'of man to man', and he seeks to justify it.
He does so by stating it as a general truth that 'The alienation
of man, in general every relation in which man stands to himself, is first realized and expressed in the relation in which man
stands to other men.' Further on he amplifies the argument as
follows:

Every self-alienation of man from himself and nature appears in the
relation in which he places himself and nature to other men
differentiated from himself. Thus, religious self-alienation necessarily
appears in the relation of the layman to the priest, or again to a
mediator, etc., since we are here dealing with the intellectual world.
In the real practical world self-alienation can only appear through
the practical real relation to other men. The means through which
alienation takes place is itself *practical*. Thus through alienated labour
man not only engenders his relation to the object and the act of
production as to powers that are alien and hostile to him; he also
engenders the relation in which other men stand to his production
and to his product, and the relation in which he stands to these other
men.[15]

Marx contends that the fundamental fact is the alienated
self-relation, but that for all practical purposes this may be
viewed as an alienated social relation. For the relation in which
man stands to himself is 'first realized and expressed in the
relation in which man stands to other men'. In the religious
sphere his alienated relation to himself as God takes practical
shape in an alienated social relation to the priest; in the economic
sphere his alienated relation to himself as producer and to
anthropological nature as his product takes practical shape in
his alienated social relation to the capitalist. A social relation 'of
man to man' thus becomes the *effective reality* of man's alienation
from himself, and the 'self-alienation process' is, so to speak,
socialized.

This position was theoretically untenable. An alienated
individual may indeed project his feeling of self-estrangement
and experience it as an estrangement from others or hostility
towards others; and this in turn may actually transform his
inter-personal relations into estranged ones. Thus if he decides
that the 'alien, hostile, powerful man' must be 'another man'
outside him, and behaves accordingly toward another actual
man outside him, hostile social relations will normally result.
Then it might be said that the alienated self-relation has found

expression as an alienated social relation. This, however, is no justification for conceiving the alienated self-relation as a social phenomenon in its essential nature.

The intra-personal situation inescapably remains the primary fact, and the alienated social relation is only a derivative fact and a result. For the theorist to ignore this is to succumb to the alienated individual's own delusion that the alien man is someone outside himself. Marx was at least obscurely aware of the shakiness of his position, for he made a note in the manuscript saying: 'We must think over the previously made statement that the relation of man to himself first becomes *objective* and *real* through his relation to another man.'[16] Evidently, he never did so.

X

COMMUNISM—THE SELF REGAINED

Human nature is the true community of man. MARX (1844)

Although Marx's dualization of man underlies his later doctrine of the class war, he does not develop this doctrine at any great length in his manuscripts. He confines himself mainly to the statement that 'the whole of society must fall asunder into two classes, property and the propertyless worker', adding at a later point that the contradiction of property and propertylessness must be grasped in dynamic terms as a 'contradiction of capital and labour'.[1]

Moreover, he has little to say here on a question that preoccupied him greatly in his later writings—the causal dynamics of the world revolution. His principal point is simply that a communist movement and communist world revolution is inevitable: 'For transcending the *ideas* of private property, the *ideas* of communism are quite sufficient. But for the transcending of real private property, a *real* communist movement is required. History will bring this, and the movement that we have already grasped in *thoughts* as a self-transcending one will work its way in reality through a very long and hard process.'[2]

Taking it for granted that the movement already grasped in thoughts must necessarily work itself out in reality, Marx devotes one manuscript ('Private Property and Communism'), and some further remarks in his manuscript on the Hegelian dialectic, to the consideration of communism itself. Although his discussion is brief, taking up only about sixteen pages, it is fuller and more concrete than anything he later wrote on this subject, and in fact is the one really serious effort he ever made to explain systematically and in some detail what communism meant to him. He considers the topic firstly in terms of the communist revolution and the immediate post-revolutionary situation, and secondly in terms of ultimate communism.

The reader who expects to find here a treatment of the questions of economic organization of society that have customarily been considered in socialist and communist theories, both before and after Marx, will be disappointed. He had not previously shown the slightest interest in communism from this point of view, nor does he now. The paper on communism does not have a word to say about questions of planning, the distribution of goods, the organization of public services, communal living arrangements, etc. And the omission of all this was no accident, for Marx did not approach the idea of communism on this plane. It no more occurred to him to investigate the distribution problem, for example, than it would occur to a Christian theologian to include in his treatise a section on the distribution problem in paradise. Marx simply takes it for granted that under communism there will be an abundance of goods for all.

His conception of communism is fundamentally philosophical or religious. It is part and parcel of the total philosophy of world history that he elaborates in the manuscripts on the model of Hegel's *Phenomenology*. If history for Marx is the developmental process or act of *becoming* of the species, communism is the state of veritable *being* that begins when history as such ends. Communism is man's post-history on earth, corresponding to the other-worldly post-history of Christian theology and to the this-worldly post-history depicted by Hegel in the closing chapter of the *Phenomenology* on 'Absolute Knowledge'. We may properly consider it a metamorphosis of the theological notion of salvation of the soul. For Marx sees the communist revolution as a revolution of self-change, and communism itself as a new state of the generic human self. If man has existed all through the act of world history in the state of self-alienation, in a dehumanized condition, communism is defined by Marx as the overcoming of alienation. It is man's 'regaining of self' (*Selbstgewinnung*), 'the reintegration or return of man to himself, transcendence of human self-alienation'.[3] Everything that Marx has to say about communism belongs to this context of thought.

[2]

Although the *Phenomenology* is its model, Marx's system differs from Hegel's in a number of important respects as a consequence of changes in the transition that have been analysed above. Following Feuerbach, Marx conceives the whole of history as a single great episode of self-externalization, alienation and transcendence of alienation. Hence it is only when seen as a whole that history is for Marx a process of man's realization of himself as man. Whereas spirit, in Hegel's system, is constantly in the process of realizing itself, constantly reappropriating its alienated objective being, the human producer in Marx's is not realizing himself but only his labour. He only externalizes himself in a world that is alien and hostile and grows increasingly so. Alienation is the hallmark of his history from beginning to end.

This history is a story of his creation of a world and loss of himself in the process. The acquisitive movement that proceeds *pari passu* in history with the productive one is a movement of the expropriation of the producer, the loss of his product to the alien power that dominates and oppresses him. His history is not a progress of the consciousness of freedom, but a progress of the consciousness of bondage, oppression, exploitation and suffering. It shows a pattern of ever increasing alienation or, as Marx was later to view it, a 'law of increasing misery'. Man does not become man but only creates the material prerequisites for it. He merely brings into being the objective setting of his future life of self-fulfillment, while growing more and more dehumanized in the process. Slaving under the taskmaster of greed, he produces a world of alien wealth, wherein, ultimately, he is to find himself.

In its delineation of the closing phase of world history, however, Marx's system comes back into line with its Hegelian model. The world communist revolution is for Marx a revolution of human self-change; it is the ultimate self-realizing act of humanity. And in so visualizing it, he was following the fundamental *schema* of the Hegelian philosophy, in which the knowing subject transcends its self-alienation by appropriating the object. Spirit, confronted by an alien and hostile objective world, changes *itself* by appropriating this world in thought. It is thus by acting upon something external, or something that falsely appears to be external, that spirit realizes its own nature.

The same idea reappears in Marx's theory of the communist revolution. Although Marx has deviated from Hegel in that he sees the acquisitive movement of world-appropriation in history as the re-realization of man, he returns to Hegel at the end. Man, who has lost the created world to his own greed, must perform an act of 'reappropriation' (*Wiederaneignung*) in order to change himself. This is Marx's definition of the communist or proletarian revolution. He holds that the only possible way for the producing man to abolish the acquisitive movement, emancipate himself from the incubus of greed, and so end his own alienation, is to carry out one, great, violent, world-wide, acquisitive exploit and expropriate the alienated world of private property from the inhuman force. In practice, this means to wrest it from the hands of the capitalist class, the collective 'alien, hostile, powerful man' in whom, as Marx sees it, the inhuman force is incarnate. The act of reappropriation, by which working man is to liberate himself from alienation, is called by Marx the 'communist action' (*Aktion*).

It is necessarily, in his view, a world revolution; it consists in the seizure of the whole alienated world at a single huge stroke. It is a world-wide proletarian action of transcendence or abolition of private property (*Aufhebung des Privateigentums*). Unlike the transcendence of the object by Hegelian spirit, which proceeds in thought and through knowing, this transcendence of the object proceeds on the plane of external action and by means of material force. It is the appropriation by the mass of proletarians of all the material objects that man has created through the ages. As Marx explains in *The Holy Family*, written shortly after completion of the manuscripts, 'since these practical results of the self-externalization of the mass exist in the real world in an external way, the mass is compelled to conquer them also in an *external* way. It cannot regard these products of its self-externalization as being simply some ideal phantasmagoria or mere externalizations of self-consciousness, and cannot seek to destroy *material* alienation through a purely *inward spiritual action*.'[4]

Marx assumes that Hegel had not only the point of view of modern political economy but also, latently, the communist point of view. The metaphysics of spirit was not simply esoteric economics; it was esoteric communism. Hegel's picture of spirit appropriating the world in thought was a mystified rendition of the proletarian act of world-appropriation. His error here, as everywhere in his system, was to picture the event idealistically or in terms of 'inward spiritual action'. The true statement is the materialist one, which translates the Hegelian transcendence of the objective world by knowing into the transcendence of the world of private property by the communist action of the proletariat. Now the reappropriation is seen not as a movement of thought but as a practical action of seizure of the alienated world of material objects. Thus does Marx apply the method of inversion of Hegel to the formulation of the idea of the communist revolution itself.

In Hegelianism, the cognitive act of appropriation of the objective world is defined in dialectical terms as the 'negation of the negation'. The knowing subject thereby abolishes itself *qua* finite being, i.e. negates itself as a negation of itself. Marx employs this same dialectical formula, *mutatis mutandis*, in his definition of the world revolution. In his alienated labour of world-creation, working man has existed only as a proletarian 'non-man' or negation of his true self. Consequently, the act by which he appropriates the alienated world of private property will be his act of self-abolition as a proletarian, or the negation of himself as a negation of himself. On the basis of this reasoning, Marx defines the communist world revolution as the 'negation of the negation'.[5]

Unlike Hegel, however, he holds that the negation of the negation does not immediately spell affirmation. For Hegel the cognitive act by which spirit negates itself as a finite being yields it the affirmative consciousness of itself as infinite being. For Marx, on the other hand, the communist action of world-appropriation does not in itself bring man the affirmative consciousness of himself as man. He credits Feuerbach with showing that the destructive process of negation of the negation is not, *per se*, an affirmation. And he says that the affirmative stage of human self-realization lies beyond the immediate revolutionary action against private property. Far from being fully human already on the morrow of the great world revolution, man, according to Marx, will exist in a temporary state of terrible degradation. The human negation of the negation produces only 'unthinking' or 'raw communism' (*der rohe Kommunismus*), in which man remains, for the moment, more than ever a negation of himself. This is the immediate post-revolutionary transitional stage that Marx later designated as the stage of the dictatorship of the proletariat.

Proudhon had viewed communism, or the communal ownership of everything, as 'oppression and slavery'. Marx's 'raw communism' closely parallels this idea, and his reference to Proudhon at this point in the manuscript suggests that he was quite aware of it. His main source of inspiration, however, was evidently the book by Lorenz von Stein to which we have referred in an earlier chapter. Stein coined the phrase 'raw communism' and defined the idea of it. He spoke of the 'French raw communism whose aspirations are not to improve the conditions of society but only to incite the different classes against one another; that kind of communism which knows very well that it leads only to an upheaval but does not know what will follow'.[6] Although he traced the ancestry of French raw communism to the Baboeuf conspiracy and Buonarroti's famous treatise about it, Stein conceived it as essentially a sub-intellectual phenomenon. The theorists of raw communism, beginning with Baboeuf and his cohorts, were merely the mouthpieces of an untutored tendency present in the dispossessed and brutalized proletarian masses. This was the tendency to put egalitarianism into practice in a wild mêlée of expropriation and destruction of property, communization of wealth and wives, etc.

Here is Marx's 'unthinking' communism, which is to prevail on the morrow of the world revolution. Raw communism will mean the promiscuous socialization of all private property, including women: 'In the same way as woman is to abandon marriage for general prostitution, so the whole world of wealth, that is, the objective being of man, is to abandon the relation of exclusive marriage with the private property owner for the relation of general prostitution with the community.'[7] Significantly, Marx even outdoes the anti-communist Stein in his negative evaluation of this state of affairs. He says that raw communism is not the real transcendence of private property but only the universalizing of it, not the overcoming of greed but only the generalizing of it, and not the abolition of labour but only its extension to all men. It is merely a new form in which the vileness of private property comes to the surface. Expressing 'envy and a desire to reduce all to a common level', it spells the total negation of the human personality: 'In completely negating the *personality* of man, this type of communism is really nothing but the logical expression of private property. General *envy*, constituting itself as power, is the disguise in which *greed* re-establishes itself and satisfies itself, only in *another* way. . . . In the approach to *woman* as the spoil and handmaid of communal lust is expressed the infinite degradation in which man exists for himself.'[8] These vivid indications from the Paris manuscripts of the way in which Marx envisaged and evaluated the immediate post-revolutionary period very probably explain the extreme reticence that he always later showed on this topic in his published writings.

The communist world revolution is for Marx a revolution of self-change, an act by which man is to end his alienation, restore his lost harmony with himself, and actualize himself as man. As we see, however, he does not conceive it directly in these terms. Self-change is not the immediate outcome, nor could it be on Marx's premise that the revolution is itself a colossal acquisitive act of violence performed in a spirit of greed, envy, hate and resentment. So he falls back upon the idea that the world revolution sets the scene for a *subsequent* self-change. But how an acquisitive action could end all acquisitive action, how the inhuman force of greed could be destroyed by a counter-force of the same character—this he never explains.

[3]

The infinite degradation under raw communism is pictured by Marx as a short stage of purgatory on the ascent of alienated man to his post-historical destiny in ultimate communism. This he discusses under the heading of 'positive humanism' or the humanization of mankind. Communism as negation of the negation is to give way in the higher stage to communism 'as *positive* transcendence of private property, of human self-alienation, and therefore as the actual appropriation of human nature through and for man', and of this Marx writes, in a burst of Hegelian lyricism, that 'It is the riddle of history resolved, and knows itself as the riddle'.[9]

The underlying assumption, as just pointed out, is that men will now be liberated from the compulsive acquisitive drive that has dominated their historical lives and turned them into alienated men. The positive transcendence of human self-alienation means to Marx, first of all, the recovery of freedom in a new non-acquisitive life of enjoyable self-activity. Having repossessed his previously enslaved inner productive powers, together with the lost world of external productive powers materialized in industry, man will be released from the suffering condition of alienated labour. Labour itself, in this sense, will be a thing of the historical past, a relic of the bygone stage of man's becoming as man. Freed at last from the lust for wealth in whose service he has laboured, he will not, however, subside into universal indolence. Instead, he will become for the first time the free conscious producing animal that it is his essence and species-character to be.

Productive activity will become joyous creation. Man will produce things spontaneously for the sheer pleasure it gives him to do so, will develop his manifold potentialities of action and response, and will cultivate his sensibilities in every sphere. He will cease to be divided against himself in his life-activity of material production, and will no longer experience this activity as activity of and for another alien, hostile, powerful man independent of him. Consequently, the products of his activity, the objectifications of himself, will no longer confront him as alien and hostile beings. They will mirror for him the joys of free self-activity instead of the agonies of alienated labour. And when he looks at himself in a world that he has created, he will no longer see before him an alienated world. As Marx puts it, the positive transcendence of private property means the 'annihilation of the *alienated* character of the objective world'.[10]

But human self-realization means much more to Marx than the return of man to himself out of his alienated labour in the life of material production. It means also the transcendence of the various subsidiary modes of production in which man has historically led a life of alienation: 'Religion, the family, the state, law, morality, science, art, etc., are only *particular* modes of production, and fall under its general law. The positive transcendence of *private property*, as the appropriation of *human* living, is, therefore, the positive transcendence of all alienation and thus the return of man from religion, the family, the state, etc., to his *human*, i.e. *social* existence. Religious alienation as such takes place only in the realm of *consciousness,* of man's inner life, but economic alienation is that of *real life*.'[11] The 'general law' of all modes of production hitherto has been the law of alienation; alienated labour has been the universal mode of production in all the realms of human life, among which the economic realm is primary. The ending of economic alienation will mean the end of the state, the family, law, morality, etc., as subordinate spheres of alienation. 'Social' man is man returned to himself out of what has historically been known as society, all of whose major institutions have been modes of alienated productive living.

What will remain is the life of art and science in a special and vastly enlarged sense of these two terms. Marx's conception of ultimate communism is fundamentally *aesthetic* in character. His utopia is an aesthetic ideal of the future man-nature relationship, which he sees in terms of artistic creation and the appreciation of the beauty of the man-made environment by its creator. The acquisitive and therefore alienated man of history is to be succeeded by the post-historical aesthetic man who will be 'rich' in a new way. Marx describes him as 'the *rich* man profoundly endowed with all the senses', adding: 'The *rich* human being is simultaneously the human being *in need* of a totality of human life-activities'.[12] In Marx's view, the relationship of this new man to nature—that is, to his own anthropological nature—will be that of an artist. Man will realize his natural tendency to arrange things 'according to the laws of beauty'. Economic activity will turn into artistic activity, with industry as the supreme avenue of creation, and the planet itself will become the new man's work of art. The alienated world will give way to the aesthetic world.

Accordingly, Marx's discussion in the manuscript on communism is largely taken up with aesthetic questions. He declares that 'The cultivation of the five senses is the work of the whole history of the world to date.'[13] The positive transcendence of private property will complete the work of history. It will mean the liberation of the human senses to appreciate man-made objects for what they inherently are rather than perceiving in them only objects of utility and potential possession. By way of illustration Marx says that the dealer in minerals sees only their market value but not the beauty and unique character of minerals; he does not and cannot know and appreciate the things in themselves so long as his perceptive faculties remain prisoners of the acquisitive attitude or, as Marx now calls it, the 'sense of having' (*der Sinn des Habens*).

Here is his master-theme again: the enemy of human self-realization is egoistic need, the drive to own and possess things. Man liberated from alienation in communism is for Marx not only a man whose productive activity has ceased to be subjugated to the acquisitive urge. His knowing activity or perception of the world has likewise been freed from it. The human senses are said to be so many different modes of 'appropriation' of external reality. In the man of the future, however, this sensory appropriation will be purified of the greed that has always in the past inhered in it and defiled it:

Private property has made us so stupid and onesided that an object is ours only when we have it, when it exists for us as capital, or when we possess it directly, eat it, drink it, wear it on our body, live in it, in short, use it. . . . For all the physical and spiritual senses, therefore, the sense of *having,* which is the simple alienation of all these senses, has been substituted. . . . The transcendence of private property is, therefore, the complete emancipation of all the human senses and attributes. . . . They relate themselves to the thing for the sake of the thing, but the thing itself is an objective human relation to itself and to man, and *vice versa.* Need or enjoyment have consequently lost their *egoistic* character, and nature has lost its mere *utility* in that using has become *human* using.[14]

This is Marx's picture of 'socialist' man, or man returned to himself 'as *social,* i.e. human man, complete, conscious and matured within the entire wealth of development to date'.[15] Man is to become 'social' or 'socialist' in the sense that he will dwell in aesthetic communion with the humanly produced world around him after he has arranged it according to the laws of beauty and trained his senses to relate to each thing for the sake of the thing. Mirroring the self-activity of the new freely creative and perceptive man, the external objects will affirm his essential nature instead of confronting him as alien and ugly denials of himself. As Marx expresses it, 'all *objects* become for him the *objectification of himself,* become objects that confirm and realize his individuality, become his objects, that is, he himself becomes the object. . . . Thus man is affirmed in the objective world not only in the act of thinking, but with *all* his senses.'[16]

All this presupposes Marx's notion that anthropological nature is the objectified self of the species. He sees the man-world relation as a social relation 'of man to man'. And communism, as the 'regaining of self', means the regaining of the alienated world-self as well as the alienated inner human self or productive powers. We may say, in fact, that for Marx communism ultimately signifies the establishment of an aesthetic community in the self-relation between man and his *alter ego* the objective world. Communism, he says, is 'fully developed naturalism as humanism, and fully developed humanism as naturalism'.[17] Man is to enter into an I-Thou relation with the human nature that exists outside himself. And this, finally, is what Marx means by 'society'. Communism is the emergence of 'society' as a communal relation between the future aesthetic man and his de-alienated world: 'Here for the first time his natural existence is his human existence and nature has become man for him. Thus, *society* is the complete essential unity of man with nature, the true resurrection of nature, the achieved naturalism of man and the achieved humanism of nature.'[18]

This entire conception of ultimate communism is fully comprehensible only against the background of the Hegelian *Phenomenology*. Marx follows the fundamental phenomenological theme straight through to the finish of his system. In terms of Hegel's formula, he views ultimate communism as the stage at which man finally comes to be at home with himself in his otherness. It is a peculiar relationship of knowing between man and his self-produced world. Unlike Hegelian knowing, which is through and through possessive and which Hegel had illustrated by saying that a dog devours things to prove that they are not absolutely self-subsistent, the Marxian knowing is scientific and sensory appreciation of things recognized as external to the perceiver. With this important difference, however, Marx reproduces in his notion of communism the Hegelian vision of the goal of history. Instead of spirit knowing itself as spirit in 'absolute knowledge', we have man knowing himself and nature as man in 'communism'.

But as Marx fully realized, man knowing himself and nature as man is not a state of affairs that would normally be describable as 'communism'. For the term 'communism' carries a stubborn connotation of *ownership*, if only by the community as a whole. The concept of communism cannot easily be divorced from the thought of public property and possession, whereas Marx conceives it to be the goal of man to transcend all possessiveness in his relations with that which lies outside himself. Things then will 'belong' to man solely in the sense that they gratify his fully cultivated senses, and the only 'having' will be a sensory and cognitive having. Consequently, the final condition of man will be beyond all ownership, beyond the property principle, and in this sense *beyond communism*. With this idea in mind, Marx closes his discussion of communism with the following statement: 'Communism is the position as negation of the negation and therefore the actual moment of human emancipation and reconquest of humanity necessary for the future historical development. Communism is the necessary form and energetic principle of the immediate future, but communism as such is not the goal of human development, the form of human society.'[19]

The Soviet editor of a Russian translation of Marx's manuscripts, published in 1956, gives a footnote to this passage saying: 'By "communism as such" Marx means raw egalitarian communism such as was propounded by Baboeuf and his followers.'[20] This is a misinterpretation of the passage, witting or unwitting as the case may be. It contradicts the fundamental idea of Marx as just explained. It might be added, however, that there is no place for this idea in the Soviet doctrine of communism, which envisages at most the 'elevation' of all property to the level of national property (*vsenarodnaia sobstvennost'*). Some recent Soviet writings have suggested that the national property will finally lose its 'state character' and become public property administered by social organizations. The Soviet theorists of communism do not foresee a stage beyond the ownership principle, however, and Marx's idea of the goal of man understandably bothers them.

PART IV

MATURE MARXISM

XI

TWO MARXISMS OR ONE?

Without German philosophy, which preceded it, particularly that of Hegel, German scientific socialism—the only scientific socialism that has ever existed—would never have come into being. ENGELS (1874)

There is an apparent gulf between the philosophical communism of Marx's manuscripts of 1844, or original Marxism as I have called it, and 'scientific socialism' as Marx and Engels expounded it in the *Communist Manifesto* of 1848 and other later writings. We seem to be confronted with two distinct Marxisms. The most conspicuous difference is that self-alienated man, who was the central subject of original Marxism, disappears from view in the later version. In fact, mature Marxism is a mental world from which 'man' seems to be absent.

Marx's first system is openly subjectivistic. It is a phenomenology of man constructed on the model of Hegel's phenomenology of spirit. Its pervasive idea is the idea of the self. It sees property as essentially a subjective phenomenon, industry as 'human psychology, sensuously considered', the objective world as man's self-objectification in productive activity, the working man as man alienated from himself, and so on. It is, further, morally or religiously meaningful in a frankly proclaimed way. The evil is alienation. The act of world history is a moral story of man's loss of himself and ultimate recovery of himself or redemption in communism.

In mature Marxism, beginning approximately with the statement of the Materialist Conception of History by Marx in *The German Ideology* (1845–6), the idea of the self seems to disappear. It turns up rather unaccountably now and then, as when Marx writes in this book: 'In revolutionary activity, change of self coincides with change of circumstances.' Nevertheless, the published formulations of Marxism do not give the impression that it has much to do with the self. Its manifest content (to revert to a phrase already used with reference to Feuerbach's and Marx's interpretation of Hegelianism) is not the self but society. This fact is epitomized in Marx's statement in the *Communist Manifesto:* 'Capital is not a personal power; it is a social power.'[1] As presented in this document, the Marxian theory of history runs exclusively in abstract social and economic categories. The realities with which it purports to deal are social-economic realities, such as the economic base of society and the ideological superstructure, the antagonistic classes into which society is said to be split, the property system by means of which the capitalist class exploits the proletarian class, and so forth. We are told that abstract 'productive powers' of society periodically rebel against abstract 'relations of production', which become 'fetters' on these powers. This is said to be happening again at the present time. Between 'labour' and 'capital', embodied in the proletariat and bourgeoisie, a mighty 'civil war' is raging across the battleground of modern society. The productive powers, vested in 'labour', are in rebellion against 'capital', which is a 'social power' or, alternatively, a 'social relation of production'. Here everything is impersonal, strictly societal.

Marx even calls into question now the concept of man's self-alienation, around which his entire thought had revolved. In *The German Ideology,* he remarks with a certain air of amused superiority that 'the philosophers' have conceived the whole historical process as a 'process of the self-alienation of "man" '.[2] Still more significantly, in the section of the *Manifesto* that treats of 'German or "True" Socialism', he writes caustically that the German *literati* have 'written "externalization of human nature" under French criticism of money-relations', and adds that German 'true socialism' has espoused 'not the interests of the proletariat but the interests of human nature, of man in general, who belongs to no class, has no reality, and subsists only in the misty realm of philosophical fantasy'.[3] Thus, the very idea of man has seemingly gone out the window along with the idea of his self-alienation. There is no 'man', Marx is saying, there are only classes. As he puts it in the sixth of the 'Theses on Feuerbach', 'Human nature is no abstraction inherent in each separate individual. In its reality it is the ensemble of the social relations.'[4]

It should be emphasized that Marx put forward this thoroughly 'socialized' or depersonalized version of Marxism in the immediate aftermath of his work on the manuscripts of 1844. This is shown by the fact that the earlier version and this one commingle in the scattered expository passages of the transitional work, *The Holy Family*, written in the following year. In other words, there was no hiatus, no gap of time during which Marx came upon and assimilated a new set of ideas unknown to him in 1844. What has just been briefly summarized is the essence of Marxism *as it crystallized in Marx's mind* during the elaboration of his phenomenology of man. When he met with Engels in Brussels in the spring of 1845, he was able to expound to his future associate the basic complex of ideas that was to become known as the Materialist Conception of History. The foundations of mature Marxism were laid in the act of creating original Marxism.*

The latter attracted little attention during the first decade or so following the publication of Marx's manuscripts in German in 1932. In recent years, however, knowledge of original Marxism has been spreading, and in various quarters interest in it has been growing. At the same time, the apparent gulf between the original philosophical Marxism and the later Marxian doctrine has created considerable perplexity. The mystery of the relation between them presently seems to be emerging as a dominant issue and focus of interest within the field of Marx scholarship. And considering that Marxism remains today much more than an antiquarian topic in the history of ideas, the discussion has inevitably fallen into the pattern of a debate as to which is the 'real Marxism'.

The world's image of Marxism has, of course, been shaped by the published formulations of the doctrine. Such habitual ways of thinking tend to resist change, particularly when institutions have come into being with a vested interest in their perpetuation. For the great majority of Marxists, and especially for the Communists, the mature system remains as always the truly serious and significant creation of Marx, and original Marxism appears at most an interesting curiosity out of his youth. Many

---

* In his preface to the 1883 German edition of the *Communist Manifesto*, Engels summarized the underlying theory of history and added: '. . . this basic thought belongs solely and exclusively to Marx'. In another preface written some years after, he repeated the summary and commented that 'when I again met Marx at Brussels, in spring, 1845, he had it ready worked out, and put it before me, in terms almost as clear as those in which I have stated it here' (*Selected Works*, vol. I, p. 25). In *Ludwig Feuerbach* he explained further: 'What I contributed—at any rate with the exception of my work in a few special fields—Marx could very well have done without me. What Marx accomplished I would not have achieved' (*ibid.* vol. II, p. 349).

Western authorities on Marx share this view although they evaluate the mature system differently. A moderate expression of the conservative position comes from Herbert Marcuse. In a major study of Hegel and the post-Hegelian movement, he gives an extensive summary of original Marxism and concludes: 'Under all aspects, however, Marx's early writings are mere preliminary stages to his mature theory, stages that should not be overemphasized.'[5]

On the other hand, a heterogeneous minority of philosophical scholars, existentialists, religious thinkers and Marxist dissenters takes the opposing position. For them the original 'humanistic' Marxism is the enduringly valuable and significant creation of Marx, and the depersonalized mature system appears to be a comedown. Those whose primary field of interest is religion find serious religious significance in the original Marxism. To existentialists who regard modern man's alienation as their central problem, the early Marx seems a distant existentialist cousin.* Finally, within the Communist movement itself, particularly in various European sections of it, the influence of original Marxism has made itself felt in recent years. A number of younger so-called 'revisionists', disillusioned by the Stalinist outcome of Russian communism, have turned to Marx's manuscripts in search of a morally meaningful Marxism.

These latter tendencies have disconcerted the official Soviet Marxists, for whom Marx's early philosophical communism was only a stepping-stone to the genuine scientific Marxism of the *Communist Manifesto*. Writing in *Kommunist*, the journal of the Central Committee of the Soviet Communist Party, the Soviet philosopher L. Pazhitnov calls the recent rise of interest in

---

* See, for example, F. H. Heinemann, *Existentialism and the Modern Predicament*, pp. 10–13. Martin Heidegger wrote in 1947 that 'Because Marx, through his experience of the alienation of modern man, is aware of a fundamental dimension of history, the Marxist view of history is superior to all other views' (quoted by Iring Fetscher, in 'Marxismusstudien', *Soviet Survey*, no. 33, July-September 1960, p. 88). In Father Jean-Yves Calvez's *La Pensée de Karl Marx*, the doctrine of alienation is viewed as the central theme of Marx's thought and as religious in significance. Jean Hyppolite argues that Marx's mature thought is incomprehensible without an understanding of original Marxism (*Études sur Marx et Hegel*, especially pp. 107–19). For Karl Löwith, the mature Marxism is a 'vulgar Marxism' of material basis and superstructure, but its 'living impulse' derives from original Marxism ('Man's Self-Alienation in the Early Writings of Marx', *Social Research*, no. 2, Summer 1954, pp. 204–5). For a survey of the literature on the early Marx, see Iring Fetscher's article cited above. See also Daniel Bell, 'In Search of Marxist Humanism,' *Soviet Survey*, no. 32, April—June 1960.

original Marxism in various quarters an 'ideological diversion'. He goes on as follows: 'The enemies of Marxism are attracted by the fact that there is not a word in the manuscripts about the revolution of the oppressed and exploited masses, not a word about the dictatorship of the proletariat. Artificially emphasizing certain not yet mature thoughts of Marx, the falsifiers try to make them the centre of gravity of the interpretation of Marxism as a whole.'[6] The reader will recognize the flagrant inaccuracy of the contention that Marx's manuscripts have nothing to say about the communist revolution, etc. The passage is worth citing simply as a summary of the official Soviet attitude toward original Marxism and those who emphasize its significance.

The problem of which is the more significant or 'real Marxism' need not detain us here. Evidently, both are real and significant. It seems advisable, therefore, to consider the question in a purely factual way by inquiring into the relation between them. We must resolve the problem of the relation between the early philosophical communism of Marx and his later so-called scientific socialism.

[2]

Marx and Engels themselves are our only authoritative sources of evidence bearing upon this problem. And when we consult their recorded opinions, we discover that they did not admit the existence of two Marxisms. What is more, their relevant statements implied a belief in the essential unity of Marxism from the manuscripts of 1844 to *Capital*. I say 'implied' because these statements did not directly refer to Marx's manuscripts. They referred to the relation between mature Marxism and preceding German philosophy, Hegel's in particular. But as we are now in a position to see, what was said about mature Marxism in this context *actually applied to original Marxism*. Had Marx and Engels supposed that there was any basic break between the Marxism of the manuscripts of 1844 and the later version, they would never have spoken as they did about the relation of the latter to Hegelianism.

In later life Marx cherished the thought of writing a short treatise on the Hegelian dialectic and his own relation to it. He wanted, as he said in a letter to Engels in 1858, to 'make accessible to the ordinary human intelligence, in two or three printers' sheets, what is *rational* in the method of Hegel but at the same time

enveloped in mysticism'.[7] However, the famous passage in the
1873 preface to *Capital* was his only further word on the matter.
A part of it has been quoted above.* The remainder reads as
follows: 'In Hegel's writings, dialectic stands on its head. You
must turn it right way up again if you want to discover the
rational kernel that is hidden away within the wrappings of
mystification.'[8] As noted earlier, Marx also observed in this
passage that he had criticized the 'mystifying aspect' of the
Hegelian dialectic nearly thirty years before, i.e. in 1844.

The cryptic reference here to his unpublished manuscripts is
entirely understandable when we recall that he did indeed
develop in them a systematic criticism of Hegel. Having turned
Hegelianism 'right way up again' by reading the *Phenomenology
of Mind* in materialistic economic terms, he proceeded to criticize
its author for representing the *Produktionsgeschichte* as a process of
spirit's becoming in terms of knowledge. This inversion of
Hegel's dialectic of history was the constitutive act of original
Marxism. And now, in 1873, Marx describes it as the constitutive
act of the mature Marxian dialectic. The plain implication is
that he considered the manuscripts of 1844 the birthplace of
mature Marxism, the founding documents of scientific socialism.

It must be noted that Marx and Engels employed the terms
'dialectic' and 'dialectical method' in a substantive as well as
methodological sense. 'Dialectic' refers to the Hegelian (or
Marxian) general conception of the historical process. Likewise,
'dialectical method' means the dialectical mode of conceiving
history. Engels, for example, expressed himself as follows when
he paraphrased in *Ludwig Feuerbach* what Marx had written in
1873 about the inversion of the dialectic: 'Thereby the dialectic
of concepts itself became merely the conscious reflex of the
dialectical motion of the real world and thus the dialectic of
Hegel was placed upon its head; or rather, turned off its head,
on which it was standing, and placed upon its feet.'[9] Clearly,
Marx and Engels are not using the term 'method' in the modern
rigorous sense when they speak of placing Hegel's 'dialectic' or
dialectical 'method' upon its feet. They are speaking of the
transformation of Hegel's dialectical mode of conceiving history
into Marx's. According to the former, history is a spiritual
process of production; according to the latter, a material
process. And the former, they say, was the 'conscious reflex' of

* See above, p. 129.

the latter, wrapped up in mystification. In other words, the Hegelian philosophy of history was a mystified economic interpretation of history—Marxism in embryo. With this idea in mind, Engels concludes *Ludwig Feuerbach* with the statement that, via Marxism, 'The German working-class movement is the inheritor of German classical philosophy.'[10]

Scientific theories normally arise after their authors have immersed themselves in the empirical data that the theory seeks to explain. But not so with the Marxian science of history according to its founders. This science came into being by means of the transformational criticism of Hegel's philosophy of history. Engels, for example, declares in *Ludwig Feuerbach* that Hegel himself brought all past philosophy to its culmination and at the same time 'showed us the way out of the labyrinth of systems to real positive knowledge of the world'. He goes on to criticize Feuerbach for casting Hegelianism aside after he had turned the weapon of criticism against it: 'Feuerbach broke through the system and simply discarded it. But a philosophy is not disposed of by the mere assertion that it is false. And so powerful a work as the Hegelian philosophy . . . could not be disposed of by simply being ignored. It had to be "sublated" ("*aufgehoben*") in its own sense, that is, in the sense that while its form had to be annihilated through criticism, the new content which had been won through it had to be saved.'[11] This, he adds, was Marx's historic accomplishment.

In 1859, Engels stated this same point still more plainly in a review of Marx's *Critique of Political Economy*. Here he said:

What distinguished Hegel's mode of thought from that of all other philosophers was the tremendous sense of the historical upon which it was based. Abstract and idealist though it was in form, yet the development of his thoughts always proceeded parallel with the development of world history and the latter is really meant to be only the test of the former. If, thereby, the real relation was inverted and stood on its head, nevertheless the real content entered everywhere into the philosophy; all the more so since Hegel—in contrast to his disciples—did not parade ignorance, but was one of the finest intellects of all time. . . . This epoch-making conception of history was the direct theoretical premise for the new materialist outlook . . ..[12]

Thus, Hegel's philosophy expressed the 'real content' of world history, albeit in an inverted idealist form. Its critical transformation by Marx yielded the scientific Materialist Conception of History.

Engels' account represents a fair summary of the genesis of original Marxism in the manuscripts of 1844. But his reference is to the genesis of the fully developed Marxism of the later writings. What he says of the rise of mature Marxism specifically applies to original Marxism. It follows inescapably that he and Marx saw in the latter simply the initial, as yet philosophically formulated version of the former. From their standpoint, there were not two Marxisms but one. Alternatively, there were two in the peculiar and limited sense in which the adult may be said to be a different person from the child. For them scientific socialism, embryonic already in Hegel's *Phenomenology*, was delivered into the world in Marx's manuscripts of 1844. The philosophical terminology of the latter was simply the umbilical cord binding the new-born child to its philosophical parent. And mature Marxism was the baby grown to adulthood. Consequently, it was perfectly proper to speak of the mature doctrine in terms applicable to original Marxism.

At the time these various statements were made by the founders, the manuscripts of 1844 had not been published, and their very existence remained unknown to the public. Consequently, it is small wonder that their followers, or many of them, despaired of making any sense out of their remarks about the genesis of scientific socialism out of German philosophy. Marx and Engels seemed to be speaking in riddles—and, indeed, they were. If Hegel had mystified the dialectic, they mystified for posterity their relationship to it. What they were saying about the manner in which Marxism arose was true. But it was specifically true of *original* Marxism, and this remained hidden in Marx's desk drawer. So the followers could only speculate in vain as to what he and Engels meant by the mysterious 'inversion' of Hegel of which they were laconically speaking from time to time. A treatise could be written on the history of these fruitless speculations, both those by Marxists and those by non-Marxist students of Marx.

Why, then, did he not make the hidden documents public? Evidently, because he realized that their publication would create more perplexities than it would dispel. Marxism as he and Engels had presented it to the world had nothing to do with man's *Selbstentfremdung*; it even, in one place, ridiculed the idea.

Its subject was not alienation but class war, not the conflict of an alienated generic man with himself but rather the conflict of classes in contemporary society. Marx no doubt felt that it would confuse and disorient the always unsufficiently class-conscious workers if he were to introduce them to the philosophically formulated first form of the creed. Besides, the essence of the original document lived on in his later writings, so why bother to publish it?

Engels maintained the same secretive attitude when the archives came into his possession after Marx's death in 1883. Some years later he made public the 'Theses on Feuerbach' as an appendix to a new edition of his own *Ludwig Feuerbach*. In 1893 a Russian visitor, Alexis Voden, suggested that Marx's other early philosophical writings also ought to be published. He reported afterwards that Engels showed embarrassment when this subject was raised, and answered that 'Marx had also written poetry in his student years, but it could hardly interest anybody'. Was not the fragment on Feuerbach 'sufficient'? And ought he not to continue work on Marx's unfinished economic writings rather than publish 'old manuscripts from publicistic works of the 1840's'? Besides, Engels concluded, 'in order to penetrate into that "old story" one needed to have an interest in Hegel himself, which was not the case with anybody then, or to be more exact, "neither with Kautsky nor with Bernstein".'[13]* This fascinating postscript to the 'old story' illustrates very clearly the dilemma in which Marx and Engels found themselves.

Inasmuch as they had withheld from the public the materials that recorded the genesis of Marxism in an inversion of Hegel's *Phenomenology*, the whole problem remained impenetrably obscure. Only by publishing the records of the vital intermediate stage, philosophical original Marxism, could the founders have explained and proved their point about the organic link of later Marxism with the Hegelian philosophy of history. Since they failed to do this, the false legend gradually arose that Marx's early philosophical period was pre-Marxist, and that Marxism itself came into being only in the aftermath

* After Engels' death the Marx archives passed into the possession of the Social Democratic Party of Germany. As I understand it, permission to make reproductions was given to representatives of the U.S.S.R. after the October Revolution of 1917, and the Russians subsequently took the initiative in publishing Marx's early philosophical writings.

of his apparent break with German philosophy in the middle 1840's. His intellectual career was divided into a pre-Marxist early philosophical period and a post-philosophical later Marxist period. A typical example of this way of thinking may be cited from a work by Paul Sweezy. After mentioning Marx's move to Paris in late 1843, he states: 'It was during the next few years, spent mostly in Paris and Brussels that he broke with his philosophic past and achieved the mature point of view from which he was to write his later economic works.'[14]

This image of Marx as a thinker who originally dabbled in German philosophy and then went on to achieve a new, mature, Marxist point of view in his later economic writings completely conflicts with the testimony from Marx and Engels that has been examined here. This testimony of the founders clearly implies that the later economic works were written from the point of view acquired by Marx in 1844 in the process of deciphering Hegelianism in economic terms, and that the post-philosophical Marx is a Marx for whom Hegelian philosophy is esoteric economics. If so, however, mature Marxism is an organic outgrowth of original Marxism, and those who see in the manuscripts of 1844 no more than 'certain not yet mature thoughts' (Pazhitnov) or 'mere preliminary stages to his mature theory, stages that should not be overemphasized' (Marcuse) are deeply in error. That they are preliminary stages is true. But according to Marx and Engels, it is true in the special sense in which it may be said that the child is a preliminary stage to the mature person. Here the essential fact is continuity in change. The preliminary stage largely predetermines the later one, and its importance cannot be overemphasized.

[3]

If we accept the belief of Marx and Engels in the essential unity of the Marxian system from 1844 onward, we still have to explain the appearance of duality. Although the original and later versions are by no means wholly dissimilar in appearance, the disappearance of man and his alienation from the mature system changes the face of Marxism so considerably as to create the impression that we are dealing with two distinct complexes of thought.

I have already suggested the explanation that seems to be

called for.* The transition to the seemingly 'dehumanized' mature Marxism actually occurred at that point in the manuscripts of 1844 where Marx decided, uncertainly but irrevocably, that man's self-alienation could and should be grasped as a social relation 'of man to man'. Only man himself can be this alien power over man, he said, but this relation of man to himself takes practical shape as a relation between the alienated worker and 'another man outside him', i.e. the capitalist. In this way the inner conflict of alienated man with himself became, in Marx's mind, a social conflict between 'labour' and 'capital', and the alienated species-self became the class-divided society. Self-alienation was projected as a social phenomenon, and Marx's psychological original system turned into his apparently sociological mature one.

One of the passages of Marx's *The Holy Family*, written just at the time of his transition from the earlier to the later formulations of the system, illustrates this point quite vividly:

The possessing class and the proletarian class represent one and the same human self-alienation. But the former feels satisfied and affirmed in this self-alienation, apprehends the alienation *as its own power,* and possesses in it the appearance of a human existence; the latter feels annihilated in this alienation, sees in it its own impotence and the reality of a non-human existence. To use an expression of Hegel's, it is a depravity in *revolt* against this depravity, a revolt necessarily aroused in this class by the contradiction between its human *nature* and its life-situation, which is a manifest, decisive and total negation of this nature.[15]

Society is here envisaged as a self-system whose inner dynamics are those of alienation. The antagonistic classes are collective expressions of the conflicting forces of the self-system. The proletariat and capitalist class, or labour and capital, are opposing sides of 'one and the same human self-alienation'.

What Marx sees in society, then, is a self-system in conflict, a split self writ large. However, he ceases from about this time to be clearly conscious of the fact that this is what he sees. To put it differently, that which he sees presents itself to him from now on simply as 'society'. Thus, in his short work *Wage Labour and Capital*, written in 1847, he asserts that 'capital and labour are two sides of one and the same relation'.[16] 'One and the same human self-alienation' has now become simply 'one and the same relation'. Marx also describes labour power as a com-

* See above, pp. 146–9.

modity that its possessor, the worker, surrenders up to capital
('the power whose slave it is'), and declares: 'But the exercise of
labour power, labour, is the worker's own life-activity, his own
life-expression. . . . Thus his life-activity is for him only a means
to enable him to exist. He works in order to live. He does not
even reckon labour as part of his life, it is rather a sacrifice of his
life.'[17] Here is the picture of alienated labour given in the manuscripts of 1844, the only difference being that Marx no longer
calls it alienated labour but simply 'wage labour' (*Lohnarbeit*).
He now apprehends the alienated self-relation as a social relation
of labour and capital, and on this basis he can say that 'Capital
is not a personal power; it is a social power.'

This makes it clear why he proceeded in the *Manifesto* to
formulate Marxism without explicit reference to the concepts
of man and his self-alienation, and why he here scornfully dismissed the whole notion of 'man in general' as unreal. For him
there was no longer any generic man, and hence no longer any
use for the idea of 'man's' self-alienation. The alienated self-
relation had transformed itself into an alienated social relation,
and 'man' was just the 'ensemble' of such relations. 'Man' had
been split in two. There were left now only the dissociated
antagonistic parts, the 'worker' and 'capitalist', neither of them
wholly human. Society itself was splitting down the centre into
two hostile 'camps' of workers and capitalists. The realities, it
appeared, were the warring classes themselves, and so it had
always been: 'The history of all hitherto existing society is the
history of class struggles.'[18] It was absurd of the German *literati*
to espouse the misty cause of 'mankind'. The only real and
pressing issue was that of which side to take, labour's or capital's,
in the ongoing class struggle of today.

Thus does the Marxism of the *Manifesto* evolve directly out
of the Marxism of the manuscripts of 1844. A system concerned
with the generic human self in its hostile relations with itself
turns into one that seems to have nothing to do with a dualized
self and everything to do with a dualized society. But this is
essentially a change of manifest content, or what Marxism seems
to be about. It affects not what Marx sees but the way in which
he sees it and, therefore, describes it. What he sees is still the
Selbstentfremdungsprozess, but he sees it as a social process.
Alienation remains his central theme, but it has gone under-
ground in his image of society.

XII

THE NEW MATERIALISM

In total contrast to German philosophy, which descends from heaven to earth, we here ascend from earth to heaven.

MARX (1846)

Marx's theory of history is frequently presented by quoting his own résumé of it in the preface to his *Critique of Political Economy*. But a theory that takes all reality as its province could not have been adequately summarized in a single paragraph. Marx had, moreover, produced a full-scale exposition of it in *The German Ideology*, a large work written jointly with Engels in 1845–6. The book was not at the time publishable, since most of it consisted of arid polemics against erstwhile Young Hegelian associates.

But the first part, written by Marx himself under the title 'Feuerbach: Opposition of the Materialist and Idealist Outlook', was a systematic statement of the developed Marxian position. Here Marx amplified in some seventy-five pages the set of eleven theses on Feuerbach written in the spring of 1845. When Engels made the theses public in 1888, he observed that he had reread the book itself and discovered how incomplete was his and Marx's knowledge of economic history at that time. He also, however, characterized it as an exposition of the Materialist Conception of History, and called the theses 'the brilliant germ of the new world-outlook'.[1] Part I of the book clearly must be classified as mature Marxism. It is now available to us, and the discussion in this chapter is based primarily upon it.

In the later preface just referred to, Marx described *The German Ideology* as the book in which he and Engels had undertaken to 'work out together the contrast between our view and the idealism of the German philosophy, and in fact to settle accounts with our former philosophic conscience'.[2] And here, indeed, we encounter a Marx who is convinced that he has made a fundamental break with his German philosophic past. For him the opposition of the 'materialist' and 'idealist' outlooks

177

is not an opposition between one position and another *within* philosophy. It is an opposition of science versus philosophy. His own new materialist position is opposed to the various idealist positions, Hegel's in particular, as a post-philosophical to differing philosophical views of the world. As all this implies, he uses the terms 'philosophy', 'science', 'materialism' and 'idealism' in a special way of his own not to be confused with the conventional usage of his time and ours.

In Marx's mind the ancient philosophical terms 'idealism' and 'materialism' have taken on unique new meanings governed wholly by the earlier thought-processes in which we have seen him engaged. To begin with 'materialism', he does not mean by this term what we are accustomed to mean when we use it in philosophical discourse. It does not have a physical or mechanical or physiological connotation, nor does it question the reality of conscious mind. It does not refer to a theory about the nature of the stuff of which the universe is composed, although Marx assumes that this is material stuff. And the term 'idealism' in his usage correspondingly differs from 'idealism' as employed in conventional philosophical discourse.

For Marx the materialist-idealist antithesis is an antithesis of approaches to the understanding of history. It is wholly a question of the nature of one's image of the human historical process, which can be seen from either of two opposite points of view. This arises from the circumstance that man, who is fundamentally a productive being, produces mentally as well as materially. As an intellectual he engages in 'mental production'; he is a 'producer of the concept'. As a worker, on the other hand, he produces non-conceptual objects in the course of what Marx variously calls the 'material life-process', 'material activity', 'material praxis', or 'material production of life'.[3] Now the idealist image of history, according to Marx, reflects the thinker's tendency to visualize it all in terms of his own activity of mental production. Thus, Hegelian idealism pictures history as essentially a process of thought-production on the part of the thinking spirit.

The idealist starts from the 'heaven' of theory and attempts to descend to the 'earth' of practice. He proceeds from man's 'sacred history' or thought-process in the effort to comprehend the historical process as a whole. The materialist, on the other hand, begins with the 'real life-process' or 'practical developmental process of man'. He takes his stand on 'earth' and adopts man's 'profane history' as the starting point for theory. Abandoning the vain effort to descend from heaven to earth, he rises from earth to heaven. He treats the sacred history as a mental reflex of the profane one, the history of mental production as an epiphenom of the history of material production. His underlying principle is that 'Life is not determined by consciousness, but consciousness by life'.[4] Marx defends it on the ground that man cannot think, and cannot live at all, without producing the material means of life. Here is the doctrine of economic base and ideological superstructure, better known in Marx's later formulation in the preface to his *Critique of Political Economy:* 'The mode of production in material life determines the general character of the social, political and spiritual processes of life. It is not the consciousness of men that determines their existence, but, on the contrary, their social existence determines their consciousness.'[5]

Thus, the dichotomy between materialism and idealism turns for Marx on the question of whether you start from earth and ascend, or start from heaven and descend, in your conception of human history. It is a question of whether you take the practical life of man or his fantasy life as the foundation for theorizing. To borrow a later expression, materialism, for Marx, is essentially and exclusively 'historical materialism'. It is a way of thinking about history that takes the practical developmental process as the primary datum and the human thought-process as its reflex. And Marx maintains that this way of thinking is radically new and unprecedented: 'In the whole conception of history up to the present this real basis of history has either been totally neglected or else considered as a minor matter quite irrelevant to the course of history.'[6]

The transition from idealism to materialism is equivalent, in Marx's view, to the transition from philosophy to science. The philosophy-science antithesis is simply the idealism-materialism antithesis regarded under the aspect of falsity and truth. As Marx expresses it: 'Where speculation ends—in real life—there real, positive science begins: the representation of the practical activity, the practical developmental process of man. Empty talk about consciousness ceases, and real knowledge has to take its place. When reality is depicted, philosophy as an independent branch of activity loses its medium of existence.'[7]

This implies a usage of 'science' and 'philosophy' no less unique than the usage of 'materialism' and 'idealism'. By 'science' (*Wissenschaft*) Marx simply means thinking that has real life as its object. Science is knowledge of the world as it is, or the clear, direct, unobstructed view of reality. And this is the materialist view, the one that focuses upon the practical developmental process as the primary datum. Scientific thinking, insofar as man or history is the object, means materialist thinking, i.e. Marxism, and what makes it scientific is nothing at all but the fact that it is true.

'Philosophy', on the other hand, means confused thinking that does not depict reality. Marx does not mean that philosophical thinking lacks a real object. All consciousness is consciousness of real life: 'Consciousness can never be anything else than conscious being (*bewusste Sein*), and the being of men is their real life-process.'[8] To illustrate the proposition, Marx says that the existence of a revolutionary consciousness or revolutionary ideas in a given epoch implies the existence of an actual revolutionary class.* Philosophical consciousness too is a reflection of reality, but through a glass darkly. It represents the real world, but not as it really is. Philosophy *qua* philosophy is idealist. It is a theoretical consciousness that takes consciousness itself rather than 'real life' to be the primary datum and so reverses the true order of priority as between life and consciousness. It sees real life through distorted idealist spectacles as a manifestation of the thought-process. Thus, Marx 'Hegelianizes' the very definition of philosophy. He says of philosophy in general what he had said earlier, in his manuscripts, of the Hegelian philosophy in particular. This he attempts to justify by saying that the Hegelian philosophy of history is the final outcome and climax of the entire human philosophical enterprise.

Generalizing the argument still further, Marx joins the philosophical false consciousness together with the religious and other non-scientific forms of consciousness under the general category of 'ideology'. Ideology is consciousness of reality in which 'men and their circumstances appear upside down as in a *camera obscura* . . .'.[9] It is, therefore, an illusory consciousness,

---

* In actual fact, of course, and as many a revolutionist has learned by experience, the existence of revolutionary ideas in a given time and place implies nothing more for certain than the existence of one or more thinkers of revolutionary ideas.

although the ideological thinker does not know it to be illusory.* The whole of German philosophy, of which Hegelianism is the finest expression, belongs to 'German ideology'. Even the Young Hegelians, who claim to have transcended Hegel, remain prisoners of illusion and purveyors of ideology. They take the religious consciousness (Feuerbach) or the critical consciousness (Bauer) or the individual's consciousness (Stirner) to be the prime datum. It is only with the attainment of genuine materialism (Marx), which sees not consciousness of any kind but 'real life' as the prime datum, that human thought ceases for the first time in history to be infected with ideology. The transition from idealism to materialism is the transcendence of philosophy and all ideology in the 'representation of the practical activity'; with this 'real positive science begins'.

Plainly, the entire reasoning process just reviewed is a restatement and generalization of the reasoning about Hegelianism in Marx's manuscripts. There he argued that the Hegelian philosophy was a false consciousness of reality in that it represented the material 'history of production' as a history of spirit's thought-production; and that Hegelianism turned upside down gave you a true consciousness of what has been and is actually happening in history. Now Marx broadens the argument. Hegelianism becomes the prototype of all ideological thinking since history began. And the transition of Marx from Hegelianism to inverted Hegelianism, now called the Materialist Conception of History, becomes the transition of mankind from the philosophical stage of mystified ideological thought to the stage of positive science. The argument has been broadened, but it is the same argument. Marx is speaking from the text of his manuscripts of 1844.

[2]

The continuity is further visible in Marx's elaboration of the doctrine of materialism in the 'Theses on Feuerbach' and *The German Ideology*. On his view, a materialist is not only one who proceeds from the practical developmental process in his con-

---

* Marx holds that the illusory ideological consciousness serves the interest of the ruling class, but he does not assume that the ideological thinker is *necessarily* a cynical paid servant of this class. Ideological thinking has an unconscious aspect as well as the conscious one. Thus, in a passage of *Ludwig Feuerbach* quoted in the previous chapter, Engels says of Hegel that 'even though unconsciously, he showed us the way out of the labyrinth of systems to real positive knowledge of the world'.

ception of history. He also proceeds from history in his conception of the world of material objects apprehended by man in sensory experience. For a materialist in Marx's peculiar sense of the term, this 'sensuous' (*sinnliche*) external world is a materialization of all past productive activity of the human race. The sensuous world around man is a nature produced by history, or in Marx's words 'an historical product, the result of the activity of a whole succession of generations . . .'.[10]

He fully recognizes the novelty of this conception in the history of materialism. Calling it the 'new materialism',[11] he criticizes all past doctrines of materialism for the failure to grasp the external material objects as materializations of human activity. This is the burden of his first thesis on Feuerbach, which reads as follows:

The chief defect of all materialism up to now (including Feuerbach's) is, that the object, reality, what we apprehend through our senses, is understood only in the form of the *object* or *sense perception*, but not as *sensuous human activity*, as *practice*, not subjectively. Hence in opposition to materialism the *active* side was developed abstractly by idealism— which of course does not know real sensuous activity (*sinnliche Tätigkeit*) as such. Feuerbach wants sensuous objects, really distinguished from the objects of thought: but he does not understand human activity itself as *objective* activity.[12]

Amplifying this criticism of past materialism in the text of *The German Ideology*, he says that Feuerbach's error was the failure to comprehend 'the sensuous world as the total living sensuous activity of the individuals composing it'.[13] He maintains that even the objects of simplest 'sensuous certainty' are actually historical products. Thus the cherry tree was transplanted to Europe by commerce only a few centuries ago, and solely by virtue of this historical fact is it given to Feuerbach's senses. Here Marx comments in an ironic footnote that Feuerbach 'cannot cope with the sensuous world except by looking at it with the "eyes", i.e. through the "spectacles", of the *philosopher*'.[14] In short, there would be no sensory world at all for the philosopher if he lacked the eyeglasses given to him through history.

As far as the nature that preceded human history is concerned, Marx goes on, it hardly exists anywhere save perhaps on a few Australian coral-islands of recent origin and does not, therefore, exist at all for Feuerbach (who lives in Germany).

Feuerbach speaks of the perceptions of natural science, but where would natural science be without industry, production, the incessant sensuous activity and creation of man? So much is this latter the basis of the whole sensuous world as it now exists that were it interrupted for only a year, Feuerbach would not only find an enormous change in the natural world but that the entire *Menschenwelt,* and his own perceptive faculties included, were missing. 'Of course, in all this', adds Marx in conclusion, 'the priority of external nature remains unassailed.'[15]

Thus does Marx restate polemically within the framework of mature Marxism the conception of the world that he had presented systematically in original Marxism. He admits in the first thesis on Feuerbach that the real affiliation of his own 'new materialism' is not with past doctrines of materialism but with a philosophy that called itself 'idealist', Hegelianism. They have in common the idea that the object or 'reality' must be understood 'subjectively', i.e. as a self-externalization of the creative subject of the historical process. They differ in that Hegelian idealism construes the world-creating activity as mental production, an ethereal activity of abstract thought, whereas Marxian materialism construes it as human activity of material production. This, of course, merely reproduces the fundamental argument of the manuscripts of 1844.

'New materialism' is simply Marx's new name for the conception of the world elaborated there. It is essentially an historical materialism, as Marx himself emphasizes when he says: 'As far as Feuerbach is a materialist he does not deal with history, and as far as he considers history he is not a materialist. With him materialism and history diverge completely . . .'.[16] With Marx, on the other hand, materialism and history converge completely in the notion that the 'sensuous' material world is a cumulative product of the human historical process. Marx has no 'dialectical materialism' as a doctrine of nature apart from history. It is precisely on account of its detachment of nature from history that he indicts the old materialism. His own 'new materialism' is dialectical in that it views the historical process, within which a man-made nature evolves, as dialectical in character. Marx's dialectics are dialectics of *history* in this comprehensive and singular sense of the word.*

* This judgment is not seriously affected by his following subsequent remark, apropos of the transformation of the medieval guildmasters into capitalists: 'Here,

'Dialectical materialism' as a theory of nature apart from human history is a development of the later, scholastic period of Marxism, which began, however, within the lifetime of the founder. We see its beginnings in the later writings of Engels. In *Anti-Dühring,* and in a set of unfinished papers published posthumously under the title *Dialectics of Nature,* he sought to supplement Marx's 'modern materialism' (as Engels still called it) with a doctrine of dialectics in nature that was a *mélange* of Hegel at his worst and the materialism of such nineteenth-century writers as Haeckel. Even in these unfinished papers, however, we find an echo of Marx's theory of the material world as a materialization of man: 'There is devilishly little left of "nature" as it was in Germany at the time when the Germanic peoples immigrated into it. The earth's surface, climate, vegetation, fauna, and the human beings themselves have infinitely changed, and all this owing to human activity, while the changes of nature in Germany which have occurred in this period of time without human interference are incalculably small.'[17] This was Engels' final obeisance to Marx's materialism.

[3]

The German Ideology not only reaffirms the first premise of original Marxism that the material world around us is a materialization of man's productive labours in history. It also reaffirms the second premise that the world so created confronts its living creators as an alien world and a gigantic fetter upon them. Thus we read here that 'man's own deed becomes an alien power opposed to him, which enslaves him instead of being controlled by him'. Marx speaks of 'the alien relation between men and what they themselves produce', and says further: 'This crystallization of social activity, this consolidation of what we ourselves produce into an objective power above us, growing out of our control, thwarting our expectations, bringing to naught our calculations, is one of the chief factors in historical development up to now.'[18] The alienated world is still his theme.

The picture up to this point has been one of continuity between original and mature Marxism. Beyond it, however, a great apparent divergence confronts us. For Marx no longer

just as in the natural sciences, we find confirmation of the law discovered by Hegel in his *Logic,* that, at a certain point, what have been purely quantitative changes become qualitative' (*Capital,* p. 319).

speaks of 'self-alienation'. He no longer, for example, explains the alien character of the objective world around us, and the object-bondage, by the alienation of man from himself in his producing activity. Instead, he offers as the explanation the fact that man produces the objective world within the 'division of labour' (*Teilung der Arbeit*): 'The social power, i.e. the multiplied productive power, which arises through the cooperation of different individuals as it is determined within the division of labour, appears to these individuals, since their cooperation is not voluntary but natural, not as their own united power but as an alien force existing outside them. . . .'[19]

'Division of labour' seems on the face of it to be a totally different idea from 'self-alienation' or 'alienated labour'. On closer analysis, however, it turns out that the transition is essentially a metamorphosis of one and the same basic idea. The lever of the metamorphosis was Marx's decision in the manuscripts of 1844 to treat man's self-alienation as a social relation between the working man and another man outside him. The alienated self-relation was thereby transformed into a social relation of production, and this was given the name 'division of labour'. Marx borrowed this term from the political economists, who meant by it simply occupational specialization. As was the case with the other key terms so borrowed, however, he enlarged upon its meaning. He interpreted the division of labour as the social expression of self-alienation. This is clear from the following passage in the manuscripts of 1844: 'The *division of labour* is the political-economic expression of the sociality (*Gesellschaftlichkeit*) of labour within alienation. Or, since labour is only an expression of human activity within externalization, an expression of life as externalization of life, the *division of labour* is nothing other than the *alienated, externalized* positing of human activity as a real species-activity or activity of man as a species-being.'[20]

Having thus originated as a concept of the 'sociality' of self-alienation in the productive process, 'division of labour' becomes the comprehensive category of mature Marxism corresponding to the category 'self-alienation' in original Marxism. The *Entfremdungsgeschichte* of the manuscripts turns into a history of the division of labour in all its ramifications and transformations. The division of alienated man against himself becomes a division of man against man, of class against class, and of the worker against himself, within the division of labour. The several non-economic spheres of alienated productive living are now called spheres of the division of labour. The outstanding example is the state. Thus, Marx writes in his *Critique of the Gotha Programme* that 'by the word "state" is meant the government machine, or the state in so far as it forms a special organism separated from society through the division of labour'. [21]

In *The German Ideology*, he traces the origin of the division of labour to the division of labour in the sexual act within the family, and so brings his theory of history into a relation of sorts with the Old Testament's. But the division of labour first truly became such, he goes on, from the moment when a division of mental and physical labour arose and with it 'the possibility, may the fact, that intellectual and material activity—enjoyment and labour, production and consumption—devolve on different individuals, and that the only possibility of their not coming into contradiction lies in the negation in its turn of the division of labour'. [22] This stage too began within the family, where wife and children became slaves of the husband and hence the first form of private property.

Thus, division of labour, as a social relation of production, is primarily a *property* relation between the producers themselves and that which they produce, on the one hand, and a non-producer on the other. It is the relation in which a producer stands in his activity to another man who does not produce but appropriates the product, or the bulk of it, as his private property. Accordingly, Marx now says of the division of labour what he had previously said of alienated labour, viz. that private property is its outgrowth and consequence: 'Division of labour and private property are, moreover, identical expressions; in the one the same thing is affirmed with reference to the activity as is affirmed in the other with reference to the product of the activity.' And further: 'The division of labour implies . . . the division between capital and labour, and the different forms of property itself.' [23]

If alienation was the general historical condition of man for original Marxism, division of labour is the general condition for mature Marxism. Each historical mode of production (*Produktionsweise*) is described by Marx as a method of human productive self-expression conditioned by the nature of the available implements of production, or by what we would call today the state of technology. Thus, modern industry is a mode of production conditioned by machine technology. Each historical mode of production has been accompanied by a particular 'form of intercourse' (*Verkehrsform*) or set of 'social relations of production.' And Marx describes every such form of intercourse or set of social relations of production as an expression of the division of labour in society. It is, in other words, a form of the relationship between non-owning producers and non-producing owners of the materials and means of production. Changes in technology bring changes in the mode of production and therewith in the concrete form of the division of labour in production. Thus, medieval agriculture, associated with landed property or the division of labour between feudal lord and serf, gives way in modern times to capitalist industry, which is associated with property in the form of capital and the division of labour between capitalist and wage worker. In *The German Ideology* Marx essays an historical survey of the forms of property in the tribal, ancient, feudal and bourgeois periods as different expressions of the division of labour determined by developments in the mode of production.

Class conflict, the theory of which he also develops here for the first time, emerges as the decisive expression of the antagonism inherent in every form of the division of labour. Having earlier viewed the self-relation in alienated labour as hostile, Marx now sees the division of labour as a hostile social relation of man to man, and class war as the multiplication of this hostility on the scale of society as a whole. The periodic past rebellions of the productive powers against the relations of productions have been rebellions of the producers against the prevailing form of the division of labour and its class of beneficiaries, and 'all collisions in history have their origin, according to our view, in the contradiction between the productive forces and the form of intercourse'.[24] Though class conflict is for Marx the supreme form of historical collision, it is by no means the only one. Since the division of labour has been ubiquitous in history, showing up within the family and between families, within the community and between communities, within the class and between classes, etc., the whole history of the race presents a panorama of contradictions. As Marx now sees it, hostility of man to man has always pervaded every pore of the social organism since the original division of labour within the family.

XIII

DIVISION OF LABOUR AND COMMUNISM

In the division of labour, man is divided. ENGELS (1878)

Original Marxism presented history as a story of man's self-alienation and ultimate transcendence of it in communism. Mature Marxism retells the tale, with added embellishments, in terms of the division of labour. It remains, however, essentially the same story. The change of manifest content, or of what Marxism seems to be about, goes along with a latent continuity of thought. Having in 1844 translated 'alienation' as 'division of labour', Marx subsequently read the division of labour as alienation. That is, he found the same meaning in the division of labour that he had previously found in the idea of alienation.

Thus, the division of labour in all its expressions is condemned as evil, and first of all on the ground that it means deprivation of freedom. Marx holds that the labour performed under every historical class division of labour in society has been essentially unfree. The social relations of production have always been coercive relations of domination and servitude. The producers have always stood in a relation of servitude to the class of those who appropriate the product as private property. And the history of this relation, from the time of primitive slave-labour to that of modern capitalist wage labour, is one of *increasing* servitude. In *The German Ideology* and elsewhere, Marx maintains that the last historical form of it is the least free, despite the legally free status of the wage worker in bourgeois society. Here, he says, labour has 'lost all semblance of self-activity'.[1] Thus, all history up to now remains for Marx a progress of human bondage. It is a story of man's ever worsening enslavement under the division of labour in society.

Marx treats the division of labour in the ordinary sense of occupational specialization as a function of the class division of society between workers and non-working property-owners (or what we may call the 'social division of labour'). He considers it under the headings of division between town and country labour, division between mental and manual labour, and finally the occupational sub-divisions within these categories. In all these forms, moreover, the division of labour is made out to be synonymous with slavery. It is the enslavement of the human being to a partial and limited sphere of activity: 'For as soon as labour is distributed, each man has a particular exclusive sphere of activity, which is forced upon him and from which he cannot escape. He is a hunter, a fisherman, a shepherd, or a critical critic, and must remain so if he does not want to lose his means of livelihood.' Further: 'The antagonism of town and country can only exist as a result of private property. It is the most crass expression of the subjection of the individual under the division of labour, under a definite activity forced upon him—a subjection which makes one man into a restricted town-animal, the other into a restricted country-animal, and daily creates anew the conflict between their interests.'[2]

Marx never abandoned this conception of occupational specialization as slavery. Indeed, it becomes an almost obsessive theme of his own later writings and also those of Engels. The following passage from the latter's *Anti-Dühring* is one of very many expressions of it:

In the division of labour, man is also divided. All other physical and mental faculties are sacrificed to the development of one single activity. This stunting of man's faculties grows in the same measure as the division of labour, which attains its highest development in manufacture. Manufacture splits up each trade into its separate fractional operations, allots each of these to an individual labourer as his life calling, and thus chains him for life to a particular detail function and a particular tool. . . . And not only the labourers, but also the classes directly or indirectly exploiting the labourers are made subject, through the division of labour, to the tool of their function: the empty-minded bourgeois to his own capital and his own thirst for profits; the lawyer to his fossilised legal conceptions, which dominate him as a power independent of him; the 'educated classes' in general to their manifold local limitations and one-sidedness, to their own physical and mental short-sightedness, to their stunted specialized education and the fact that they are chained for life to this specialized activity itself—even when this specialized activity is merely to do nothing.[3]

Engels credits the earlier utopian socialists with the discovery of the evil of occupational specialization. This is, indeed, one of the few genuine points of contact between Marx and his socialist predecessors, especially Charles Fourier. But they were not the principal source of his view.

His position grows out of and presupposes the philosophical conception of man presented in the manuscripts of 1844. Man was defined as a free conscious producer in need of a 'totality of human life-activities'. This in turn was Marx's translation into anthropological terms of the Hegelian concept of *Geist*, which Hegel had seen as 'manifesting, developing and perfecting its powers in every direction which its manifold nature can follow'.*
And from this definition of the species-character of man it followed that man cannot realize his human nature so long as he is a specialized animal bound down to some one occupation all his life. He cannot be free without the opportunity to cultivate his manifold creative faculties in every possible direction. Somewhat inexplicably in the absence of an explicit restatement of this position, Marx and Engels in their later writings present occupational specialization under the division of labour as evil, unnatural and enslaving.

In fact, all the symptoms that Marx had previously treated under the heading of 'alienation' are now attributed to the disease of division of labour. Occupational specialization is seen as something that defeats the self-realization of man, something that dehumanizes him. In *The Poverty of Philosophy* (1847), the division of labour is said to contradict the 'integral development of the individual'.⁴ In *Wage Labour and Capital*, Marx writes that the capitalist wage labourer 'becomes transformed into a simple, monotonous productive force that does not have to use intense body or intellectual faculties'.⁵ In *Wages, Price and Profit* (1865) he says that the worker in modern machine industry 'is a mere machine for producing alien wealth, broken in body and brutalized in mind'.⁶ Here once again is the tormented man of the manuscripts of 1844, who mortifies his body and ruins his spirit in productive activity performed under compulsion of greed. The difference is that the latter is now defined as the greed of *another* man separated from the worker by the social division of labour.

In *Wage Labour and Capital*, which outlines the argument later amplified at great length in *Capital* itself, Marx constructs his peculiar conception of capitalism as a system of ever intensifying

* See above, p. 47.

division of labour within the division of labour. That is, within the social division of labour between wage worker and capitalist, the former is subjected to greater and greater division against himself through specialization. Within the enslavement of wage labour to the capitalist greed for profit, labour is also subjected to increasing slavery of specialization. And this situation worsens in a vicious circle. Competition among capitalists for economic survival impels one or more to raise productivity of labour by introducing new machinery, which intensifies the division of labour in the factory. Others are compelled to follow suit, so that 'division of labour is necessarily followed by greater division of labour, the application of machinery by still greater application of machinery, work on a large scale by work on a still larger scale'. This, says Marx, is 'the law which gives capital no rest and continually whispers in its ear: "Go on! Go on!" '.[7] So goes the self-destructive inner dialectic of capitalist production as represented by Marx in *Capital*. The upward curve of technological progress is simultaneously a downward curve of dehumanization of the worker under the division of labour. This in turn is a prime component of the increasing misery that Marx sees as the efficient cause of the proletarian revolution.

In Chapter XII of *Capital*, he gives a short economic history of society under the aspect of ever increasing occupational specialization. He traces the phenomenon from its simple beginnings in the family and the primitive community through handicraft production in the guilds to the modern 'manufacturing division of labour'. The tale reaches its frightful climax when manufacturing, dating from the middle sixteenth century, becomes 'machinofacture' at the close of the eighteenth. Marx writes of the manufacturing division of labour: 'It transforms the worker into a cripple, a monster, by forcing him to develop some specialized dexterity at the cost of a world of productive impulses and faculties. . . . Having been rendered incapable of following his natural bent to make something independently, the manufacturing worker can only develop productive activity as an appurtenance of the capitalist workshop. Just as it was written upon the brow of the chosen people that they were Jehovah's property, so does the division of labour brand the manufacturing worker as the property of capital.'[8] Thus, increasing subordination of labour to specialization means increasing subordination of labour to capital, which again means

its increasing subordination to specialization, and so on in a
vicious circle.

Not content with telling the story of man's decline and fall
under the division of labour, Marx gives also, mostly in foot-
notes, a rambling history of opinions about it. In various ways
he damns those who have praised the division of labour, and
praises those who have damned it. He finds an ancient theoretical
advocate of it in Plato, whose *Republic* was just 'an Athenian
idealization of the Egyptian caste system'. He says that political
economy, itself a product of the manufacturing period, generally
approves of the division of labour, but that Adam Smith, who
praised the phenomenon at the start of *The Wealth of Nations*,
condemns it later in the book. As usual, Hegel grasped the
crucial point. He held 'extremely heretical views concerning the
division of labour', as shown by the remark in his *Rechtsphilosofie*:
'When we speak of educated men, we mean, primarily, those
who can do everything that others do.'[9]

[2]

Marx makes small reference to the state in his theory of history.
As indicated earlier, he sees the governmental machine as one
of the countless expressions of the division of labour, its officials
being subjugated to the specialized activity of governing. Moreover, he considers that the state *qua* state is authoritarian in
nature whatever the formal facade of democracy, and therefore
questions the very idea of a 'free state'.[10] But the authoritarianism
of the state is not what preoccupies him in his doctrine of history
as the evolution of human bondage.

He is concerned with servitude under the division of labour
generally, and sees the realm of production as its primary sphere.
Marx, in fact, tends to take the term 'political economy' quite
literally, and to incorporate his political theory within his
economic theory. The social relations of production are themselves the principal power relations. Not only is the ruling class
a ruling class by virtue of being a possessing and exploiting class;
its exercise of power is manifested primarily in the activity of
exploiting. Otherwise expressing it, the prime object of rule is
labour itself, and the prime locus of domination and servitude is
the social division of labour. From Marx's point of view, the state
is essentially a defence mechanism by which the beneficiaries of
this division strive to perpetuate it. It is a glorified police force

standing guard over the real imprisonment of man within the division of labour in production.

All this particularly applies to Marx's picture of modern bourgeois society. He argues that the capitalist *qua* capitalist is the despotic ruling authority here: 'The power that used to be concentrated in the hands of Asiatic and Egyptian kings or of Etruscan theocrats and the like, has in modern society been transferred to the capitalists—it may be to individual capitalists; or it may be to collective capitalists, as in joint-stock companies.'[11] Thus, relations of domination and servitude that in past ages were more narrowly political in mode of expression have now been incorporated directly into the productive process, which represents a completely *politicalized economy*. Marx speaks, for example, of 'the capitalist form of production and the *politico-economical conditions* appropriate to that form of production', adding that the latter are 'diametrically opposed to all . . . revolutionary ferments, and to their aim—the abolition of the old division of labour'.[12]*

The politicalized economy is pictured as totally authoritarian. It is variously described in *Capital* as the 'despotism of capital', 'autocracy of capital' and 'dictatorship of capital'. Its 'politico-economical conditions' are likened repeatedly to those of a military dictatorship, with a capitalist generalissimo ruling from a distance via officer-managers and sergeant-foremen. We read in the *Communist Manifesto*, for example, that 'Masses of labourers, crowded into the factory, are organized like soldiers. As privates of the industrial army they are placed under the command of a perfect hierarchy of officers and sergeants. Not only are they slaves of the bourgeois class, and of the bourgeois state; they are daily and hourly enslaved by the machine, by the over-looker, and, above all, by the individual bourgeois manu-facturer himself. The more openly this despotism proclaims gain to be its end and aim, the more hateful and the more embittering it is.'[13] As for the factory code, this is simply the document 'in which capital formulates its autocracy over its workers—in a private legislative system, and without the partition of authority and the representative methods so much loved by the bour-geoisie . . .'.[14]

Thus, the regime under which the mass of men spend their waking hours is the despotic regime of the factory, outside which

* Italics added.

something approaching anarchy prevails. What renders the
dictatorial methods necessary, according to Marx, is not the
nature of the 'associated labour process' in modern industry. It
is rather the antagonism inherent in the social division of labour
between capitalist and worker, and the latter's resentment of his
increasing torment under bondage to a minute specialized
operation. The proletarian subjects of the autocracy of capital
become more and more rebellious against their 'politico-
economical conditions' as these become more and more intolerable. In all this the state remains in the background, its
function being to suppress revolts against the economic autocracy. Consequently, Marx imagines that the state will become
the immediate object of attack at the final point of world-
revolutionary crisis when the subjects rise up. They must over-
power the guard force in order to free their creative powers
from the existing despotic regime of production: 'In order,
therefore, to assert themselves as individuals, they must overthrow the state.'[15]

Marx believes that the state will live a short post-revolutionary
after-life as a dictatorship of the proletariat, and will then pass
out of existence along with the despotism of capital and all
associated manifestations of the division of labour in society. He
only mentions the proletarian dictatorship two or three times in
the later writings, and generally has little to say about the
transitional period beyond emphasizing that it witnesses the
Aufhebung of private property. As suggested earlier, this is
possibly to be explained by his reluctance to repeat in public
what he had written privately in 1844 on 'raw communism' as a
state of infinite human degradation. He prefers to speak about
that which, in his view, lies beyond it: 'When, in the course of
development, class distinctions have disappeared, and all production has been concentrated in the hands of a vast association
of the whole nation, the public power will lose its political
character. . . . In place of the old bourgeois society, with its
classes and class antagonism, we shall have an association in
which the free development of each is the precondition for the
free development of all.'[16]

[3]

The discussion of communism in *The German Ideology* is briefer
than that in the manuscripts of 1844, but fuller than anything

to be found in the later writings. As in the earlier longer discussion, Marx here visualizes the communist revolution itself as a world-wide act of seizure and socialization of the productive powers materialized in industry. Moreover, he continues to conceive of this event as the great divide between history as the becoming of the species and post-history as its mature being. The difference, again, is a difference in the formula employed to express the idea. Instead of saying as before that the communist revolution means the transcendence of self-alienation, he says that it means the transcendence of the division of labour.

The theory of history now makes reference to a number of past revolutionary appropriations at points of transition from epoch to epoch, e.g. from feudalism to capitalism. Marx contrasts the future communist revolution with them on the ground that they brought only changes in the *form* of the division of labour, whereas it will abolish the phenomenon. He says that all earlier revolutionary appropriations were restricted in that 'individuals whose self-activity was restricted by a crude instrument of production and a limited intercourse appropriated this crude instrument of production, and hence merely achieved a new state of limitation. Their instrument of production became their property, but they themselves remained determined by the division of labour and their own instrument of production'. The communist revolution, on the other hand, abolishes the divided mode of productive activity: 'In all revolutions up till now the mode of activity always remained unscathed, and it was only a question of a different distribution of this activity, a new distribution of labour to other persons, whilst the communist revolution is directed against the preceding *mode* of activity, does away with *labour*, and abolishes the rule of all classes with the classes themselves. . . .'[17]

In original Marxism, Marx had argued, in opposition to Hegel, that man cannot get over his alienation by a cognitive act of appropriation but must practically appropriate the alienated world of productive powers. He now repeats the argument, substituting division of labour for alienation and not making explicit reference to Hegel: 'The transformation, through the division of labour, of personal powers (relationships) into material powers, cannot be dispelled by dismissing the general idea of it from one's mind, but only by the action of individuals in again subjecting these material powers to them-

selves and abolishing the division of labour.'[18] The terminology
has changed but the idea has not. The recovery of the alienated
world of 'material powers' still means to Marx the ending of
object-bondage and the repossession by working man of his lost
faculties of productive self-expression in industry: 'The appropriation of these powers is nothing more than the development
of the individual capacities (*Fähigkeiten*) corresponding to the
material instruments of production. The appropriation of a
totality of instruments of production is, for this very reason, the
development of a totality of capacities in the individuals themselves.'[19]

The communist revolution thus remains a revolution of self-
change in its essential meaning to Marx, and he says so in the
third thesis on Feuerbach and the formula of *The German
Ideology* cited earlier: 'In revolutionary activity, change of self
coincides with change of circumstances.' This cryptic sentence
presupposes the entire Marxian *Weltanschauung* as originally
expressed in the manuscripts of 1844. The 'change of circumstances' is the change in the relation of working man to the
world of externalized productive powers, which had been lost
to him through alienation (division of labour) but are now
restored to him by the revolutionary act of counter-appropria-
tion. Since the powers of production materialized in industry are
his powers, i.e. his own faculties for creative expression of himself,
the recovery of them is his 'regaining of self'. He is now the
master rather than the servant of his own externalized nature—
his anthropological nature.

This is the concealed background of a famous later statement
by Engels about communism: 'The whole sphere of the conditions of life which environ man, and which have hitherto ruled
man, now comes under the dominion and control of man, who
for the first time becomes the real, conscious Lord of Nature. . . .
The extraneous objective forces that have hitherto governed
history pass under the control of man himself. . . . It is the
ascent of man from the kingdom of necessity to the kingdom of
freedom.'[20] To the reader unfamiliar with the entire background of Marx's thought, it may seem that this refers to the
mastery of nature by means of technology. In actuality, it refers
to the mastery of technology as man's own nature outside himself. The kingdom of necessity is the alienated world of history,
the realm of object-bondage. The 'extraneous objective forces'

over which man is to become lord in the kingdom of freedom are understood as the externalized forces of the species-self. The nature to which man will no longer be subservient is his own nature.

Returning to the discussion in *The German Ideology*, Marx continues to suppose that the external change of self will bring internal change of self as well. The repossession of the productive powers materialized in industry will liberate those that lie within man, and labour as hitherto known will give way to free, spontaneous creativity along all possible lines. Thus, communism means 'the transformation of labour into self-activity', and 'Only at this stage does self-activity coincide with material life, which corresponds to the development of individuals into complete individuals and the casting off of all natural limitations.'[21] Marx illustrates the casting off of limitations by saying that 'in communist society, where nobody has one exclusive sphere of activity but each can become accomplished in any branch he wishes, society regulates the general production and thus makes it possible for me to do one thing today and another tomorrow, to hunt in the morning, fish in the afternoon, rear cattle in the evening, criticize after dinner, just as I have a mind, without ever becoming hunter, fisherman, shepherd or critic'.[22]* Man will cease to be divided against himself in slavery to some one specialized mode of activity.

Having translated 'alienation' as 'division of labour', Marx could no longer discuss the revolution of self-change under the heading of 'positive transcendence of human self-alienation'. That is why we find no treatment of communism in the later writings comparable in length to the manuscript of 1844 on communism. After *The German Ideology*, Marx confines himself to occasional brief allusions to the ultimate stage in which man is to be reintegrated with his human nature externally and internally. It is notable, however, that self-realization in free-

---

* It may be noted that Soviet official Marxism does not find this fundamental idea of Marx's acceptable. Thus the Party's theoretical journal *Kommunist* (no. 12, August, 1960, p. 117) cites with approval the following passage from the unpublished work of a Soviet economist, V. M. Kriukov: 'An unintelligent person and philistine might form his own picture of communism approximately as follows: you rise in the morning and ask yourself, where shall I go to work to-day—shall I be chief engineer at the factory or go and head the fishing brigade? Or shall I run down to Moscow and hold an urgent meeting of the presidium of the Academy of Science?' *Kommunist* comments: 'It will not be so.' But the view of the 'unintelligent person and philistine' is not so far from Marx's as stated in *The German Ideology* and other writings.

dom, i.e. the transcendence of self-alienation, is the invariable theme of these laconic utterances. Instead of living labour being as before a means to increase accumulated labour, he writes in the *Manifesto,* accumulated labour will become 'but a means to widen, to enrich, to promote the existence of the labourer'. [23] Observing in *Capital* that the material life-process of society will become 'a process carried on by a free association of producers, under their conscious and purposive control', he describes this process as one 'wherein material wealth exists to promote the developmental needs of the worker', and says further that 'the detail worker, who has nothing more to perform than a partial social function, shall be superseded by an individual with an all-round development, one for whom various social functions are alternative modes of activity'. [24]

Thus, the communist idea remains fundamentally psychological in content for the mature Marx. Instead of man being subordinate to the process of production, the process of production becomes subordinate to man and turns into pleasureable self-activity. Liberated from the drive for accumulation, man produces in order to realize his nature as a being with manifold creative capacities requiring free outlet in a 'totality of human life-activities'. Engels echoes the theme in *Anti-Dühring,* saying that 'the former division of labour must disappear' and that, as a result, 'productive labour, instead of being a means to the subjection of men, will become a means to their emancipation, by giving each individual the opportunity to develop and exercise all his faculties, physical and mental, in all directions'. Moreover, 'in time to come there will no longer be any professional porters or architects, and . . . the man who for half an hour gives instructions as an architect will also push a barrow for a period, until his activity as an architect is once again required. It is a fine sort of socialism that perpetuates the professional porter!' [25]

The future free creative life within the walls of the factory presented a difficult problem in this connection. As already indicated, Marx believed that the fall of the despotism of capital would release the detail worker to become an individual with an all-round development. The despotic regime of the factory would vanish with the underlying antagonism between capitalist and worker, and the old division of labour would vanish with it. Yet it was impossible to imagine any factory regime, no matter how freely cooperative, without specialization. The complete individuals could hardly be pictured as wandering from machine to machine or from workshop to workshop just as they had a mind, although they could be seen as rotating jobs.*

In the unfinished third volume of *Capital*, Marx adumbrates an interesting solution for this dilemma. The inspiration lies in original Marxism, in which the advent of communism was viewed in terms of the transformation of the alienated man of history into an aesthetic man whose world is a sphere and object of art. Marx suggests that the future social regulation of production in industry, and the exercise of authority requisite in it, will be artistic in essence. The co-operative labours in the factory 'necessarily require for the connection and unity of the process one commanding will, and this performs a function, which does not refer to fragmentary operations, but to the combined labour of the workshop, in the same way as does that of a director of an orchestra'.[26] The old authoritarianism of the factory regime, based on servitude under the division of labour, would be supplanted by a free conscious discipline such as that which prevails in a symphony orchestra. Authority would no longer be authoritarian when it had become a matter of artistic discipline on the part of workers expressing themselves in the factory as performers in an orchestra. As we saw, original Marxism had nothing to say about practical economic arrangements under communism. If mature Marxism has next to nothing to add, the main reason is that Marx continued to think of communism in terms of the transformation of economics into aesthetics.

Nor did the distribution problem figure in his thinking in any important way. His best known reference to it comes in the *Critique of the Gotha Programme*:

In a higher phase of communist society, after the enslaving subordination of the individual to the division of labour, and therewith also the antithesis between mental and physical labour, has vanished; after labour has become not only a means of life but life's prime want;

* In a short polemical article of 1872 against the anarchist current in socialism, Engels argued that an authoritarian regime in the factory is inherent in machine technology: 'The automatic machinery of a big factory is much more despotic than the small capitalists who employ workers have ever been.... Wanting to abolish authority in large-scale industry is tantamount to wanting to abolish industry itself, to destroy the power loom in order to return to the spinning wheel' ('On Authority', in *Selected Works*, vol. I, p. 637). There is clearly some inconsistency between this position and Marx's.

after the productive forces have also increased with the all-round development of the individual, and all the springs of cooperative wealth flow more abundantly—only then can the narrow horizon of bourgeois right be crossed in its entirety and society inscribe on its banners: From each according to his ability, to each according to his needs![27]

The main part of the sentence seems at first glance to be the old French socialist slogan with which it closes, and the reader may naturally infer that distribution according to need is the essence of the communist idea according to Marx. As mentioned earlier, however, this whole passage appears in the midst of a passionate tirade against 'vulgar socialism' and its 'presentation of socialism as turning principally on distribution'. For Marx socialism or communism does not turn principally on distribution. It turns on deliverance from the 'enslaving subordination of the individual to the division of labour', and the resulting 'all-round development of the individual'. What may seem two casually inserted subordinate clauses to the reader form the heart of the sentence for the author.

[4]

When Marx in 1844 posited the alienated self-relation as an alienated social relation of production, the division of alienated man against himself became, as we have seen, the social division of labour. The image of species-man in conflict with himself turned into Marx's later image of society engulfed in class war. Accordingly, the abolition of the social division of labour means to him the elimination of all the antagonisms that have always pervaded every pore of society. It signifies the advent of harmony and unison within humanity at large, the emergence of a unified society consisting of a vast association of 'complete individuals'. In place of the conflict-free generic man of the manuscripts of 1844, we have the classless society of the later Marxist writings.

Man returned to himself out of alienation has become society returned to itself out of the division of labour, and this is Marx's definition of 'communist society'. The content of the idea remains, however, the same as before. The undivided society is the no longer divided species-self or 'social man' of the manuscripts of 1844, as Marx cryptically indicates in the tenth thesis on Feuerbach: 'The standpoint of the old materialism is *civil* society; the standpoint of the new materialism is *human society* or socialized humanity' (*vergesellschaftete Menschheit*).[28] Socialized humanity is humanity brought back into total harmony with itself by the abolition of the antagonism inherent in the social division of labour. All subordinate expressions of the division of labour, and the antagonism inherent in it, vanish along with the basic one. Socialized humanity is not only a classless but also a stateless, law-less, family-less, religion-less and generally structure-less collectivity of complete individuals who live in harmony with themselves, with each other, and with the anthropological nature outside them. It hardly needs pointing out that this society without social structure is not a social order in any very meaningful sense of that term.

The community with which Marx was chiefly concerned, in the final analysis, was the community of man with his internal and external human nature. As he himself said in 1844, 'Human nature is the true community of man.' His doctrine does not construe socialism as a quest for community-forms in the field of society. It is understandable, therefore, that he never ceased to scorn the 'utopian socialism' that concerned itself with the devising of changes in the structure of society. In the end, he found himself at odds with some of his own followers in the Social Democratic Party of Germany on this issue. Utopian socialism was raging in the party, he complained in a letter of 1877. Numerous members of it were 'playing with fancy pictures of the future structure of society'.[29]

On very few occasions did he himself attempt to say something concrete about the future order. One was in *The Civil War in France*, written in 1871 on the occasion of the suppression of the Paris Commune. This tract was provoked from Marx under pressure of a particular unanticipated political event. In one passage he allowed that communism would be a system under which 'united cooperative societies are to regulate the national production under a common plan'. In the very next breath, however, he lapsed back into his usual antipathy toward any discussion of communism as a social system. Speaking of the working class, he said: 'They have no ideals to realize, but to set free the elements of the new society with which old collapsing bourgeois society is pregnant.'[30] By the 'elements of the new society' he meant the creative powers of man, now shackled, as he saw it, to the lust for money. The elements of the new society were elements of human nature.

The difference between Marx and those among his followers whom he berated for playing with fancy pictures of the future structure of society is not that they were utopians and he was not. The difference is that their utopias were envisagements of the good society in terms of concrete socio-economic arrangements, whereas his was an envisagement of an entire 'new state of the world' (as he had once called it), characterized essentially by self-change on the scale of all humanity. His utopia was the world of human self-realization in freedom which would result, as he saw it, from the communist revolution's abolition of the division of labour in all its manifold enslaving forms.

XIV

THE WORLD AS LABOUR AND CAPITAL

Accumulate! Accumulate! That is Moses and all the prophets!
MARX (1867)

'When it becomes possible to hold fast to a commodity as exchange-value, or to exchange-value as a commodity, the greed for money awakens. . . . Modern society which, when still in its infancy, pulled Pluto by the hair of his head out of the bowels of the earth, acclaims gold, its Holy Grail, as the glittering incarnation of its inmost vital principle.'[1] So writes Marx in *Capital*, and we immediately recognize the master-theme of original Marxism. Here again we read that money is the universal power that not even the most sacrosanct things can withstand, and the radical leveller that effaces all distinctions. Marx even supports his point in the manner of 1844 by a quotation of the same lines from *Timon of Athens:* 'Thus much of this will make black, white; foul, fair; wrong, right; base, noble; old, young; coward, valiant.'[2]

The book is about economics—but what is economics? To Marx it is that which he has always considered it to be: the theology of the worldly god.* *Capital* treats of capitalism as a quasi-religious phenomenon. It tells a story of working man divided against another man who is dominated by a maniacal money-worship. Their struggle—the warfare of labour and capital—mounts in intensity to a final wild crescendo of violence, and Volume One—the only part of *Capital* that Marx completed and published—closes with the revolutionary *dénouement*: 'The knell of capitalist property sounds. The expropriators are expropriated. . . . It is a negation of a negation.'[3] 'Negation of a negation' was from the start, as we have seen, Marx's dialectical formula for the communist revolution of self-change.

---

* The theological essence of political economy is a recurrent theme in Marx's later writings as well as the earlier ones. In a footnote in *Capital* (p. 56), for example, he quotes his own earlier statement that the political economists, who treat capitalist institutions as the only natural ones, 'resemble the theologians, who also establish two kinds of religion. Every religion but their own is an invention of men, while their own religion is an emanation from God' (*The Poverty of Philosophy*, p. 131).

The book can also, it is necessary to add, be read as a straight
treatise of economics, and many have done so. It then appears
as an infinitely tortuous, unsuccessful endeavour to demonstrate
the *a priori* inevitability of a falling rate of profit and various
consequences in the way of intensified exploitation of the labour
force. But unless we grasp it as drama, and in fact as one of the
most dramatic books of modern times, we shall comprehend
neither the powerful influence that it has exerted upon history
nor its basic underlying significance. It is, moreover, drama in
the tragic mood, and it may be pertinent to add that its author
was all his life a lover of Aeschylean and Shakespearean tragedy.

It may be said without much exaggeration that Marx was one
of those thinkers who spend their lives writing a single important
book under a number of different titles. In this instance, even
the titles show a certain continuity. He started out in the summer
of 1844 to write a systematic *Kritik* of political economy.
Resuming the work in the later 1840's, he wrote up the results
in 1857-8 in a huge new set of manuscripts on the *Kritik* of
political economy.* In the following year he published in book
form an elongated preface to the theory under the title of
'contribution' to the *Kritik* of political economy. And when the
book was finally finished in 1867 and published under the title
of *Capital*, it was sub-titled *Kritik* of political economy. This
major work of Marx's is simply the form in which he completed
the book he started to write in the manuscripts of 1844.

The continuity of titles reflects an underlying continuity of
idea and intent. Having had only the sketchiest preliminary
acquaintance with political economy when he first created
Marxism, Marx went on in the later years to digest mountains of
economic literature—the 'economic filth' as he often called it in
letters to Engels. And he enlarged the literature of economics
with much material of his own that has been of interest to
economists in one way or another and has influenced subsequent
thinking about the economic aspects of society and history. Yet
he never became a political economist as such; he always
remained a *critic* of political economy. Thus, his design in *Capital*
was not to show how capitalism works but how forces immanent
in it work its destruction inevitably.

From this point of view *Capital* is the attempted proof of a

---

* These have been published recently under the title of *Grundrisse der Kritik der
Politischen Ökonomie* (Dietz Verlag, Berlin, 1953). The materials cover 1100 pages.

preconception. Marx had postulated in the manuscripts of 1844 that the communist revolution grasped 'in thoughts' must necessarily work itself out also 'in reality'. His understanding of this necessity was explained in various writings of the middle 1840's. In *The Holy Family*, for example, he said that it was not a question of what this or that proletarian or the proletariat as a whole conceives as a goal, but of what the proletariat would be driven involuntarily to do by virtue of its life-situation in society. *The German Ideology* was more specific, envisaging the future situation as follows: 'Thus things have now come to such a pass that the individuals must appropriate the existing totality of productive forces, not only to achieve self-activity but also merely to safeguard their very existence.'[4] The first purpose of *Capital* was to demonstrate how and why things must inevitably come to 'such a pass'. That is why Marx addressed himself in it not to history as a whole but specifically to the modern capitalist period.

The object was to write the obituary of capitalism in advance of its decease. But this is not the only sense in which *Capital* is a book of criticism of political economy rather than of political economy as such. From the start Marx conceived the idea of a *Kritik* of political economy on the analogy of Feuerbach's *Kritik* of theology and religion via Hegelianism. Political economy was presumed to be a science of the earthly accumulation of capital corresponding to the accumulation of spiritual capital in heaven, i.e. to man's externalization of himself in the image of God and his resulting self-estrangement. The criticism of it would consist in showing, in terms of the political economist's own conceptual categories such as labour and capital, that man is similarly alienated from himself when, under the domination of egoistic need, he externalizes his productive power in the form of money. This is the standpoint from which Marx proceeded in the creation of original Marxism. And this, *mutatis mutandis,* is the standpoint from which he wrote *Capital*.

It is not, therefore, surprising that before we come to the end of the introductory part. 'Commodities and Money', we find him returning to his starting point: the analogy between economics and religion. This is preceded by an analysis of the nature of the commodity, of which Marx says that, though it seems at first a simple humdrum thing, it really is full of metaphysical subtleties and theological whimsies. As a useful object or use-value, a commodity is the embodiment of a certain quantity of concrete human labour in a material substratum supplied by nature. As an exchange-value or 'phenomenal' value-form, on the other hand, it is an objectification of 'abstract labour' or a 'mere jelly of undifferentiated human labour', this being defined as so much expenditure of 'social average labour power'. Commodities *qua* commodities are 'crystals of this social substance'.[5]

As such, Marx says, they are 'social hieroglyphs' that mirror the character of the labour itself as an attribute of its reifications. The mystery of the commodity-form is that 'the social relation of the producers to the sum total of their own labour presents itself to them as a social relation, not between themselves, but between the products of their labour'. Marx goes on: 'To find an analogy we must enter the nebulous world of religion. In that world, the products of the human mind become independent shapes, endowed with lives of their own, and able to enter into relations with men and women. The products of the human hand do the same thing in the world of commodities (*Warenwelt*). I speak of this as the *fetishistic character* which attaches to the products of labour, so soon as they are produced in the form of commodities.' A little further on, he explains that the fetishistic character of commodities is manifest in the fetishistic character of money, which is 'the direct incarnation of all human labour'.[6]

Marx's use of the term 'fetishism' (*Fetischismus*) dates all the way back to the manuscripts of 1844, where he wrote: 'The nations which are still dazzled by the sensuous splendour of precious metals, and are therefore still fetish-worshippers of metal money, are not yet fully developed money-nations.— Contrast of France and England. The extent to which the solution of theoretical riddles is the task of praxis and effected through praxis . . . is shown, for example, in *fetishism*. The sensuous consciousness of the fetish-worshipper is different from that of the Greek, because his sensuous existence is still different.'[7] Without abandoning this premise that theoretical riddles have their solution in praxis (which changes the form of consciousness by changing the underlying life-conditions), Marx has extended the notion of fetishism to the 'fully developed money-nations' and made modern capitalist man the supreme example of the fetish-worshipper. But the basic idea behind the doctrine of the fetishistic character of commodities was formulated already in

1843 in the essay 'On the Jewish Question', where Marx wrote: 'Money is the alienated essence of man's work and his being. This alien being rules over him and he worships it.'

Like the alienated man of the manuscripts of 1844, the fetish-worshipper of *Capital* lives in a world of the creations of his own hand. Marx does not question, any more than he had done previously, the antecedent existence of a non-human nature. But this he sees as merely the material presupposition of the human history of production. Thus, the earth itself is defined as the most general instrument of production 'since it provides the worker with the platform for all his operations, and supplies a field for the employment of his activity'.[8] The non-human nature is the platform for the labour process in history, and the receptacle of raw materials that are worked up into use-values and then enter into exchange as commodities. These material wrappings of this or that amount of abstract human labour, as Marx describes them, form in their cumulative entirety a nature produced by history, a world of commodity-fetishes that lord it over their bemused creators. He calls it a world of alien wealth. Like the *Sachenwelt* of original Marxism, this *Warenwelt* is the producers' alienated being and governs them instead of being governed by them. The terminology has changed somewhat, but the *Weltanschauung* has not.

[2]

Capital is concerned not with the labour process as such but with the capitalist labour process, which Marx describes as 'a unity of the labour process and the process of creating surplus value' (*Verwertungsprozess*).[9] The labour process itself is simply purposive activity carried on for the production of use-values, and is the perennial condition imposed by nature on human life. The capitalist labour process, on the other hand, has as its aim neither the production of use-values nor the profit to be made on any given transaction, but the 'expansion of value' (*Verwertung des Werts**) or 'never ending process of profit-making itself'. Marx illustrates this fundamental distinction by reference to Aristotle's contrast of 'economics', or the art of producing useful

---

* The important term *Verwertung* appeared already in the manuscript on 'Alienated Labour', where Marx wrote that the (inner) world of man is devalued in proportion as the world of things expands in value—*Mit der Verwertung der Sachenwelt nimmt die Entwertung der Menschenwelt in direktem Verhältnis zu* (*MEGA*, III, p. 82). *Capital* represents a vast amplification of this proposition.

things, and 'chrematistics' or money-making. 'And chrematistics appear to turn upon money', Aristotle had written in *De republica*, 'for money is the beginning and end of this kind of exchange. Therefore wealth, as chrematistics strive to attain it, is unlimited.' Just so, says Marx, the aggrandizement of value as capital is an end in itself and 'has no limits'. The motive force of capitalist production is a 'passionate hunt for value' or 'urge towards absolute enrichment' (*absolute Bereicherungstrieb*).[10] The labour process in the capitalist form is productive activity performed as wage labour in the service of a drive to infinite accumulation of capital.

Given Marx's assumptions, the accumulation of capital must be a process of creation of surplus value. He has assumed, first of all, that labour power, defined as the 'life energies' or aggregate of bodily and mental capacities exercised by a human being in the production of use-values, is the sole 'value-creating substance'. A measure of 'dead labour', or the value already stored up in the materials and implements consumed in the labour process, is transferred to the emergent new products. But it is only the addition of 'living labour' to the dead that creates new value. In Marx's vivid phrase, 'By transforming money into commodities which form the material elements of a new product or serve as factors in the labour process, and by incorporating living labour power with their dead substance, the capitalist transforms value (past labour, objectified labour, dead labour) into capital, into self-expanding value, into a monster quick with life, which begins to "work" as if love were breeding in its body.'[11]

This is the value-creating process, whose prolongation beyond a certain point makes it a process of creating surplus value (*Mehrwert*). Here again the reasoning turns wholly on the initial assumptions, from which it follows that the accumulation of capital results from a greater or lesser discrepancy between the value of the living labour power expended in the capitalist labour process and the value that the labour power creates in this process. The labour power is the proletarian wage worker's sole commodity, and its value as such has to be determined in the same manner as that of any other commodity, i.e. by the amount of abstract labour stored up in it. This means in practice the quantity of means of subsistence requisite to keep the worker alive and working and to enable him to reproduce his kind. But the use of this commodity for a day by the capitalist purchaser of it yields a greater quantity of new value than the subsistence wage that this commodity is worth. The excess of the former over the latter is surplus value, which belongs to the purchaser of the labour power. It is a function of the surplus labour time, meaning that elastic part of the working day during which the worker goes on producing after he has produced the equivalent of the value of his labour power for a whole day.

Marx treats capitalist production as a process of self-aggrandizement of capital via the extraction of the maximum possible surplus value from the living labour power consumed in the process.* He says that 'the end and aim, the driving force, of capitalist production is an endeavour to promote to the uttermost the self-expansion of capital, this meaning the production of the largest possible amount of surplus value, and therefore the maximum possible exploitation of labour power by the capitalist'.[12] Marx distinguishes two ways of maximizing surplus value: increasing 'absolute surplus value' by further prolongation of the working day, and increasing 'relative surplus value' by reduction of the labour time requisite for reproducing the value of the labour power itself. The reduction of necessary labour time is achieved by raising labour productivity through the introduction of more and more machinery, and therewith more and more minute division of labour, into the labour process. It is the development along this latter line that explains for Marx the necessity of a falling rate of profit. *Capital* is largely taken up with an extended exposition of the two methods of maximizing surplus value. Both result in the more and more intensified exploitation of living labour, more and more suffering, labour torment and enslavement.

In considering the former of the two, Marx ascribes to 'capital' an inherent tendency to appropriate the whole twenty-four hours of theoretically possible labour time minus the miserable modicum absolutely required to keep the 'embodiment of

---

* M. M. Bober suggests that wage labour is the distinguishing mark of capitalism according to Marx (*Karl Marx's Interpretation of History*, p. 177). This is true, but wage labour in turn is defined by Marx as labour expended in the capitalist quest for surplus value. His conception of capitalism is, therefore, inseparable from his notion of the peculiar motivating force of the process. It might be added that Chapters IX, X, and XI of Bober's book contain an admirably clear exposition of the purely economic aspect of Marx's theory of capitalism. Any reader unfamiliar with the argument of *Capital* from that point of view may profitably consult them.

labour power' alive. Capital, 'in its unbridled passion for self-expansion', develops a 'greed for surplus labour', an 'impulse to suck labour dry', or a 'vampire thirst for the living blood of labour'.[13] Feeding on living labour like a vampire-bat, this blind, ruthless, insatiable and diabolically sadistic force of greed confiscates 'every atom of freedom' both in bodily and intellectual activity:

> Obviously, therefore, throughout his working life, the worker is to be nothing but labour power; all his available time is, by nature and by law, to be labour time, is to be devoted to promoting the self-expansion of capital. . . . In its blind, unbridled passion, its were-wolf hunger for surplus labour, capital is not content to overstep the moral restrictions upon the length of the working day. It oversteps the purely physical limitations as well. It usurps the time needed for the growth, the development, and the healthy maintenance of the body. . . . Capital does not enquire how long the embodiment of labour power is likely to live. Its only interest is in ensuring that a maximum amount of labour power shall be expended in one working day.[14]

Marx accompanies this characterization of capital with long quotations from British factory inspectors' reports on horrible cases of exploitation of child labour and women's labour in the early and middle nineteenth century.

The other path by which capital proceeds in the 'unbridled passion' for surplus value is that of increasing mechanization of the labour process, which means to Marx, as we have seen, increasing dehumanization of the worker. The devices for raising labour productivity by introducing a more and more minute division of labour are so many torture devices that 'mutilate the worker into a fragment of a human being, degrade him to become a mere appurtenance of the machine, make his work such a torment that its essential meaning is destroyed; estrange him from the intellectual potentialities of the labour process in very proportion to the extent to which science is incorporated into it as an independent power'. They 'distort the conditions under which he works, subjecting him, during the labour process, to a despotism which is all the more hateful because of its pettiness'.[15]

Increasingly, then, the workers became 'living appendages' of a lifeless mechanism—the factory. Labour at the machine prohibits free bodily and mental activity, says Marx over and over, and even the lightening of it 'becomes a means of torture, for the machine does not free the worker from his work, but merely deprives his work of interest'. He goes on: 'All kinds of capitalist production, in so far as they are not merely labour processes, but also processes for promoting the self-expansion of capital, have this in common, that in them the worker does not use the instruments of labour, but the instruments of labour use the worker. . . . Through its conversion into an automaton, the instrument of labour comes to confront the worker during the labour process as capital, as dead labour, which controls the living labour power and sucks it dry. The divorce of the intellectual powers of the process of production from the manual labour, and the transformation of these powers into powers of capital over labour, are completed . . . in large-scale industry based upon machine production.'[16]

Here is Marx's description of the 'despotism of capital' or 'autocracy of capital'. The scene is the factory—a place of detention ruled by a dictatorial *Nicht-Arbeiter* through his militarized minions. Massed inside are a great number of machines, each one feeding upon and slowly destroying its living appendages, who exist only to promote the self-expansion of capital and only so long as they continue to promote it. The instruments of labour that they themselves have created are instruments of torture and tyranny turned against them. Each worker is enslaved to a minute, mindless operation that he is forced to repeat endlessly. His every movement is performed at the coercive behest of an 'alien will'. And the unseen dictatorial power, whose will this is, continually contrives to prolong the torture by a few more minutes beyond the monstrous portion of the twenty-four hours already given over to it. Clearly, the 'despotism of capital' is Marx's portrait of hell.

If we enlarge the portrait to universal proportions, we have his image of the world as a whole. *Capital* would have been more accurately entitled *The World as Labour and Capital*. What it essentially depicts is a universal labour process performed under a universal despotism of capital. For Marx the whole earth is the scene of a process of production motivated by capital's 'boundless drive for self-expansion' (*massloser Trieb nach Selbstverwertung*). It is continually spurred on and accelerated by a werewolf hunger for surplus value. And the vast world of materialized labour that emanates from this process confronts the exploited and enslaved producers as a world of capital—a werewolf-world. Not only does their labour power itself belong to its purchaser—capital. The great bulk of all that it produces is turned into dead capital, which weighs down upon its creators 'like an incubus'. The continually expanding mass of dead capital in the form of machines dominates and oppresses the living embodiments of labour power, and the more they produce under the despotism of capital the more it expands and crushes them. They are thus driven deeper and deeper into an abyss of servitude, degradation and misery from which there is no escape but world-wide rebellion against capital, the overthrow of the despotism, and the seizure of the materialized productive powers. To epitomize the whole idea, Marx reverts once again in the latter part of the book to the Feuerbachian analogy: 'Just as, in the sphere of religion, man is dominated by the creature of his own brain; so, in the sphere of capitalist production, he is dominated by the creature of his own hand.'[17] And again at the close of the unfinished manuscript of the third volume of *Capital*, he defines capitalism as follows: 'This is a special form of the development of the productive powers of labour, in such a way that these powers appear as self-dependent powers of capital lording it over labour and standing in direct opposition to the labourer's own development.'[18]

[3]

Marx was a man of one fundamental fixed idea, and what has been summarized in the preceding section is simply the final expression of it. His *Kritik* of political economy first took shape in 1844 as a philosophical conception according to which man loses himself in the historical act of producing a world in alienated labour, meaning productive activity performed under the compulsion of greed. As we see, it remained this in essence when Marx brought forth the completed version in *Capital* twenty-three years after. Superficially, it appears a different system, for Marx no longer uses 'self-alienation' as his key term. But this is a change in manifest content; it does not affect the underlying substance and inspiration of his thought. What was manifest in the original system remains latent in the mature one, and in various ways just pointed out it even appears on the surface. In sum, having postulated in the manuscripts of 1844 that man's self-alienation in productive activity is a 'fact of political economy', Marx proceeded to elaborate his economics as economics of self-alienation.

The basic underlying continuity is visible, on the one hand, in his concept of capital, which is simply the name now given to what he had called in the manuscripts a passion of greed. The infinite *Habsucht* of which he had spoken in 1844 becomes the boundless drive for self-expansion in value. Capital in the physical sense of means of production is seen as the material expression of a dynamic force or life-urge towards self-aggrandizement in terms of wealth. Starting as before with Adam Smith's notion of capital as command over labour, which he now alters to read command over *unpaid* labour, Marx posits a 'passionate hunt for value' or 'urge towards absolute enrichment' as the force behind it. The command over unpaid labour becomes for him the means of extracting unlimited surplus value to gratify this urge.

Marx still sees in money the power over all things, and in the acquisitive mania a will-to-power in pecuniary guise.* The self-expansion of capital is a movement of world conquest: 'Accumulation is a conquest of the world of social wealth. It increases the mass of human material exploited by the capitalist, and thus amplifies his direct and indirect *dominion (Herrschaft)*.' At this point Marx inserts a lengthy footnote on Luther's study of the usurer, which 'shows forcibly that the love of power is an element in the impulse to acquire wealth'. And he proceeds to quote Luther as saying that the usurer 'wants to be God over all men'.[19] The same applies to Marx's capitalist. His life-urge to absolute enrichment is an urge to become the Absolute in terms of the power that wealth commands.

This is an economic concept in name only. The word comes from Adam Smith and the political economists; the idea, from Hegel and the world of German philosophy. Marx's *Kapital* is just as much a citizen of this world as, for example, Schopenhauer's *Wille* or Nietzsche's *Wille zur Macht*, with which it has obvious affinities. But the immediate affiliation of the idea is Hegelian. The *absolute Bereicherungstrieb* is a translation in economic terms of the drive to infinite self-enrichment that Hegel ascribes to spirit, which is insatiably greedy to appro-

* See above, pp. 138-9.

priate all things cognitively as 'property of the ego' and thus to assert its power over them. The Hegelian dialectic of aggrandizement, whereby spirit is driven to infinitize itself in terms of knowledge, reappears in Marx's mature thought as a dialectic of the self-expansion of capital—a movement of self-infinitizing in terms of money. Hegel's *Logic*, which he reread while working on *Capital*, remained for him always the 'money of the spirit'. He saw in Hegel's 'epistemological totalitarianism' (as it has been called here) a mystified expression of a monetary totalitarianism in capitalist production. That is why Marx, unlike most others of his erstwhile Young Hegelian circle, never ceased to be a fascinated devotée of Hegelian dialectics, and an irascible opponent of all those who in the later years tended to dismiss the dialectical idea as a 'dead horse'. On the other hand, it may also cast light on his inability to write the short treatise showing 'what is rational' in the dialectic, but 'enveloped in mysticism'. For the dialectic remained so enveloped in Marx's mind.

The passion of greed was described in the manuscripts of 1844 as an inhuman force that holds sway over everything. In *Capital* this proposition is reiterated in conjunction with a great mass of factual data from the history of capitalism during the Industrial Revolution. At the same time, the inhumanity of the inhuman force is drawn with a descriptive power far surpassing that shown in the original sketch. There Marx was content simply to identify the force as something utterly alien that renders all productive activity *'nicht freiwillig'*, causes the producer to mortify his body and ruin his spirit, and reduces him to the depths of self-alienation. Now he gives us a graphic portrait of it. The force takes shape in the pages of *Capital* as an absolutely vicious monster that literally swallows up its victims, devouring the living blood of labour and growing more and more thirsty for this sustenance the more it drinks of it. Like Hegel's cunning deity, which actualizes itself by the destructive using up of mankind, the monster does no work but only subsists and grows bloated on the labour power of the masses, who grow progressively more dehumanized in the process. The victim, having 'sold' his productive powers to the inhuman force, is reduced to 'living raw material' or 'personified labour time'.[20] He is slowly and agonizingly destroyed in the monster's deadly embrace, becoming a mere machine broken in body and brutalized in mind. At the end, however, he rebels.

This drama at the heart of *Capital* is, in its latent content, a drama of the inner life of man, of the self in conflict with itself. It is a representation of man being dehumanized and destroyed by a tyrannical force of acquisitiveness that has arisen and grown autonomous within him. The force controls his movements, usurps his life-energies, torments him mercilessly, drives him relentlessly to aggrandizement for the sake of aggrandizement, and ruins his life. At the same time, the dehumanized victim of the compulsive drive towards absolute enrichment is aware of his 'dehumanization' and rebels against the force responsible for reducing him to this state. No work of literature or psychiatry known to this writer has portrayed with comparable descriptive power the destructive and dehumanizing essence of the neurotic process of self-alienation. No one has shown more graphically than Marx what slavery and misery man may endure when he comes under the sway of the drive to infinite self-aggrandizement.

Marx showed at times a dim realization that he was dealing with a servitude within man and a conflict of the alienated self with itself. He said, for example, in his speech of 1856 on the anniversary of the *People's Paper:* 'At the same pace that mankind masters nature, man seems to become enslaved to other men *or to his own infamy.*'[21]* But this was, at best, a slip of the tongue. The ostensible subject of *Capital* is capitalism. The process depicted in it is not identified as the self-alienation process but as the process of capitalist production in modern society. Instead of the *Selbstentfremdungsprozess* of original Marxism, we have the *Selbstverwertungsprozess* of mature Marxism. This is shown as a social drama of enslavement of man to *another* man rather than 'to his own infamy'. The change, however, is merely a metamorphosis. It results from Marx's fateful decision in 1844 to treat self-alienation as being, for all practical purposes, a social relation of man to man.

As the reader will recall, he postulated a reality behind the alienated man's relation to himself as to 'another, hostile, powerful man, independent of him'. Thereby the alien inner man was personified in the capitalist. Self-alienation was socialized, i.e. treated as a social relation of production between worker and capitalist, and Marx started down the road to *Capital* with its projection of the neurotic process of self-alienation as the

* Italics added.

process of capitalist production. At the time, he tried to justify his procedure by laying it down as a general maxim that the relation in which a man stands to himself is first 'realized and made objective' in the relation in which he stands to another man outside him—from which it follows that self-alienation may rightly be seen as a social relation. Curiously, he repeats this maxim for no apparent purpose in a footnote in the early part of *Capital*. Here he writes: 'Since the human being does not come into the world bringing a mirror with him, nor yet as a Fichtean philosopher able to say "I am myself"', he first recognizes himself as reflected in other men. The man Peter grasps his relation to himself as a human being through becoming aware of his relation to the man Paul as a being of like kind with himself. Thereupon Paul, with flesh and bone, with all his Pauline corporeality, becomes for Peter the phenomenal form of the human kind.'[22]

In effect, Marx personified in the capitalist the alien power within the alienated man that divided him against himself. *Capital* offers abundant explicit testimony to this. Who or what is the capitalist? 'As capitalist', answers Marx, 'he is only personified capital (*nur personifiziertes Kapital*). His soul is the soul of capital (*Seine Seele ist die Kapitalseele*). But capital has but a single life-urge, the urge to self-expansion. . . .'[24] Thus, the capitalist is greed incarnate, the personification of the life-urge to material self-aggrandizement. As Marx expresses it in another passage, 'only in so far as the increasing appropriation of abstract wealth is the sole motive of his operations does he function as a *capitalist*, or as personified capital endowed with will and consciousness'.[24]

At a later point he says that the capitalist must spend as well as accumulate, and that his drive to absolute enrichment therefore coexists with a prodigal extravagance. 'Therewith, in the capitalist's breast there develops a Faustian conflict between the passion for accumulation and the desire for enjoyment.' But the former remains always his 'ruling passion': 'Only in so far as the capitalist is personified capital has he a historical value. . . . Only as the personification of capital is the capitalist respectable.'[25] Marx adds, it is true, that the acquisitive mania is the effect of the social mechanism (i.e. competition) in which the capitalist is only the driving wheel. As we have seen, however, it is the driving wheel that makes Marx's social mechanism what it is. The whole system collapses without the werewolf hunger for surplus value as a postulate.

The capitalist and worker of *Capital* are personifications of the dissociated antagonistic forces in Marx's original self-alienated man. The capitalist, as just shown, is the personification of the life-urge to self-aggrandizement in terms of wealth. He is the *Kapitalseele* incarnate, capital in human form, the monster personified. The worker on the other hand, is the embodiment of living labour power, creative capacity in human form, personified labour time. Neither is *man*, although the essential human attribute—creativity—remains with the worker. Accordingly, Marx considers the worker to be the incarnation of the real self. But it cannot become human until it is emancipated from its incubus—'personified capital endowed with will and consciousness'.

XV

THE MYTH AND THE PROBLEM
OF CONDUCT

*The theoretical conclusions of the Communists are in no way
based on ideas or principles that have been invented, or discovered,
by this or that would-be universal reformer. They merely express,
in general terms, actual relations springing from an existing class
struggle, from a historical movement going on under our very eyes.*

MARX (1848)

Marxism, as we have seen, did not arise out of an empirical
study of economic processes in modern society. Marx had next
to no direct knowledge of workers and working conditions, and
had only just begun the study of political economy, at the
moment of creation of his economic interpretation of history.
The path by which he arrived at it was the path of transformation
of Hegelianism on which he had been travelling ever since 1841.
Marxism was the final outcome in his mind of the movement of
thought set going by Feuerbach's suggestion that Hegelianism
was no mere philosopher's fantasy but a mystified reflection of
the actual state of affairs in the world. According to Feuerbach,
all one had to do to speculative philosophy in order to reach the
simple daylight of reality was to turn its gaze 'from the internal
towards the external'. Marx proceeded to do this in his own way,
and the final result was his projection of man's self-alienation as
an impersonal social process. Truly, Marxism may be seen as
Hegelianism inverted. Speaking very broadly, the relation
between them may be described as follows: Hegel represents the
universe as a subjective process; Marx, turning the system
around, ends up by representing a subjective process as the
universe—the social cosmos.

Having arrived at this point, Marx maintained that he had
gone beyond philosophy, and in a very significant sense he was
right. But beyond to what? He claimed direct insight into
'reality', and on this ground described his own representation of
it as real positive science. Now it is quite true that he had an

arresting vision of something real. Were this not so, incidentally, Marxism could scarcely have achieved any large influence in the world and drawn followers after the manner of religious movements from time immemorial. But the reality that Marx apprehended and portrayed was *inner reality*. The forces of which he was aware were subjective forces, forces of the alienated human self, conceived, however, and also perceived, as forces abroad in society. Insofar as this determined his thinking, it was not 'real positive science' at which he had arrived out of Hegelianism. Instead, he had gone beyond philosophy into that out of which philosophy, ages ago, originated—myth. For this is the decisive characteristic of mythic thought, that something by nature interior is apprehended as exterior, that a drama of the inner life of man is experienced and depicted as taking place in the outer world.

In this modern instance of it, an historic sequence was reversed. Whereas philosophy had once arisen against a background of myth, here myth arose against a background of philosophy—the Hegelian philosophy. A phenomenology of spirit, in which the world was consciously represented as a subjective process of realization of a world-self, became first a new phenomenology in which Marx pictured the world as a process of realization of a human species-self. This was done consciously and without mystification, and original Marxism remained fundamentally on the ground of philosophical thought. At a decisive point in it, however, Marx made the transition to the mythic mode of thought. The subjective process of *Entfremdungsgeschichte* was embodied in an image of society. And Marx went on to elaborate the Materialist Conception of History as the doctrinal enclosure of a mythic vision in which the dualism of conflicting forces of the alienated self was apprehended as a dualism of social forces, a class struggle in society, a warfare of labour and capital. From this standpoint it might be said that mature Marxism is mystified original Marxism. The classic vehicle of this mystification is *Capital*.

In forming his concept of society, Marx started with Hegel's picture of 'civil society' as a multitude of egoistic human atoms competing in the marketplace. He then sought the 'anatomy' of civil society in political economy, but the anatomy of political economy, in turn, was given in the idea of 'political-economic alienation'. The consequence was original Marxism's image of the alienated species-man, or the species of alienated men. The mass of self-estranged humanity was then split by Marx into two great classes of 'workers' and 'capitalists', and the process of alienated labour was projected as the 'life-process of society', whose productive powers embodied in the worker element are exploited for the infinite aggrandizement of capital as embodied in the capitalist element.

Conflicting forces of the alienated self were thus conceived as external social forces, and Marx's image of society took final shape as an image of self-become-society. Society, in other words, was envisaged as a self-system whose inner dynamics are those of alienation. Marx indicates this in a statement quoted earlier from *The Holy Family*, where the two opposing classes are described as opposing sides of 'one and the same human self-alienation'. However, at about this time he ceases to realize that what he sees in society is self-alienation externalized. Instead of calling capital and labour two sides of 'one and the same human self-alienation', he calls them simply 'two sides of one and the same relation'. What Marx actually sees is an inner reality, a subjective world, but he does not see it as subjective, and of course does not describe it as such. He has entered completely into the vision. In its latent content the 'relation' remains a self-relation, but in manifest content it is now a pure social-economic relation. The outcome is that what Marx *represents* as a social system in conflict bears the *characteristics* of a self-system in conflict.

In the end, however, the latent content of his thought-process registered dimly in the manifest content. I have suggested that what he actually *saw* in society was alienated man writ large. This thesis finds confirmation in *Capital*. What Marx saw in society shaped the image of it drawn here, and this is, in the final analysis, an image of society as a split personality. Having at first housed the antagonistic selves of alienated man in antagonistic social classes, he now pictures the classes in the form of selves. The aggregate of capitalists and the aggregate of workers are depicted as collective personifications of the conflicting life-forces of capital and labour. There emerges in *Capital* a vision of class-divided society as two great class-selves at war—the infinitely greedy, despotic, exploiting, vicious, werewolf-self of capital (*Kapitalseele*) on the one hand, and the exploited, enslaved, tormented, rebellious productive self of labour on the other. Marx calls the collective capital-personality by various ironic names, such as 'Monsieur Capital' or 'My Lord Capital'.[1] The collective labour-personality is called the 'Collective Worker' (*Gesamtarbeiter*). It is the 'totality' of the labour force of society, and the individual worker is 'an organ of the Collective Worker'.[2] Thus, society is a self-system after all, a collective dual personality.

Its life-process as it takes form in Marx's main work is an inner drama projected as a social drama. The *dramatis personae* are My Lord Capital and the Collective Worker. These are the only 'people' in Marx's social universe.* The social scene is a great arena whereon the collective capital-personality and the collective labour-personality fight out the war of the self in terms of such issues as the length of the working day. My Lord Capital has a vampire thirst for the living blood of labour. He is insatiably greedy to incorporate it all as his own substance. He will stop at absolutely nothing to extract a little more of the life-energies of labour in his unbridled passion for self-expansion. But My Lord Capital undermines himself: 'Fanatically bent upon the expansion of value, he relentlessly drives human beings to production for production's sake, thus bringing about a development of social productivity and the creation of those material conditions of production which can alone form the real basis of a higher type of society, whose fundamental principle is the full and free development of every individual.'[3]

Producing under the relentless compulsion of My Lord Capital's drive for surplus value, the Collective worker sinks deeper and deeper into an abyss of misery in accordance with the 'absolute general law of capitalist accumulation', which Marx formulates as follows: 'The accumulation of wealth at one pole of society involves a simultaneous accumulation of poverty, labour torment, slavery, ignorance, brutalization, and moral degradation, at the opposite pole—where dwells the class that produces its own product in the form of capital.'[4] Eventually,

---

* As G. D. H. Cole expresses it, 'In essence, there is but one product, but one gigantic associated capitalist and but one many-handed labourer yoked to the task of creating Surplus Value.' Commenting, he says that for Marx 'not individuals, but only social classes possess ultimate reality'. He adds: 'It is impossible thoroughly to understand Marx's thought without appreciating this mystical view of reality' (*Capital*, Introduction, p. xxviii). The essential point, it seems to me, is not that Marx views social classes rather than individuals as possessing ultimate reality, but that his image of society is the image of a collective dual personality.

Marx postulates, a point is reached at which the despotism of capital becomes absolutely unbearable. Then the knell of private property sounds, the Collective Worker wrests the world of alien wealth away from My Lord Capital, the monster is thereby destroyed, and all hostilities cease. Liberated from capital's drive to self-expansion, labour ceases to be labour and turns into spontaneous human productive living. The historical world of capital and labour becomes, in the end, a world that knows neither capital nor labour, a world of 'full and free development of every individual'.

This is Marx's myth of the warfare of labour and capital. It is through and through a moralistic myth, a tale of good and evil, a story of struggle between constructive and destructive forces for possession of the world. Its underlying moral theme is the theme of original Marxism: man's division against himself and dehumanization under the despotism of greed, and his final emancipation of himself and his productive activity from this despotism by the seizure of the alienated world of private property. The difference is that the alienated man has been bifurcated. The conflicting subjective forces of creativity and the will to infinite self-aggrandizement are seen and shown as class forces clashing across the battleground of society.

It is readily understandable in this light why Marx dismissed the slogan of 'fair distribution' as 'obsolete verbal rubbish',* and violently rejected all suggestion that the struggle raging in the world had something to do with distributive justice. Justice connotes a rightful balance, a delimitation of mutual claims, a settlement. This idea was wholly inapplicable to the conflict situation in the world as Marx envisaged it. No rightful balance could conceivably be struck, no delimitation of mutual claims achieved, between forces representing *man split in two*. The only possible solution of such a conflict was the ending of it by abolition of the force that made two hostile entities out of one, i.e. labour and capital out of man. No wonder, then, that Marx regarded as a grotesque joke such socialist slogans of the day as 'a fair day's wage for a fair day's work', and derided the idea of justice. He continually insisted that the struggle between labour and capital was a mortal combat and could only be ended by the destruction of capital. The issue for Marx was not justice but man's loss of himself under enslavement to an *unmenschliche*

* See above, pp. 19-20.

Macht, and his recovery of himself by the total vanquishment of this force. The ending of the worker's material impoverishment was incidental to the real goal—the ending of his dehumanization.

The moral structure of Marx's myth is related to that of Hegel's philosophical religion of self in an important way that remains to be noted. Hegel, it will be recalled, built an *apologia* of pride, a doctrine of the beneficence of moral evil, into his philosophy of history as the self-realization of God. The process by which humanity transcends human limitations on the path to absolute knowledge is seen as a destructive one, but Hegel justifies the crimes committed and the suffering caused on the ground that man in the end becomes God, or alternatively that God in the end overcomes all self-estrangement and becomes fully himself and free. For Marx, on the contrary, the self-infinitizing movement of capital is dehumanizing. Instead of liberating man, it prevents him from realizing his human nature in free productive activity. As suggested earlier, a basic shift of moral position, associated in part with Feuerbach's influence, is reflected in this.

It must now be added, however, that Marx remains faithful to the Hegelian scheme in that he too represents the destructive process as the decisive cause of the constructive outcome. Thus, in the important passage of *Capital* quoted above he holds that the acquisitive fanaticism is itself responsible for creating those new conditions of social wealth in which this fanaticism will no longer exist. Moreover, ever increasing suffering under the despotism of capital is seen as the change-producing factor, the motive force of the overthrow of the despotism. Capital becomes, therefore, the agency of capital's own destruction, and Hegel's notion of moral evil as the prime beneficent force in history lives on in Marx's thought. He sees in the dehumanization process itself the means of man's ultimate humanization. He entrusts to the force of greed that he recognizes as absolutely evil the decisive responsibility for ensuring the triumph at the end of that which is constructive and good. In a significant sense My Lord Capital is the hero as well as the villain of Marx's mythic narrative.*

* In *Ludwig Feuerbach* Engels made explicit the underlying presupposition concerning the historical beneficence of moral evil. Criticizing Feuerbach's ethics of love as quite 'shallow' in comparison with Hegel's view, he wrote: 'With Hegel evil is the form in which the motive force of historical development presents itself. This contains the twofold meaning that, on the one hand, each new advance necessarily

[2]

One of the characteristics of true mythic thinking is that the thinker is not aware of it as mythical. For him it is a revelation of what empirically *is*. The inner process that the myth represents as outer is actually perceived to be taking place in the outer world. It fills the field of mental vision as an overwhelmingly immediate and tangible presentation of external reality.* To describe and depict it appears, then, as no more than the true empiricism, and to act in terms of it the utmost realism. So it was with Marx. Now that reality had been grasped, he said, philosophy—speculative thought—had lost its medium of existence. It had given way to 'real positive science', which would consist in the transcription of the apprehended reality. The 'reality' to which he referred was something that he actually saw in a vision of the kind just described.

What he beheld in the vision was a process or movement, a movement of the social world. In one place he called it 'the real historical movement which is turning the world upside down'.[5] Elsewhere he described it as a 'real social movement which already, in all civilized countries, proclaims the approach of a terrible upheaval'.[6] It must be emphasized that he was not using the term 'movement' in the sense meant when we speak, for example, of communism as a world-wide movement. He was not referring to any such circumscribed socio-political fact as an organized mass movement of people to gain certain objectives. He was speaking of the process projected in *Capital*, the movement of class-divided society to the final point of crisis and convulsion at which the Collective Worker would rise up in awful wrath and destroy My Lord Capital.

appears as a sacrilege against things hallowed . . . and that, on the other hand, it is precisely the wicked passions of man—greed and the lust for power—which, since the emergence of class antagonisms, serve as levers of historical development—a fact of which the history of feudalism and of the bourgeoisie, for example, constitutes a single continual proof. But it does not occur to Feuerbach to investigate the historical role of moral evil' (*Selected Works,* vol. II, pp. 345–6).

* According to Ernst Cassirer, it is characteristic of mythic consciousness that 'the entire self is given up to a single impression, is "possessed" by it . . .'. Mythic consciousness, he suggests, lacks the 'free ideality' of theoretical thinking. 'Here thought does not confront its data in an attitude of free contemplation . . . but is simply captivated by a total impression' (*Language and Myth,* pp. 33, 57). Speaking of mythic presentations, the authors of another study write: 'They are products of imagination, but they are not mere fantasy. . . . True myth presents its images and its imaginary actors, not with the playfulness of fantasy, but with a compelling authority' (Henri and H. A. Frankfort, *Before Philosophy,* p. 15).

It was a visible presence before his mind. This is reflected in his continual references to it as a movement taking place 'under our very eyes'. The frequency with which this expression appears in his writings after 1844 is remarkable. In the *Manifesto* he speaks of 'an historical movement going on under our very eyes'.[7] In *The Poverty of Philosophy* he says that socialists need not concern themselves with devising programmes for the future, but 'have only to give an account of what passes before their eyes and to make of that their medium'.[8] Again, in *Herr Vogt* he writes that it 'is not a matter of bringing some utopian system or other into being but of consciously participating in the historical revolutionary process of society which is taking place before our very eyes'.[9]

So overpoweringly vivid and compelling was Marx's vision of the 'real social movement' that he feared the final upheaval would come before he had completed the grand demonstration of it in *Capital*. 'I am working like mad all through the nights at putting my economic studies together so that I may at least have the outlines clear before the deluge comes', Marx asserted to Engels on 8 December 1857.[10] He was working like mad to forestall the world cataclysm with his book about it. He was afraid that the world would turn upside down before he had shown how and why it would happen. In a letter written in 1858, he said: 'I have a presentiment that now, when after fifteen years of study I have got far enough to have the thing within my grasp, stormy movements from without will probably interfere. Never mind. If I get finished so late that I no longer find the world ready to pay attention to such things, the fault will obviously be my own.'[11] These statements, written in the relatively tranquil 1850's, tell little about the actual social world of Europe at that time. They reveal a great deal, however, about the inner world that Marx apprehended as outer.

True, the European scene in those years did not present a picture of perfect calm. There had been the revolutionary events of 1848, and the ensuing period saw its share of strikes, labour unrest, commercial slumps and international episodes. These were mostly minor events at best. Significantly, Marx admitted and even emphasized this fact. For him, however, these minor events were signs and symbols of the reality that he beheld in the vision. He saw it manifesting itself in them. In his speech on the anniversary of the *People's Paper* in 1856, he used a geological metaphor to convey this: 'The so-called revolutions of 1848 were but poor incidents—small fractures and fissures in the dry crust of European society. However, they denounced the abyss. Beneath the apparently solid surface, they betrayed oceans of liquid matter, only needing expansion to render into fragments continents of hard rock.'[12] For Marx it did not matter at all that Europe showed little obvious turbulence. Even 'poor incidents' denounced the abyss, told of what was really happening. He heard the rumblings of the world-historical volcano in every manifestation of unrest on the surface of European society. This was an outgrowth of the fact that his central vision of the world was projective in character.

Capital contains a great wealth of factual data culled from records of the economic and social history of early modern capitalism. Marx piles quotation on quotation from the reports of British factory inspectors and commissions of inquiry on conditions in the factories and factory towns of nineteenth century England. These conditions were very often so frightful as to justify his typical comment, in this case on a report dealing with child labour in a match factory, that: 'Dante would have found the worst horrors of his Inferno surpassed in this manufacture.'[13] The total picture that emerges out of Marx's careful collation of these accounts is a picture of total frightfulness. This explains the credibility to many of his mythic image of society. *Capital*'s actual subject is not an external Inferno, but the internal Inferno in alienated man. But it is illustrated with documentary material from the history of the terrible exploitation of factory workers under the conditions of the Industrial Revolution. It is in great measure this documentation of myth with materials from economic history that made Marxism an influential force in the world.

Having projected the conflict between the exploiting and exploited selves onto the field of society at large, Marx grew marvellously alive and sensitive to everything in the past or present social environment that could be assimilated into the vision, interpreted in its terms—and absolutely blind to everything else. All evidence of actual economic oppression and exploitation of workers by employers, all empirical social material that could be used to document and dramatize the warfare of My Lord Capital and the Collective Worker, was grist for his scholarly mill. Whatever could not be so used, fitted into the picture, squared with the mythic vision, he never noticed. Thus, he failed to see that the frightful factory conditions detailed in *Capital* were changing for the better during the long years of his work on the book. During the 1850's and 1860's, when living standards were slowly getting better for the majority of workers, he went on labouring in the library to prove with irrefutable logic that they had to get worse. His mind was monopolized by the myth, and this made no provision for serious amelioration of workers' conditions before the world revolution.

None of what has been said here is meant to deny that Marx's vision corresponded to certain socio-economic actualities of his time and after. Were that not so, it would be very hard to explain why the *Weltanschauung* of the *Communist Manifesto* and *Capital* has seemed to many people in different times and places to be relevant to social reality as given in their experience. In speaking of Marx's 'myth of the warfare of labour and capital', I am not at all suggesting that there have been no class antagonisms in modern society, that strife between wage workers and capitalist employers is some sort of chimera. Manifestly, these things are facts of social history and contemporary life. Capital and labour have fought their battles in various forms and at different levels of intensity in all industrial societies. The argument of these pages is not that warfare between labour and capital is *per se* a myth, or that *Capital* lacked any meaningful resemblance to the society it purported to describe. It is, rather, that Marx projected upon the real conflicts of that society a conflict out of the inner life of man. His representation of this conflict was shaped by the whole preceding development of German philosophy as we have traced it, and also, presumably, by his own experience as a person beset by acute inner conflict and tending unconsciously to seek some solution, such as by projection. The mythic quality of the resulting portrayal of capitalist society is most clearly seen in its dramatic character.

[3]

Why take part in the class struggle? This question has been addressed to Marx and Marxism over and over again by philosophical critics. It is formulated in various ways. Some inquire why a thinker who regards the victory of the proletariat to be historically preordained should actively promote it. If it is bound to happen anyhow, why bother? Alternatively, it is asked why, given the fact that he disclaimed any general ethical norm and asserted his position to be that of 'real positive science', Marx took the side of the proletariat. What ground had a scientist to be partisan? Thought bogs down in these questions, and tends to conclude with a confession of the hopelessness of trying to understand Marx's reasoning process as it related to practical action.* It is indeed quite hopeless unless this reasoning process is comprehended as that of a mind possessed by a mythic vision of the world as just defined.

For the mythic thinker there is no problem of conduct in the sense in which the moral philosopher understands it. There is, in other words, no question of what manner of life is best for man to lead and why, and consequently no search for an ethical principle of conduct as the solution of the question. The proper and worthy mode of conduct is as overwhelmingly plain as the reality luminously present before his mind in the myth. The answer to the question as to what should be done is given in the vision of what is happening in the world. This, as suggested above, is a vision of the inner as outer. A drama of the inner life of man is externalized and experienced as taking place in the outer world. The conflict of good and evil forces of the self, its constructive and destructive powers, appears to be resolving itself externally. For Marx the outer reality is social reality, and the conflict appears as a war of classes into which society has split. The contending forces of good and evil are respectively the productive powers, lodged in the proletariat, and the inhuman force of capital incarnate in the bourgeoisie, which is the collective *Personifikation des Kapitals* (to use Marx's own phrase).

Why the problem of conduct is resolved in the mythic vision itself, resolved without ever arising as a subject of inquiry, is obvious. The thinker himself is intensely involved in the drama that appears to be taking place in the world outside him. Were this not so, he would never have engaged in the myth-making act in the first place. Once he has done so, however, his involvement becomes an involvement in what is now apprehended as a world-conflict. The moral drama of the self has its locus for him in the movement of the world wherein it appears writ large. The whole world, or alternatively the world of society, has become the battlefield on which the war of the self is being waged, on which

* See, for example, G. D. H. Cole, *Socialist Thought: The Forerunners*, p. 277.

the good forces are fighting for their life against the evil ones. Since it is *his* conflict that is being enacted out there, the thinker naturally feels impelled to do his part, help the good forces along, urge them to battle, cheer their victories, bemoan their setbacks, and in general give them all manner of active support. He wants to join the fray, and bids others to do the same. The point is to *participate* in the action already going on, as he sees it, outside him.

This is the special logic (or 'psycho-logic') of mythic thinking as it relates to practical action. The answer to the question as to what should be done is given in the mythic vision itself, and can be summed up in a single word: 'Participate!' In so far as the mythic thinker gives any recognition at all to the problem of conduct, he answers immediately, emphatically and categorically in this vein. So Marx, as noted above, says that it is not a matter of bringing some utopian system or other into being (i.e. of defining a social goal and purposefully endeavouring to realize it) but simply of 'consciously participating in the historical revolutionary process of society which is taking place before our very eyes'. Here the participation takes the form of 'revolutionary praxis'. To engage in practical revolutionary action on the side of the proletariat is to promote, help along and accelerate the 'real historical movement which is turning the world upside down'. Moreover, since the theory of revolution is simply the 'literary expression'[14] of this movement, revolutionary praxis is the conscious enactment of the theory, and Marx is convinced that all 'theoretical' problems have their solution in social praxis.* This is his celebrated doctrine of the unity of theory and practice. Not pragmatism but mysticism is its foundation.

If the projection of an inner moral drama upon the outer world is the essence of myth, the urge and injunction to 'participate' is the origin of ritual. Later the ritual activity may come to be performed as a merely symbolic re-enactment of the events recounted in the mythic narrative. But it is not so in the beginning. Originally the call to participate expresses the mythic thinker's passionate felt need to accelerate the ongoing drama of events as he experiences it in the vision.† This imperative of

---

* See above, p. 102.

† One school of thought is inclined to give ritual precedence over myth. Lord Raglan, for example, writes that a myth 'is simply a narrative associated with a

participation is categorical. The mythic thinker cannot or will not reason with you about it. All he can do is to point to the world and say: 'Can't you *see* what is happening?' He knows that if you *do* see, you will, just as he does, act accordingly. Therefore, his supreme concern is just to make everybody see what is going on under their eyes, to communicate the vision in an image of the world-process, e.g. a *Capital*. This, he may feel, is the most effective way in which he himself can actively participate.

Thus, Marx sees his paramount practical task as that of making the good forces more fully conscious of the nature, conditions and prospects of the conflict, more clearly aware of the total evilness of the evil forces against which they are pitted, more cognizant of the utter hopelessness of any compromise solution in terms of justice, which would imply a delimitation of mutual claims and a cessation of hostilities. He wants everybody on his side to understand that there is no substitute for unconditional victory of the good forces and total defeat of the evil ones. Anyone who takes the idea of justice at all seriously (Proudhon, for example) becomes the butt of his bitter abuse and invective. Further, he wants to buoy the good forces up with firm confidence in their ultimate triumph, and so concludes the *Communist Manifesto* by telling the proletariat that it has nothing to lose but its chains and a world to win. He wants to organize and direct these forces, to provide generalship for them in the ongoing conflict and impending final battle, and so helps found an International Workingmen's Association and immerses himself in the practical politics of world revolution. For it is 'the practical and violent action of the masses alone by which these conflicts can be resolved'.[15] Only by a mass revolutionary praxis that consummates the historical movement of the world can the war of the self be won. For Marx, then, the active promotion of the inevitable found its rationale in the idea of shortening the 'birth pangs' of a new state of the world that in turn meant to him a new *state of self*. And siding with the pro-

rite', and Stanley Hyman says that 'myth tells a story sanctioning a rite' (T. A. Sebeok, ed., *Myth: A Symposium*, pp. 76, 90). It seems, however, that this theory would apply only to the later stages, when the original relation of thought and action may indeed be reversed, with the myth becoming a sanction for an established rite. Thus, if for Marx the imperative of participation sprang from the mythic vision of the warfare of labour and capital, nowadays Marx's myth is largely a narrative associated with the rites of Communist single-party politics.

letariat meant siding with the force in the world that was fighting *his war*. For him the proletariat remained always what he had once called it, the material weapon of philosophy or reality striving toward thought. But this was *his* thought.

The immense distance of the standpoint of the mythic consciousness from that of moral philosophy as an activity of free critical inquiry into values is perfectly plain. Not only are they far apart; they are irreconcilably in conflict. Presupposing as it does a suspension of commitment in the matter of what is good and what is evil, moral philosophy *per se* bespeaks—to the visionary Marx—a perverse blindness to what is happening in the world. No one who saw what he sees could possibly consider the problem of conduct to be intellectually problematic. Hence the very idea of moral philosophy became anathema to Marx. He could not abide it and displayed towards it an attitude of utter contempt. His cardinal concern, as a totally committed mythic thinker, was simply to elaborate the vision, to make others see what he saw. He knew that if he could only make them more 'conscious' of it, then they too—or many of them— would participate more actively. There was no question whatever of propounding some normative principle of life and conduct. What Marx produced, therefore, in *Capital* was not a book of ethics but a book of revelation. As such, however, this bible of Marxism, as it is justly called, is moralistic from beginning to end.

Marx's mythic vision of the world movement died with him, although he attempted to perpetuate it in writings that were to become sacred texts of real social movements carrying on in his name. The story of the different interpretations of its meaning which have arisen within these movements would be the subject of an independent study. Suffice it to say that Marx's myth of the warfare of labour and capital has meant many things to many people. Some of the followers, contrary to all Marx's explicit statements on this point, assumed that the moral message had to do with justice and injustice. Others understood in various ways that it had to do with freedom and bondage. Finally, some among the literal-minded intellectuals of the movement, especially at the close of the nineteenth century, assumed that there was no moral theme in it at all. This is understandable when we consider that Marx offered the myth as real positive science, and economic science at that, and accompanied the statements of it with the most emphatic disclaimers of ethical purport. Hence the irony and the paradox that some years after the founder's death, Karl Kautsky, the leader of orthodox Marxism in Germany, turned to the naturalist Darwin for a moral message that he presumed to be missing in the writings of his teacher—the moralist Marx.

CONCLUSION

MARX AND THE PRESENT AGE

And the relation to himself a man cannot get rid of, any more than he can get rid of himself, which moreover is one and the same thing, since the self is the relationship to oneself.

SOREN KIERKEGAARD

Although Marx has been dead for not far short of a century now, adequate assessment of him probably remains a matter for the future. If importance may be measured by impact, he is certainly one of the most important minds of modern times. One manifestation of this impact is the multitude of movements, both ruling and non-ruling, which profess Marxism in one or another version as their creed. Being the most powerful prophet of the new nineteenth-century religion of socialism, Marx found followers for whom his ideas became a belief-system and the basis of a new culture. Through the Marxist group that came to power in the Russian Revolution of 1917 his teaching proved instrumental in the rise of Communism as a new socio-cultural formation which in a variety of forms now covers about a third of the earth. He would doubtless repudiate very much of what his future Communist followers have said and done in his name, and might not always find it easy to recognize *his* Marxism in such offshoots as 'Marxism-Leninism' or 'Mao Tse-tung Thought'. But of how many prophets and progenitors of new cultures could something similar not be said?

Marx's intellectual influence is also still widespread outside those countries where Marxism is a state ideology. It is not clear to what extent this would have been so, however, had it not been for the discovery of the early Marx some decades ago. For some persons, it is true, the strength of Marx lies in the economic interpretation of history and the class analysis of society and politics; and from their viewpoint his middle and later writings, and those of Engels, form the main part of what is perennially valuable in Marxism. On the other hand, Marx's treatment of capitalism, and particularly his dialectic of capitalism's inevitable revolutionary breakdown, has lost its cogency. Although poverty and economic injustice remain serious in many of the industrially advanced countries and in places are acute, capitalist economies have not obeyed Marx's 'absolute general law of capitalist accumulation'. They have not, moreover, begot their own negations in a cataclysmic final episode, but have tended to evolve under various social pressures into mixed economies with more or less extensive welfare arrangements, and working classes have grown less proletarian as a result.

Marx saw the world proletarian revolution as the pathway of man's entry into a post-historical existence radically different in character from life as hitherto known. The miscarriage of his economics of proletarian revolution necessarily calls into question his confidence that such a global post-history is man's destiny. As a programmatic idea, however, this conception is more meaningful now than at the time of its enunciation. Marx, it will be recalled, defined history as collective man's 'act of becoming', the long and painful growing up of the human species. Capitalism evoked his grudging enthusiasm in the *Manifesto* precisely because of its role as the mighty accelerator of the developmental process: it was revolutionizing technology and creating the productive forces capable of sustaining the species in a life no longer given over to the further amassing of productive forces. There is no reason to believe that Marx envisaged this future condition as one of static perfection. Its definitive features were, rather, that man in the mass would achieve mastery of his surroundings and collective life-process, and 'labour' in the historic sense of drudgery would give way to the productive self-expression of fully developed human beings seeking exercise of their diverse and many-sided talents. If in his later writings Marx no longer used the phrase 'positive humanism' to describe the post-historical state of affairs, he never ceased to conceive it in these terms. Instead of sacrificing themselves in order to create the material prerequisites of an authentically human existence, future generations would actually experience such an existence. The species' arduous growth-process would terminate in its maturity. Human *being* would take the place of historical *becoming*.

The present-day relevance of this way of thinking requires little explanation. In the second half of the twentieth century it has become increasingly plain that man, who inhabits a small planet with finite space and finite resources, is in a crisis of growth—and of the growth-thinking that has naturally attended and reinforced the historical striving for growth in all its forms. Growth of population, growth of technology, growth of pollution and growth of social complexity are so many interrelated aspects of the crisis. Some of the eminent minds of the present age have responded by advocating an orientation toward what is variously called a 'steady-state economy' (Lewis Mumford), a 'stable-state society' (Jacques Monod) and a 'developed society' (Kenneth Boulding). The implication seems to be that in order to bring the situation under control, we shall have to institute some kind of global management of human affairs and check the rampant growth along many lines that is endangering the human enterprise, which is not of course to deny that poverty and misery in many less developed lands will require, among other things, greater production for a time to meet essential needs.

In order to bring growth under control, growth-thinking will have to be transcended. It is in this context that Marx's conception of post-history becomes meaningful. He offers little if any practical guidance on solving the crisis. Because of his impassioned anti-Malthusianism, stemming from the desire to explain poverty by the dynamics of capitalism rather than, as Malthus did, by the multiplying of people, he left no Marxist legacy of awareness of the population danger. He did not anticipate the problems of pollution and exhaustion of natural resources. Although extremely sensitive to the compulsions of industrial technology under capitalism, he was insensitive to the compulsions inherent in the technological process *per se*. But all this having been noted, the decisive fact is that Marx advanced a philosophical conception of man and history that does not value growth for its own sake. He envisaged collective man as master of his circumstances and living in a developed society at the end of history. More significant in some ways than practical solutions is the philosophical guidance embodied in this utopia. Ironically, his Russian Communist disciples, for whom Marxism itself became in part a gospel of economic growth in the effort to 'overtake and outstrip' industrially more advanced countries, have as much to learn from him in this respect as do the rest of us. In terms of ultimate values, five-year plans and great leaps forward are no more in the spirit of Marx than the fanatic capitalist 'production for production's sake' that he decried in *Capital*.

Paradoxically, then, the aspect of Marx's thought that is most live and relevant to the concerns of people in our time is the utopian aspect, the part relating to the post-revolutionary future. There is still a further respect in which this is true. For Marx, as we have seen, the world revolution would be the universal act of human self-change. It would liberate the creative powers from the acquisitive mania, and men would finally become whole and harmonious as productive beings realizing themselves in a totality of life-activities and aesthetic appreciation of their surroundings. They would arrange their no longer alienated world according to the laws of beauty, and labour in the historical sense would be abolished. As Marx put it in a passage of *Capital* quoted earlier, the 'higher type of society' would have as its principle the 'full and free development of every individual'. This higher type of society was only an abstract postulated setting of a new mode of human life. In the unfinished third volume of *Capital*, Marx called it the 'realm of freedom'. There would remain, he said, a minimal realm of necessity or amount of work that must be done, although the producers would 'accomplish their task with the least expenditure of energy and under conditions most adequate to their human nature and most worthy of it'. He then went on: 'Beyond it begins that development of human power, which is its own end, the true realm of freedom, which, however, can flourish only upon that realm of necessity as its basis. The shortening of the working day is its fundamental premise.'[1]

Marx's aesthetic utopia, his vision of the abolition of labour in a post-historical world in which human existence would take on the character of creative leisure and artistic expression, was astonishingly modern in a way. It anticipated the rise of this possibility as a result of the technological revolution of the twentieth century. Automation and the unlocking of the productive powers of the atom have begun to pose the question of a profound reorientation of man's existence on this planet, a reorientation from the work-centred life to a different kind of life. In a sense, it might be said that the problem of the *good* life may become inescapable for a growing proportion of mankind. The revolution involved is not a political one but rather a revolution of man's attitude towards himself and the purposes of his existence, a revolution of values. If economic labour is largely abolished by the technological revolution in its later phases, what use will men make of the unprecedented freedom to do what they want to do as distinguished from what they have to do? What kind of living will take the place of a large part of what has been called working for a living? Will the post-compulsion world be one in which people realize their creative potentials as free human beings, or will it be one of unutterable tedium? The next stage of history may conceivably carry out an experiment on human nature and give the answer to these questions.

Although his idea of the abolition of labour, and with it the old rigid divisions of labour, may, therefore, have been prophetic, Marx's thought as a whole is not seriously related to the issues just posed. Indeed, it never occurred to him to pose them. He did not see that the shortening of the working day might, beyond a certain point, prove the opposite of a blessing, that it might become the 'premise' not of men's joyful realization of themselves in manifold creative and artistic ways but of their unhappiness in a life of deadening diversions. For him the ascent of man from the realm of economic necessity to that of freedom was the 'riddle of history resolved', whereas in actuality it represents no more than a chance to start resolving it. The only problem freedom can solve is that of bondage; otherwise it represents not a solution but merely an opportunity. The real growing up of the race, the emergence of man from his historical growth-process into adulthood, will only take place if this opportunity is realized and worthy solutions of the problem of human existence in freedom are found.

It was not want of foresight but preoccupation with bondage that kept Marx from asking whether the advent of freedom might not bring a host of new problems—the dilemmas of freedom. He could no more bring himself to ask this question than a person enduring constant severe pain could worry over the possibility of becoming bored with life after the pain has been relieved. Being a suffering individual himself, who had projected upon the outer world an inner drama of oppression, he saw suffering everywhere.* Accordingly, relief from the suffering, liberation from bondage, was all that really mattered. What blocked the entry of man into the realm of freedom was not the

* Marx also suffered from physical complaints, and even remarked, on completion of *Capital*, that the bourgeoisie would remember his carbuncles. He probably made this statement in a jocular vein. In any event, it must not be taken seriously, as though the carbuncles could explain *Capital*.

continuing necessity to work for a living, but the continuing compulsion to work under the despotism of greed.

If the shortening of the working day was the premise of the future flourishing of freedom, what was the premise of the shortening of the working day? For Marx it was the abolition of the monstrous force that made the working day so long and hellish and kept lengthening it little by little as the progress of technology made possible its shortening. So the reduction of economic necessity was wholly linked in his mind with the ending of the torment of dehumanization caused by the acquisitive passion. The point was to liberate man from *alienated* labour, and it was only from this standpoint that Marx considered the problem of man's self-realization in freedom. He was pre-occupied with the removal of a block to the rise of the problem, and tended to equate this precondition of a solution with the solution itself. In short, human self-alienation and the over-coming of it remained always the supreme concern of Marx and the central theme of his thought.

In this too, however, he was very modern and in advance of his time. Although the theme of self-alienation is of age-old and universal human interest, there are many signs of its emergence as one of the most prominent subjects of conscious concern to twentieth-century man, especially in the West. This undoubtedly explains the interest that Marx's manuscripts of 1844 have aroused in recent years among Western thinkers. The relevance of Marx's central theme to our problems in the present age is obvious. The question is whether he has anything valid and important to say to us about human self-alienation and the means of overcoming it.

In considering the question, we must not isolate original from mature Marxism, as though the explicit philosophy of alienation presented in the early writings were Marx's final contribution to the subject. As I have sought to show here, the development of Marx's thought from the early philosophical to the later mythic stage was prefigured in the manuscripts of 1844 themselves. *Capital* was the logical fruition of all his thought from the begin-ning, when he set the 'realization of philosophy' as the task for the next stage of history and defined the proletariat as the 'material weapon' of philosophy or alienated man striving to overcome his alienation. This alienated species-man of original Marxism is writ large in *Capital*'s image of a conflicting social system. The dissociated selves of the original alienated man appear here as the monstrously greedy My Lord Capital and the enslaved and exploited Collective Worker. The raging inner conflict in the system between capital and labour is a representation in impersonal terms of the warring forces of the alienated personality: the urge to self-aggrandizement on the one hand, and the creative powers on the other. The self-destructive dialectic of the system reflects the dynamics of the alienated personality, which is enslaved and tormented by its own compulsive aggrandizing tendency and finally rebels against it.

This was, I have argued, a mythic picture of society in that a drama of the inner life of man was superimposed upon the facts of outer social reality. But a critique of Marx's treatment of alienation cannot stop short at the point of stating that it culminated in mythic thought. For mythic thought may be a vehicle of moral truth. It has been said of myth that 'Its ultimate end is not wishful distortion of the world, but serious envisagement of its fundamental truths; moral orientation, not escape.'* Our concluding question, then, is this: To what extent did Marx's thought on alienation, including the mythic part, envisage fundamental truth and offer moral orientation?

He had something valid and important to say, I think, on the question of the ground or cause of alienation. He found this in the aggrandizing tendency, the self-infinitizing movement that may arise in man, calling it 'capital'. And this brought him, unwittingly, into some positive relation to the Hebraic-Christian religious tradition, which had been founded upon the condemnation of human self-aggrandizement or pride. Unlike Hegel, for whom man was alienated from himself in the degree to which he still fell short of being the Absolute, Marx held, in effect, that man is alienated from himself as a consequence of striving for the Absolute. In the process he has lost his humanity, becoming *Unmensch* ruled over by an *unmenschliche Macht*. Hegel only rationalized alienation; Marx recognized it. To his credit as a moral thinker, he recognized the inhuman force as inhuman and enslavement to it as enslavement rather than a higher form of freedom. The latent presence of this recognition in the depths of Marx's myth probably helps to explain the power of attraction it has exerted on many.

The recognition was not, however, a clear one, and the lack of

* Susanne K. Langer, *Philosophy in a New Key* (New York, 1951), p. 153.

clarity is evident in Marx's definition of alienation as fundamentally a phenomenon of the economic life or 'fact of political
economy'. We have retraced here the steps that led him to
this idea. Hegel had presented history as a process of the self-
alienation and self-realization of God in the person of mankind.
Feuerbach construed this as a mystified revelation of the
universally self-estranged condition of man himself in the life of
religion, and Marx, following Feuerbach's example, drew the
same conclusion in a different way. Positing that 'Hegel has
the point of view of modern political economy', he construed the
Hegelian philosophy of history as a revelation of the self-
estranged condition of mankind in the economic life. Both
Feuerbach and Marx Hegelianized humanity. That is, they took
Hegel's category of alienation to be universally operative in the
collective life of man. The one located the neurotic process in
religion, which he saw as a phenomenon of human self-worship.
The other located it in economics, which he saw as a practical
religion of money-worship. As a consequence, the one found
self-alienation to be the essence of Christianity, and the other
found it to be the essence of capitalism.

In its intrinsic nature, however, self-alienation is neither a fact
of religion nor a fact of political economy. It may find *expression*
in the economic life or in religion, just as it may also find expression in politics, war and every other human pursuit. Thus, a
given alienated individual may develop a compulsive urge
towards absolute enrichment, and for him the economic life
will indeed be a practical religion of money-worship and a sphere
of 'alienated labour'. But his alienation only becomes in a derivative way an economic fact. Inherently or in itself it is a fact of the
life of the self, i.e. a spiritual or, as we say today, psychological
fact. It is a sickness of the self growing out of and reflecting a
man's confusion of humanity in his own person with deity, his
quest to actualize himself as a supra-human absolute being.
Alienation is the counterpart of egoism in this sense. It is not,
therefore, a general condition of humanity. Man is not born
alienated, although he is born with a potentiality of becoming an
alienated individual. No matter how many individual men may
belong to this category, it is always an individual matter.

Marx originally had within his grasp, or at any rate within
easy reach, the truth that alienation is essentially a fact of the
life of the individual human self. This is shown by his very first

statement about it, the statement of 1843 that man is alienated from himself when he produces under the compulsion of 'egoistic need'. But he failed to trace this egoism to its real source within the personality of the alienated individual himself. It became for him a kind of disembodied inhuman force ruling over everything. First he universalized it, making out both the egoistic need and the resulting alienation to be a *species* phenomenon, and then he split the species and made one section's alienation the consequence of the other's egoistic need. He was never clear about the source of this egoistic need, but suggested in *Capital* that money is the cause of the greed for money and that competition is responsible for the maniacal, specifically capitalist form of it, the 'werewolf hunger for surplus value'. And he never seems to have asked himself what would prevent the inhuman force from rising again to estrange man from himself on the yonder side of history. These were so many different manifestations of Marx's failure to grasp clearly the phenomenon with which he was working.

Not having located the 'egoistic need' within the personality of the alienated individual person, he also failed to understand that it is only there, and by the individual's own moral effort, that the egoism can be undone and the revolutionary 'change of self' achieved. If the starting point is the moral rebellion against alienated living and the force that condemns him to this servitude (as Marx indicates in his image of the proletarian as dehumanized man no longer willing to be dehumanized), the ensuing revolutionary movement of emancipation is its direct moral continuation. It is essentially a work of self-clarification and *self-changing*. Its tools are the power of understanding, the urge to be free, and the willingness to be merely human. Its dialectic is a Socratic dialectic of 'Know thyself.' The 'revolution' or real change of self that emerges in and through this movement of emancipation, is, likewise, a moral revolution. The change of 'circumstances' with which it coincides is a change of the self's character, meaning the habitual circumstances within the self that have been shaped by alienated living and stand in the way of its freedom, the inner autocracy or coercive system. Such a revolution within the self cannot occur or start in a violent catastrophic episode. It is the outcome of a gradual process, and *is* this process taken as a whole. Alternatively, it is the merely theoretical point of culmination of the whole slow growth of inward freedom and repossession of the productive powers of the self which takes place in the movement and by the labour of self-liberation.

The foregoing exposition, drawing as it does upon Marx's own terms and concepts, suggests that a true understanding of the means of transcending alienation was a possible achievement for him. Yet it also makes clear that he did not arrive at such an understanding. In a very important sense, moreover, his whole system and myth represented a flight from it, a search for a way of transcendence that would entail no moral work of self-liberation on the part of the alienated individual. Magnifying the problem to the proportions of humanity in general, Marx exempted alienated man in particular from all moral responsibility for striving to change himself. Self-change was to be reached by a revolutionary praxis that would alter *external* circumstances, and the war of the self was to be won through transference of hostilities to the field of relations between man and man. Men were told, in effect, that violence against other men was the only possible means by which they themselves could become new men. Not moral orientation but escape was the burden of this message. Marx created in Marxism a gospel of transcendence of alienation by other means than those which alone can encompass the end, a solution that evades the solution, a pseudo-solution. As such Marxism was a miscarriage. At best it was one of the grand aberrations of the human mind on its long and continuing journey toward self-clarification.

The decisive act of escape was the division of the original alienated man into two men. Only so long as an alienated man can find in himself the courage to recognize that the 'alien power' against which he rebels is a power within him, that the inhuman force which makes his life a forced labour is a force of the self, that the 'alien, hostile, powerful man' is an inner man, the absolute being of his imagination, has he hope of transcending his alienation. To set it apart from himself and outside himself as 'another man' is to resign this hope. It is the ultimate evasion—the escape into insanity. This, philosophically speaking, was the meaning of Marx's differentiation of the alien power from alienated man and envisagement of it as 'personified capital endowed with will and consciousness'. Society was split into two collective personifications of the forces at war in the self, and Marx lost conscious hold on the concept of self-alienated man. Here the myth was born, and with it the illusion that self-change could be accomplished through the ritual of participation in an historical revolutionary movement of society 'taking place before our very eyes'.

The moral escapism at the core of Marx's thought finds expression, finally, in this conception of the means of self-change. Collectivizing the process and evading the issue of individual responsibility for self-liberation, he ended up by invoking one set of destructive passions to destroy another. Dispossessed by capital of his productive powers, dehumanized man was to be motivated by wrath, hatred, envy and greed in the war to reappropriate them. The lust for power was to be annihilated by a counter-lust for power, and greed by a counter-greed. It is true, as Marx said in his unpublished papers, that man on the morrow of such a revolution would exist in a state of 'infinite degradation', but groundless to suppose that such degradation must be the beginning of his radical self-reform. There could be no greater confession of failure on Marx's part than this mode of envisagement of the moral revolution of self-change that he had postulated as the goal for man. The failure was not, of course, Marx's alone, for much of modern thought prepared the way for it. It only brought into sharp focus the wider failure of modern thinkers to comprehend certain fundamental truths of the inner life of man that were discovered and enunciated ages ago in different parts of the world, and later lost sight of. More recently, insight into these truths has been recovered by a depth psychology that drew some of its inspiration, paradoxically, from the German philosophical movement of which Marx was a representative.

REFERENCES

INTRODUCTION (pp. 11–27)

1. *Paths in Utopia,* p. 10.
2. *Braun's Archiv für Sociale Gesetzgebung und Statistik,* vol. v, 1892, p. 489.
3. *Historical Materialism and the Economics of Karl Marx,* pp. 113–17 passim.
4. *Ethics and the Materialist Conception of History,* p. 202.
5. K. Marx and F. Engels, *Selected Works,* vol. I, p. 360 (hereafter cited as *Selected Works* I or *Selected Works* II).
6. K. Marx and F. Engels, *Historisch-Kritische Gesamtausgabe, erste Abteilung,* vol. v, p. 227 (hereafter cited as *MEGA,* followed by the volume number. The separately published parts of vol. I will be cited as I/1 and I/2).
7. *Ibid.* pp. 396, 397.
8. *Capital,* p. 671.
9. *Ibid.* p. 188.
10. Marx/Engels, *Kleine Ökonomische Schriften,* p. 412.
11. *Selected Works* II, p. 23.
12. *Ibid.* pp. 20, 23, 24.
13. *The Open Society and its Enemies,* vol. II, p. 192.
14. *The Heavenly City of the Eighteenth-Century Philosophers,* pp. 10, 17.
15. *Critique of Political Economy,* p. 13.
16. *German Ideology,* p. 198; *MEGA,* v, p. 193.
17. *German Ideology,* p. 199.
18. *MEGA,* III, p. 446.
19. *Ibid.* p. 448.

I. THE SELF AS GOD IN GERMAN PHILOSOPHY (pp. 31–44)

1. *Faust* (Part I), trans. Philip Wayne, pp. 52, 54, 91.
2. *The Sickness Unto Death,* p. 207.
3. *Fundamental Principles of the Metaphysic of Ethics,* pp. 61, 62.
4. *Ibid.* p. 58.
5. *Ibid.* pp. 77–8.
6. *Kant's Critique of Practical Reason,* p. 322.
7. *Fundamental Principles of the Metaphysic of Ethics,* p. 21.
8. *Kant's Critique of Practical Reason,* p. 321.
9. *Ibid.* p. 219.
10. *Ibid.* pp. 292, 293.
11. *Ibid.* p. 293.

12. *Early Theological Writings,* pp. 176, 162–3 (the latter passage appears in the more literal translation given by Walter A. Kaufmann in 'Hegel's Early Antitheological Phase', *The Philosophical Review,* January 1954, pp. 12–13).
13. *Early Theological Writings,* pp. 178, 181.
14. *Ibid.* pp. 211, 212, 244.
15. *Ibid.* pp. 264–5.
16. *Ibid.* p. 266.
17. *Ibid.* p. 311.
18. *Ibid.* p. 314.
19. *The Phenomenology of Mind,* p. 750 (hereafter cited as *Phenomenology*).
20. *Early Theological Writings,* p. 14.
21. *Ibid.* p. 35.
22. *Ibid.* p. 53.
23. G. W. F. Hegel, *The Logic of Hegel,* p. 55.

II. HISTORY AS GOD'S SELF-REALIZATION (pp. 45–56)

1. *The Logic of Hegel,* p. 74.
2. *Phenomenology,* p. 807.
3. *Hegel's Philosophy of Mind,* p. 176.
4. *Phenomenology,* pp. 85, 86.
5. *Ibid.* p. 801.
6. *Philosophy of History,* p. 73.
7. *Ibid.* p. 19.
8. *Ibid.* pp. 73–4.
9. *The Logic of Hegel,* p. 335.
10. *Philosophy of History,* p. 55.
11. *Phenomenology,* p. 203.
12. *The Logic of Hegel,* p. 88.
13. *Phenomenology,* p. 137.
14. *Ibid.* p. 97.
15. *The Logic of Hegel,* p. 62.
16. *Hegel's Science of Logic,* vol. I, p. 143.
17. *The Logic of Hegel,* p. 49.
18. *Philosophy of History,* p. 17.
19. *The Logic of Hegel,* p. 66.
20. *Philosophy of History,* p. 104.
21. *Ibid.* p. 78.
22. *Phenomenology,* p. 801.
23. *The Logic of Hegel,* p. 105.
24. *Lectures on the History of Philosophy,* vol. III, pp. 551, 552, 554.

III. THE DIALECTIC OF AGGRANDIZEMENT (pp. 57–69)

1. *The Logic of Hegel*, pp. 148–50.
2. *The Vocation of Man*, p. 174.
3. *Hegel's Science of Logic*, vol. I, p. 62.
4. *The Logic of Hegel*, pp. 175, 177.
5. *Ibid.* p. 178.
6. *Ibid.* p. 54.
7. *Foundations of Democracy*, published as part II of *Ethics*, vol. LXVI, October 1955, no. I, p. 15.
8. *Phenomenology*, p. 782.
9. *Hegel's Philosophy of Right*, p. 232.
10. *Ibid.* p. 236.
11. *The Logic of Hegel*, p. 150.
12. *Philosophy of History*, p. 69.
13. *Early Theological Writings*, p. 38.
14. *The Logic of Hegel*, pp. 351–2.
15. *Philosophy of History*, p. 31.
16. *Ibid.* p. 33.
17. J. Loewenberg, in Introduction to *Hegel Selections*, p. xl.
18. *Phenomenology*, p. 135; *Philosophy of History*, pp. 21, 26–7.
19. *Philosophy of History*, pp. 21, 66–7.
20. *Ibid.* pp. 32, 67.
21. *Ibid.* p. 20.
22. *Ibid.* p. 32.
23. 'Beyond Good and Evil', p. 202, in *The Philosophy of Nietzsche*.

IV. PHILOSOPHY REVOLTS AGAINST THE WORLD (pp. 73–84)

1. *MEGA*, II, p. 428.
2. *MEGA*, I/I, p. 10.
3. *Karl Marx: His Life and Work*, p. 379.
4. *MEGA*, I/2, p. 42.
5. *MEGA*, I/I, p. 63.
6. *Ibid.* pp. 64, 131.
7. *Ibid.* pp. 64, 65.
8. *Ibid.* p. 132.
9. *Ibid.* p. 573.
10. *Ibid.* pp. 609–10.
11. *Ibid.* p. 175.
12. K. Marx and F. Engels, *Selected Correspondence*, p. 233 (hereafter cited as *Selected Correspondence*).
13. *Selected Works*, II, p. 333.
14. *MEGA*, III, p. 316.
15. *Essence of Christianity*, pp. xxxiv, xxxv.

16. *MEGA*, III, p. 160.
17. *Kleine Philosophische Schriften*, p. 58.
18. *Ibid.* pp. 122, 123.
19. *Essence of Christianity*, p. 230.
20. *Kleine Philosophische Schriften*, pp. 72, 73, 122–3.

V. METAPHYSICS AS ESOTERIC PSYCHOLOGY
(pp. 85–94)

1. *Kleine Philosophische Schriften*, p. 56.
2. *Essence of Christianity*, p. 228.
3. *Ibid.* p. 230.
4. *Kleine Philosophische Schriften*, p. 73.
5. *Essence of Christianity*, pp. 29, 30, 31.
6. *Ibid.* p. xvi.
7. *Ibid.* p. 26.
8. *Ibid.* p. 33.
9. *Ibid.; Kleine Philosophische Schriften*, p. 110.
10. *Essence of Christianity*, p. 47.
11. *Ibid.* p. 127.
12. *Ibid.* pp. 196, 73.
13. *Ibid.* pp. 217–8.
14. *Kleine Philosophische Schriften*, p. 159.
15. *Ibid.* p. 169.
16. *Ibid.*
17. *Ibid.* p. 196.

VI. MARX AND FEUERBACH (pp. 95–105)

1. *MEGA*, III, p. 34.
2. *German Ideology*, pp. 3, 39.
3. *Selected Correspondence*, p. 169.
4. *MEGA*, I/I, pp. 426–7, 406–7.
5. *MEGA*, III, p. 370.
6. *Ibid.* p. 231.
7. *Ibid.* p. 168.
8. *MEGA*, I/I, p. 608.
9. *Ibid.* p. 607.
10. *Ibid.*
11. *Ibid.* p. 615.
12. *German Ideology*, p. 37.
13. *Ibid.* pp. 33, 34.
14. *MEGA*, I/I, p. 608.
15. *German Ideology*, p. 198.
16. *MEGA*, I/I, pp. 607, 608.
17. *Hegel's Philosophy of Right*, pp. 189, 267.

18. *MEGA*, i/i, p. 434.
19. *Ibid.* p. 436.
20. *Ibid.* pp. 586, 598.
21. *Ibid.* p. 584.
22. *Ibid.* p. 599.

VII. THE RISE OF PHILOSOPHICAL COMMUNISM
(pp. 106–120)

1. *MEGA*, i/i, p. 601.
2. *Critique of Political Economy*, p. 11.
3. *What is Property?*, p. 257.
4. *Ibid.* pp. 251, 249.
5. *Ibid.* pp. 271, 248.
6. *Sozialistische Aufsätze*, p. 167.
7. *Ibid.* pp. 166, 165.
8. *Ibid.* p. 170.
9. *MEGA*, i/i, pp. 601, 603.
10. *Ibid.* p. 605.
11. *Ibid.*
12. *Ibid.* p. 601.
13. *Ibid.* p. 573.
14. *Ibid.* pp. 616, 620.
15. *Ibid.* pp. 619–20.
16. *From Hegel to Marx*, p. 191.
17. *Der Socialismus und Communismus des heutigen Frankreichs*, pp. 39, 51.
18. *Hegel's Philosophy of Right*, pp. 150, 277.
19. *Der Socialismus und Communismus des heutigen Frankreichs*, p. 9.
20. *MEGA*, i/i, pp. 618, 620.
21. *MEGA*, iii, pp. 206, 212.
22. *MEGA*, i/i, p. 621.
23. *MEGA*, iii, p. 157.

VIII. WORKING MAN AS WORLD CREATOR (pp. 123–135)

1. *MEGA*, iii, pp. 34, 35.
2. *Ibid.* p. 34.
3. *Ibid.* pp. 151, 153.
4. *Ibid.* p. 155.
5. *Ibid.* pp. 167, 156.
6. *Ibid.* p. 156.
7. *Ibid.* p. 92.
8. *Ibid.* p. 157.
9. *Ibid.* pp. 152–3, 170.
10. *Ibid.* pp. 155–6.

11. *MEGA*, III, p. 155.
12. *Ibid.* p. 158.
13. *Ibid.* p. 164.
14. *Capital*, p. 873.
15. *MEGA*, III, p. 117.
16. *Ibid.* pp. 121, 122.
17. *Ibid.* p. 89.
18. *Ibid.* pp. 84, 122.
19. *Ibid.* pp. 88–9.
20. *Ibid.* p. 93.
21. *Ibid.* pp. 89, 86.
22. *Ibid.* p. 83.
23. *Ibid.* p. 161.
24. *Ibid.* pp. 155, 85.
25. *Ibid.* p. 88.
26. *Ibid.*
27. *Ibid.* pp. 94, 86.
28. *Ibid.* pp. 85–6.

IX. ALIENATION AND MONEY-WORSHIP (pp. 136–149)

1. *MEGA*, III, pp. 91–2.
2. *Ibid.* p. 89.
3. *Ibid.* pp. 81–2.
4. *Ibid.* pp. 145, 147–8.
5. *Ibid.* p. 130.
6. *Ibid.* p. 136.
7. *Ibid.* p. 86.
8. *Ibid.* p. 83.
9. *Ibid.* p. 154.
10. Karen Horney, *Neurosis and Human Growth*, pp. 159, 160, 166.
11. *MEGA*, III, pp. 89–90.
12. *Ibid.* p. 90.
13. *Ibid.* pp. 90–1.
14. *Ibid.* p. 152.
15. *Ibid.* pp. 89, 91.
16. *Ibid.* p. 90.

X. COMMUNISM—THE SELF REGAINED (pp. 150–161)

1. *MEGA*, III, pp. 81, 111.
2. *Ibid.* p. 134.
3. *Ibid.* pp. 113–14.
4. *Ibid.* p. 254.
5. *Ibid.* p. 134.
6. *Der Socialismus und Communismus des heutigen Frankreichs*, p. xv.

7. *MEGA*, III, p. 112.
8. *Ibid.* pp. 112, 113.
9. *Ibid.* p. 114.
10. *Ibid.* p. 166.
11. *Ibid.* p. 115.
12. *Ibid.* pp. 121, 123.
13. *Ibid.* p. 120.
14. *Ibid.* pp. 118–19.
15. *Ibid.* p. 114.
16. *Ibid.* p. 119.
17. *Ibid.* p. 114.
18. *Ibid.* p. 116.
19. *Ibid.* p. 126.
20. *Iz rannikh proizvedenii*, p. 663.

XI. TWO MARXISMS OR ONE? (pp. 165–176)

1. *Selected Works* I, p. 47.
2. *German Ideology*, p. 68.
3. *Selected Works* I, p. 58.
4. *German Ideology*, p. 198.
5. *Reason and Revolution*, p. 295.
6. 'U istokov revoliutsionnogo perevorota v filosofii', *Kommunist*, no. 2, February 1958, p. 88.
7. *Selected Correspondence*, p. 102.
8. *Capital*, p. 873.
9. *Selected Works* II, p. 350.
10. *Selected Works* I, p. 364.
11. *Selected Works* II, p. 333.
12. *Selected Works* I, p. 372.
13. *Vospominaniia o Markse i Engel'se*, p. 345 (noted by Daniel Bell in *Soviet Survey*, April-June 1960, p. 28).
14. *The Theory of Capitalist Development*, p. 13.
15. *MEGA*, III, p. 206.
16. *Selected Works* I, p. 93.
17. *Ibid.* p. 82
18. *Ibid.* p. 34.

XII. THE NEW MATERIALISM (pp. 177–187)

1. *Selected Works* II, p. 325.
2. *Critique of Political Economy*, p. 13.
3. *German Ideology*, pp. 64, 42.
4. *Ibid.* p. 15.
5. *Critique of Political Economy*, pp. 11–12.
6. *German Ideology*, p. 30.

7. *German Ideology*, p. 30.
8. *Ibid.* p. 14.
9. *Ibid.*
10. *Ibid.* p. 35.
11. *Ibid.* p. 199.
12. *Ibid.* p. 197.
13. *Ibid.* p. 37.
14. *Ibid.* p. 35.
15. *Ibid.* pp. 36–7.
16. *Ibid.* pp. 37–8.
17. *Dialectics of Nature*, p. 306.
18. *German Ideology*, pp. 22, 25, 23.
19. *Ibid.* p. 24.
20. *MEGA*, III, p. 139.
21. *Selected Works* II, p. 31.
22. *German Ideology*, p. 21.
23. *Ibid.* pp. 22, 65.
24. *Ibid.* p. 73.

XIII. DIVISION OF LABOUR AND COMMUNISM
(pp. 188–202)

1. *German Ideology*, p. 66.
2. *Ibid.* pp. 22, 24.
3. *Herr Eugen Dühring's Revolution in Science*, pp. 435–6 (hereafter cited as *Anti-Dühring*).
4. *Poverty of Philosophy*, p. 157.
5. *Selected Works* I, p. 102.
6. *Ibid.* p. 439.
7. *Ibid.* p. 100.
8. *Capital*, pp. 381–2.
9. *Ibid.* pp. 383, 385, 388.
10. *Selected Works* II, p. 29.
11. *Capital*, p. 350.
12. *Ibid.* p. 527.
13. *Selected Works* I, p. 41.
14. *Capital*, p. 453.
15. *German Ideology*, p. 78.
16. *Selected Works* I, p. 54.
17. *German Ideology*, pp. 67, 69.
18. *Ibid.* p. 74.
19. *Ibid.* p. 66.
20. *Selected Works* II, pp. 140–1.
21. *German Ideology*, pp. 67–8.
22. *Ibid.* p. 22.

23. *Selected Works* I, p. 48.
24. *Capital*, pp. 54, 685, 527.
25. *Anti-Dühring*, pp. 438, 299.
26. *Capital*, vol. III, p. 451.
27. *Selected Works* II, p. 23.
28. *German Ideology*, p. 199.
29. *Selected Correspondence*, p. 350.
30. *Selected Works* I, p. 523.

XIV. THE WORLD AS LABOUR AND CAPITAL
(pp. 203–217)

1. *Capital*, p. 113.
2. *Ibid.*
3. *Ibid.* p. 846.
4. *German Ideology*, p. 66.
5. *Capital*, pp. 6–7.
6. *Ibid.* pp. 45–6, 47, 49.
7. *MEGA*, III, p. 133.
8. *Capital*, p. 173.
9. *Ibid.* p. 192.
10. *Ibid.* pp. 137, 138.
11. *Ibid.* p. 189.
12. *Ibid.* pp. 346–7.
13. *Ibid.* pp. 235, 237, 239, 259, 270.
14. *Ibid.* pp. 268–9.
15. *Ibid.* p. 713.
16. *Ibid.* pp. 451–2.
17. *Ibid.* p. 685.
18. *Capital*, vol. III, pp. 1026–7.
19. *Capital*, p. 651.
20. *Ibid.* pp. 347, 244.
21. *Selected Works* I, p. 359.
22. *Capital*, p. 23.
23. *Das Kapital*, p. 241.
24. *Capital*, p. 138.
25. *Ibid.* pp. 650, 651, 652, 653.

XV. THE MYTH AND THE PROBLEM OF CONDUCT
(pp. 218–232)

1. *Capital*, pp. 677, 708.
2. *Ibid.* pp. 551, 552.
3. *Ibid.* p. 651.
4. *Ibid.* p. 714.
5. *Selected Correspondence*, p. 15.

6. *German Ideology*, p. 191.
7. *Selected Works* I, p. 46.
8. *Poverty of Philosophy*, p. 136.
9. *Herr Vogt*, p. 35.
10. *Selected Correspondence*, p. 225.
11. *Ibid.* p. 224.
12. *Selected Works* I, p. 359.
13. *Capital*, p. 248.
14. *Selected Correspondence*, p. 17.
15. *Ibid.* p. 16.

CONCLUSION (pp. 233–243)

1. *Capital*, vol. III, pp. 954–5.

LIST OF BOOKS CITED

BECKER, CARL L., *The Heavenly City of the Eighteenth-Century Philosophers*. New Haven: Yale University Press, 1932.

BOBER, M. M., *Karl Marx's Interpretation of History*. Cambridge: Harvard University Press, 1950.

BUBER, M., *Paths in Utopia*. London: Routledge & Kegan Paul, 1949.

CALVEZ, JEAN-YVES, *La Pensée de Karl Marx*. Paris: Editions du Seuil, 1956.

CARR, E. H., *Karl Marx: A Study in Fanaticism*. London: J. M. Dent & Sons, 1934.

CASSIRER, ERNST, *Language and Myth*, trans. Susanne K. Langer. New York: Harper & Brothers, 1946.

COLE, G. D. H., *A History of Socialist Thought*, vol. I, *The Forerunners, 1789–1850*. London: Macmillan Company, 1953.

COOPER, R., *The Logical Influence of Hegel on Marx*. University of Washington Publications in the Social Sciences, vol. II, no. 2. Seattle, 1925.

CROCE, BENEDETTO, *Historical Materialism and the Economics of Karl Marx*. New York: Macmillan Company, 1914.

ENGELS, F., *Dialectics of Nature*. Moscow: Foreign Languages Publishing House, 1954.

ENGELS, F., *Herr Eugen Dühring's Revolution in Science (Anti-Dühring)*. Moscow: Foreign Languages Publishing House, 1947.

FEUERBACH, LUDWIG, *The Essence of Christianity*. New York: Harper & Bros., 1957.

FEUERBACH, LUDWIG, *Kleine Philosophische Schriften* (1842–1845), ed. Max Gustav Lange. Leipzig: Verlag Felix Meiner, 1950.

FICHTE, J. G., *The Vocation of Man*. La Salle, Illinois: The Open Court Publishing Company, 1955.

FRANKFORT, HENRI and H. A., *Before Philosophy*. Penguin Books, 1949.

GOETHE, *Faust* (Part I), trans. Philip Wayne. Penguin Books, 1949.

HEGEL, G. W. F., *Early Theological Writings*, trans. T. M. Knox. Chicago: University of Chicago Press, 1948.

HEGEL, G. W. F., *Lectures on the History of Philosophy*, trans. Elizabeth S. Haldane and Frances H. Simson, vol. III. London: Kegan Paul, 1896.

HEGEL, G. W. F., *The Logic of Hegel*, translated from *The Encyclopaedia of the Philosophical Sciences* by William Wallace. London: Geoffrey Cumberlege, 1950.

HEGEL, G. W. F., *The Phenomenology of Mind*, trans. J. B. Baillie. London: George Allen & Unwin, 1931.

HEGEL, G. W. F., *The Philosophy of History*, trans. J. Sibree. New York: Dover Publications, 1956.

Hegel Selections, ed. J. Loewenberg. New York: Charles Scribner's Sons, 1929.

Hegel's Philosophy of Mind, translated from *The Encyclopaedia of the Philosophical Sciences* by William Wallace. Oxford: The Clarendon Press, 1894.

Hegel's Philosophy of Right, trans. T. M. Knox. Oxford: The Clarendon Press, 1953.

Hegel's Science of Logic, trans. W. H. Johnston and L. G. Struthers, vol. i. London: George Allen & Unwin, 1951.

HEINEMANN, F. H., *Existentialism and the Modern Predicament*. New York: Harper Torchbooks, 1958.

HESS, MOSES, *Sozialistische Aufsätze 1841–1847*, ed. Theodor Zlocisti. Berlin: Welt-Verlag, 1921.

HOOK, SIDNEY, *From Hegel to Marx: Studies in the Intellectual Development of Karl Marx*. New York: The Humanities Press, 1950.

HORNEY, KAREN, *Neurosis and Human Growth: The Struggle Toward Self-Realization*. New York: W. W. Norton & Co., 1950.

HYPPOLITE, JEAN, *Études sur Marx et Hegel*. Paris: Librairie Marcel Rivière et Cie, 1955.

KANT, IMMANUEL, *The Fundamental Principles of the Metaphysic of Ethics*. New York: Appleton-Century-Crofts, 1938.

Kant's Critique of Practical Reason and Other Works on the Theory of Ethics, trans. Thomas Kingsmill Abbott. London: Longmans, Green & Co., 1909.

KAUTSKY, KARL, *Ethics and the Materialist Conception of History*. Chicago: Charles H. Kerr, 1907.

KIERKEGAARD, SØREN, *The Sickness Unto Death*, trans. Walter Lowrie. Princeton: Princeton University Press, 1951.

LENIN, V. I., *Selected Works*, vol. ii. Moscow: Foreign Languages Publishing House, 1947.

LINDSAY, A. D., *Karl Marx's Capital: An Introductory Essay*. London: Geoffrey Cumberlege, 1947.

LOVEJOY, A. O., *The Great Chain of Being*. Cambridge: Harvard University Press, 1948.

MARCUSE, H., *Reason and Revolution: Hegel and the Rise of Social Theory*. New York: Humanities Press, 1954.

MARX, K., *Capital*, trans. Eden and Cedar Paul. London: J. M. Dent & Sons, 1933.

MARX, K., *Capital*, vol. iii, ed. F. Engels. Chicago: Charles H. Kerr, 1909.

MARX, K., *A Contribution to the Critique of Political Economy.* Chicago: Charles H. Kerr, 1904.

MARX, K., *Herr Vogt.* London: Petsch & Co., 1860.

MARX, K., *Das Kapital,* vol. I. Berlin: Dietz Verlag, 1957.

MARX, K., *The Poverty of Philosophy.* Chicago: Charles H. Kerr, undated.

MARX, K., *A World Without Jews,* trans. Dagobert D. Runes. New York: Philosophical Library, 1959.

MARX, K. and ENGELS, F., *The German Ideology,* parts I and III, ed. R. Pascal. New York: International Publishers, 1939.

MARX, K. and ENGELS, F., *Historisch-Kritische Gesamtausgabe. Erste Abteilung,* vol. I–V, eds. D. Rjazanov and V. Adoratski. Berlin: Marx-Engels Verlag G.M.B.H., 1927–1932.

MARX, K. and ENGELS, F., *Iz rannikh proizvedenii.* Moscow: Gosudarstvennoe Izdatel'stvo Politicheskoi Literatury, 1956.

MARX, K. and ENGELS, F., *Kleine Ökonomische Schriften.* Berlin: Dietz Verlag, 1955.

MARX, K. and ENGELS, F., *Selected Correspondence 1846–1895.* New York: International Publishers, 1942.

MARX, K. and ENGELS, F., *Selected Works,* in two volumes. Moscow: Foreign Languages Publishing House, 1958 (vol. I) and 1951 (vol. II).

MAYER, GUSTAV, *Friedrich Engels: A Biography.* New York: Alfred A. Knopf, 1936.

NIETZSCHE, F., *The Philosophy of Nietzsche.* New York: Modern Library, 1932.

POPPER, K. R., *The Open Society and Its Enemies,* vol. II, *The High Tide of Prophecy: Hegel, Marx and the Aftermath.* London: George Routledge & Sons, 1945.

PROUDHON, P. J., *What Is Property? An Inquiry into the Principles of Right and Government,* trans. Benjamin R. Tucker, London, 1902.

RÜHLE, OTTO, *Karl Marx: His Life and Work,* trans. Eden and Cedar Paul. London: George Allen & Unwin, 1929.

SEBEOK, THOMAS E., ed., *Myth: A Symposium.* Bloomington: Indiana University Press, 1958.

SHISKIN, A., *Osnovy kommunisticheskoi morali.* Moscow: Gosudarstvennoe Izdatel'stvo Politicheskoi Literatury, 1955.

SMITH, ADAM, *An Inquiry into the Nature and Causes of the Wealth of Nations.* New York: The Modern Library, 1937.

STACE, W. T., *The Philosophy of Hegel.* Dover Publications, 1955.

STEIN, LORENZ VON, *Der Socialismus und Communismus des heutigen Frankreichs.* Leipzig: Otto Wigand, 1848.

Sweezy, Paul, *The Theory of Capitalist Development: Principles of Marxian Political Economy.* New York: Oxford University Press, 1942.

Vospominaniia o Markse i Engel'se. Institute of Marx-Engels-Lenin-Stalin. Moscow: Gosudarstvennoe Izdatel'stvo Politicheskoi Literatury, 1956.

INDEX

alienated labour, *see* alienation

alienation, 34, 165, 197, 205; and capitalism, 212; and class war, 176; and communism, 117–18; and division of labour, 185; and greed, 137–9; and Marxism, 97, 165, 172–4, 176, 237–42; and political economy, 106, 110–11, 119, 145–6, 219; and proletariat, 113–14; and revolution, 100–102, 105; and the state, 102–5

    as deprivation of freedom, 133–5; as social phenomenon, 146–9, 175–6, 215–16, 220

    Feuerbach's view of, 83–4; Hegel's view of, 49–52, 55; Marx on, 99, 100–102, 106, 111, 125–8, 133–5, 145–9; psychiatric view of, 144–5; transcendence of, 151, 156–61

Anti-Dühring, by Engels, 189, 198

Aristotle, 207–8

art: and communism, 157–9, 235; and human nature, 134; and industry, 199

atheism: and Hegel, 47; Marx's, 22, 74

Aufhebung, 51, 59, 91, 153, 194, 236

Augustine, St, 23

Baboeuf, François-Noel (Gracchus), 114, 155, 161

Bauer, Bruno, 73, 75, 111

Becker, Carl, 23

Bell, Daniel, 168 n.

Bentham, Jeremy, Marx on, 17–18

Bernstein, Eduard, 173

Bober, M. M., 209 n.

Buber, Martin, 12

Calvez, Jean-Yves, 168 n.

Capital, by Marx, 13, 15, 17, 21, 129, 142, 169, 184 n., 190–2, 198, 199, 203–17 *passim*, 219, 220, 225, 226, 227, 231, 233, 235, 237 n., 240

capital: as philosophical concept, 213–14; as social power, 176; autocracy of, 193–4, 211–12, 243; definition of, 213; Marx's idea of, 138, 141

capitalism: and alienation, 215; and division of labour, 190–1; and religion, 212; as religious phenomenon, 203; Marx's conception of, 209, 234, 239

Carr, E. H., 17 n.

Cassirer, Ernst, 224 n.

Christianity, 32, 46; and Marxism, 22–5; Feuerbach's relation to, 93–4, 239; Hegel's relation to, 39–40, 43, 69, 75–6, 83; Hess on, 110; Kierkegaard's view of, 32; Marx on, 112

civil society, 103–4, 106–8, 219

Civil War in France, by Marx, 201

class struggle, 146–7, 150, 173, 176, 187, 220, 227

Cole, G. D. H., 130–1 n., 221 n., 228 n.

communism, 112, 235; aesthetic character of, 157–9; and alienation, 117–18; and distribution, 200; and division of labour, 200; and freedom, 196; and Hegel, 153; and humanism 110, 156–9; and proletariat, 115, 117; and social institutions, 201

    as naturalism, 159–60; as negation of negation, 154–6, 160; as transcendence of alienation, 151

    beyond property principle, 160–1; Feuerbach on, 91; not goal of human society, 160; philosophical, 26–7, 107–8, 110, 113, 117, 165, 169; Proudhon on, 109; raw, 154–5, 161, 194; Soviet view of, 161

Communist Manifesto, by Marx and Engels, 15, 23, 165, 166, 167 n., 168, 176, 193, 198, 225, 227, 230

Cooper, Rebecca, 17 n.

criticism: as a weapon, 80; of political economy, 119–20, 125, 204; of politics, 102–3; of religion, 75–6, 80, 84, 91, 99–100, 102; slogan of, 73–4; transformational, 85–7, 97–8, 103, 171

Critique of the Gotha Program, by Marx, 19, 186, 199

Critique of Political Economy, by Marx, 23, 106, 125, 171, 177, 179

Critique of Practical Reason, by Kant, 89 n.

Croce, Benedetto, 12–13

Darwin, Charles, 232

Das Kapital, see *Capital*

democracy, Marx on, 104

De republica, by Aristotle, 208